Religion, Economics, and Demography

This book is a gem that deserves wide attention from social and behavioral scientists, policymakers, and citizens –and indeed, anyone who is interested in understanding the role of religion in contemporary American society. Evelyn Lehrer is a superb scholar, who blends sound economic theory and reasoning, rigorous analyses of excellent data, and thoughtful, nuanced interpretation. Taken together, the essays in this volume build a compelling case for the important –yet often ignored –in fluence of religion on educational attainment and earnings, marriage and family life, and a host of population processes and outcomes. Lehrer has made a landmark contribution to the exciting literature that is emerging at the interface of religion and economics.

Christopher G. Ellison
Elsie and Stanley E. Adams, Sr. Centennial Professor
Sociology and Religious Studies
The University of Texas at Austin

Using the tools of economics, this book analyzes how religion affects decisions and outcomes in a wide range of areas, including education, employment, family size, entry into cohabitation and formal marriage, the choice of spouse, and divorce.

In each case, the relationships are rigorously quantified based on multivariate statistical analyses of large scale U.S. data. The results show, for example, that when people marry outside their faith, there is an increase in the probability of divorce, the magnitude of the adverse effect depending in part on the ecumenical/exclusivist nature of the two religions. Other analyses show that youth who grow up with some religion in their lives are less likely than their counterparts with little or no religious involvement to drop out of high school or enter cohabiting arrangements at a young age. Overall, both religious affiliation and the extent of participation in religious activities are found to have far-reaching implications for economic and demographic behavior.

The book contains a wealth of data illustrating how the religious and secular realms of people's lives are intimately intertwined. With its economic perspective, it offers new ways of thinking about these relationships, and is a valuable resource for students and scholars interested in the role of religion in education, work, and the family.

Evelyn L. Lehrer is currently Professor of Economics at the University of Illinois in Chicago, USA.

Routledge Frontiers of Political Economy

1 **Equilibrium versus Understanding**
Towards the rehumanization of
economics within social theory
Mark Addleson

2 **Evolution, Order and Complexity**
*Edited by Elias L. Khalil and
Kenneth E. Boulding*

3 **Interactions in Political Economy**
Malvern after ten years
Edited by Steven Pressman

4 **The End of Economics**
Michael Perelman

5 **Probability in Economics**
Omar F. Hamouda and Robin Rowley

6 **Capital Controversy, Post-Keynesian
Economics and the History of
Economics**
Essays in honour of Geoff Harcourt,
volume one
*Edited by Philip Arestis, Gabriel
Palma and Malcolm Sawyer*

7 **Markets, Unemployment and
Economic Policy**
Essays in honour of Geoff Harcourt,
volume two
*Edited by Philip Arestis, Gabriel
Palma and Malcolm Sawyer*

8 **Social Economy**
The logic of capitalist development
Clark Everling

9 **New Keynesian Economics/Post
Keynesian Alternatives**
Edited by Roy J. Rotheim

10 **The Representative Agent in
Macroeconomics**
James E. Hartley

11 **Borderlands of Economics**
Essays in honour of Daniel R.
Fusfeld
*Edited by Nahid Aslanbeigui and
Young Back Choi*

12 **Value, Distribution and Capital**
Essays in honour of Pierangelo
Garegnani
*Edited by Gary Mongiovi and
Fabio Petri*

13 **The Economics of Science**
Methodology and epistemology as if
economics really mattered
James R. Wible

14 **Competitiveness, Localised Learning
and Regional Development**
Specialisation and prosperity in
small open economies
*Peter Maskell, Heikki Eskelinen,
Ingjaldur Hannibalsson, Anders
Malmberg and Eirik Vatne*

15 **Labour Market Theory**
A constructive reassessment
Ben J. Fine

16 **Women and European Employment**
Jill Rubery, Mark Smith, Colette Fagan and Damian Grimshaw

17 **Explorations in Economic Methodology**
From Lakatos to empirical philosophy of science
Roger Backhouse

18 **Subjectivity in Political Economy**
Essays on wanting and choosing
David P. Levine

19 **The Political Economy of Middle East Peace**
The impact of competing trade agendas
Edited by J.W. Wright Jnr

20 **The Active Consumer**
Novelty and surprise in consumer choice
Edited by Marina Bianchi

21 **Subjectivism and Economic Analysis**
Essays in memory of Ludwig Lachmann
Edited by Roger Koppl and Gary Mongiovi

22 **Themes in Post-Keynesian Economics**
Essays in honour of Geoff Harcourt, volume three
Edited by Claudio Sardoni and Peter Kriesler

23 **The Dynamics of Technological Knowledge**
Cristiano Antonelli

24 **The Political Economy of Diet, Health and Food Policy**
Ben J. Fine

25 **The End of Finance**
Capital market inflation, financial derivatives and pension fund capitalism
Jan Toporowski

26 **Political Economy and the New Capitalism**
Edited by Jan Toporowski

27 **Growth Theory**
A philosophical perspective
Patricia Northover

28 **The Political Economy of the Small Firm**
Edited by Charlie Dannreuther

29 **Hahn and Economic Methodology**
Edited by Thomas Boylan and Paschal F. O'Gorman

30 **Gender, Growth and Trade**
The miracle economies of the postwar years
David Kucera

31 **Normative Political Economy**
Subjective freedom, the market and the state
David Levine

32 **Economist with a Public Purpose**
Essays in honour of John Kenneth Galbraith
Edited by Michael Keaney

33 **Involuntary Unemployment**
The elusive quest for a theory
Michel De Vroey

34 **The Fundamental Institutions of Capitalism**
Ernesto Screpanti

35 **Transcending Transaction**
The search for self-generating markets
Alan Shipman

36 **Power in Business and the State**
An historical analysis of its concentration
Frank Bealey

37 **Editing Economics**
Essays in honour of Mark Perlman
Hank Lim, Ungsuh K. Park and Geoff Harcourt

38 **Money, Macroeconomics and Keynes**
Essays in honour of Victoria Chick,
volume one
*Philip Arestis, Meghnad Desai and
Sheila Dow*

39 **Methodology, Microeconomics
and Keynes**
Essays in honour of Victoria Chick,
volume two
*Philip Arestis, Meghnad Desai and
Sheila Dow*

40 **Market Drive and Governance**
Reexamining the rules for economic
and commercial contest
Ralf Boscheck

41 **The Value of Marx**
Political economy for contemporary
capitalism
Alfredo Saad-Filho

42 **Issues in Positive Political Economy**
S. Mansoob Murshed

43 **The Enigma of Globalisation**
A journey to a new stage of
capitalism
Robert Went

44 **The Market**
Equilibrium, stability, mythology
S.N. Afriat

45 **The Political Economy of Rule
Evasion and Policy Reform**
Jim Leitzel

46 **Unpaid Work and the Economy**
Edited by Antonella Picchio

47 **Distributional Justice**
Theory and measurement
Hilde Bojer

48 **Cognitive Developments in Economics**
Edited by Salvatore Rizzello

49 **Social Foundations of Markets,
Money and Credit**
Costas Lapavitsas

50 **Rethinking Capitalist Development**
Essays on the economics of Josef
Steindl
*Edited by Tracy Mott and
Nina Shapiro*

51 **An Evolutionary Approach to Social
Welfare**
Christian Sartorius

52 **Kalecki's Economics Today**
*Edited by Zdzislaw L. Sadowski and
Adam Szeworski*

53 **Fiscal Policy from Reagan to Blair**
The left veers right
Ravi K. Roy and Arthur T. Denzau

54 **The Cognitive Mechanics of
Economic Development and
Institutional Change**
Bertin Martens

55 **Individualism and the Social Order**
The social element in liberal thought
Charles R. McCann Jnr

56 **Affirmative Action in the United
States and India**
A comparative perspective
Thomas E. Weisskopf

57 **Global Political Economy and the
Wealth of Nations**
Performance, institutions, problems
and policies
Edited by Phillip Anthony O'Hara

58 **Structural Economics**
Thijs ten Raa

59 **Macroeconomic Theory and
Economic Policy**
Essays in honour of Jean-Paul
Fitoussi
Edited by K. Vela Velupillai

60 **The Struggle Over Work**
The "end of work" and employment
alternatives in post-industrial
societies
Shaun Wilson

61 **The Political Economy of Global Sporting Organisations**
John Forster and Nigel Pope

62 **The Flawed Foundations of General Equilibrium Theory**
Critical essays on economic theory
Frank Ackerman and Alejandro Nadal

63 **Uncertainty in Economic Theory**
Essays in honor of David Schmeidler's 65th Birthday
Edited by Itzhak Gilboa

64 **The New Institutional Economics of Corruption**
Edited by Johann Graf Lambsdorff, Markus Taube and Matthias Schramm

65 **The Price Index and its Extension**
A chapter in economic measurement
S.N. Afriat

66 **Reduction, Rationality and Game Theory in Marxian Economics**
Bruce Philp

67 **Culture and Politics in Economic Development**
Volker Bornschier

68 **Modern Applications of Austrian Thought**
Edited by Jürgen G. Backhaus

69 **Ordinary Choices**
Individuals, incommensurability, and democracy
Robert Urquhart

70 **Labour Theory of Value**
Peter C. Dooley

71 **Capitalism**
Victor D. Lippit

72 **Macroeconomic Foundations of Macroeconomics**
Alvaro Cencini

73 **Marx for the 21st Century**
Edited by Hiroshi Uchida

74 **Growth and Development in the Global Political Economy**
Social structures of accumulation and modes of regulation
Phillip Anthony O'Hara

75 **The New Economy and Macroeconomic Stability**
A neo-modern perspective drawing on the complexity approach and Keynesian economics
Teodoro Dario Togati

76 **The Future of Social Security Policy**
Women, work and a citizens basic income
Ailsa McKay

77 **Clinton and Blair**
The political economy of the Third Way
Flavio Romano

78 **Marxian Reproduction Schema**
Money and aggregate demand in a capitalist economy
A.B. Trigg

79 **The Core Theory in Economics**
Problems and solutions
Lester G. Telser

80 **Economics, Ethics and the Market**
Introduction and applications
Johan J. Graafland

81 **Social Costs and Public Action in Modern Capitalism**
Essays inspired by Karl William Kapp's Theory of Social Costs
Edited by Wolfram Elsner, Pietro Frigato and Paolo Ramazzotti

82 **Globalization and the Myths of Free Trade**
History, theory and empirical evidence
Edited by Anwar Shaikh

83 **Equilibrium in Economics**
Scope and limits
Edited by Valeria Mosini

84 **Globalization**
State of the art and perspectives
Edited by Stefan A. Schirm

85 **Neoliberalism**
National and regional experiments
with global ideas
*Edited by Ravi K. Roy, Arthur T.
Denzau and Thomas D. Willett*

86 **Post-Keynesian Macroeconomics**
Essays in honour of Ingrid Rima
*Edited by Mathew Forstater, Gary
Mongiovi and Steven Pressman*

87 **Consumer Capitalism**
Anastasios S. Korkotsides

88 **Remapping Gender in the
New Global Order**
*Edited Marjorie Griffin Cohen and
Janine Brodie*

89 **Hayek and Natural Law**
Eric Angner

90 **Race and Economic Opportunity in
the Twenty-first Century**
Edited by Marlene Kim

91 **Renaissance in Behavioural
Economics**
Harvey Leibenstein's impact on
contemporary economic analysis
Edited by Roger Frantz

92 **Human Ecology Economics**
A new framework for global
sustainability
Edited by Roy E. Allen

93 **Imagining Economics Otherwise**
Encounters with identity/difference
Nitasha Kaul

94 **Reigniting the Labor Movement**
Restoring means to ends in a
democratic labor movement
Gerald Friedman

95 **The Spatial Model of Politics**
Norman Schofield

96 **The Economics of American
Judaism**
Carmel Ullman Chiswick

97 **Critical Political Economy**
Christian Arnsperger

98 **Culture and Economic Explanation**
Economics in the US and Japan
Donald W. Katzner

99 **Feminism, Economics and Utopia**
Time travelling through paradigms
Karin Schönpflug

100 **Risk in International Finance**
Vikash Yadav

101 **Economic Policy and Performance in
Industrial Democracies**
Party governments, central banks
and the fiscal-monetary policy mix
Takayuki Sakamoto

102 **Advances on Income Inequality and
Concentration Measures**
*Edited by Gianni Betti and
Achille Lemmi*

103 **Economic Representations**
Academic and everyday
Edited by David F. Ruccio

104 **Mathematical Economics and the
Dynamics of Capitalism**
Goodwin's legacy continued
*Edited by Peter Flaschel and
Michael Landesmann*

105 **The Keynesian Multiplier**
*Edited by Claude Gnos and
Louis-Philippe Rochon*

106 **Money, Enterprise and Income
Distribution**
Towards a macroeconomic theory
of capitalism
John Smithin

107 **Fiscal Decentralization and Local
Public Finance in Japan**
Nobuki Mochida

108 **The "Uncertain" Foundations of
Post-Keynesian Economics**
Essays in exploration
Stephen P. Dunn

109 **Karl Marx's Grundrisse**
Foundations of the critique of
political economy 150 years later
Edited by Marcello Musto

110 **Economics and the Price Index**
S.N. Afriat and Carlo Milana

111 **Sublime Economy**
On the intersection of art and
economics
*Edited by Jack Amariglio, Joseph W.
Childers and Stephen E. Cullenberg*

112 **Popper, Hayek and the Open Society**
Calvin Hayes

113 **The Political Economy of Work**
David Spencer

114 **Institutional Economics**
Bernard Chavance

115 **Religion, Economics, and
Demography**
The effects of religion on education,
work, and the family
Evelyn L. Lehrer

Religion, Economics, and Demography

The effects of religion on education, work, and the family

Evelyn L. Lehrer

Routledge
Taylor & Francis Group

LONDON AND NEW YORK

First published 2009 by Routledge
2 Park Square, Milton Park, Abingdon, Oxon OX14 4RN

Simultaneously published in the USA and Canada
by Routledge
711 Third Avenue, New York, NY 10017

*Routledge is an imprint of the Taylor & Francis Group,
an informa business*

First issued in paperback 2011

Typeset in Times New Roman by
RefineCatch Limited, Bungay, Suffolk

British Library Cataloguing in Publication Data
A catalogue record for this book is available from the British Library

Library of Congress Cataloging in Publication Data
Lehrer, Evelyn L.
Religion, economics and demography : an economic perspective on the
role of religion in education, female employment, fertility, cohabitation,
marriage and divorce / Evelyn L. Lehrer.
p. cm.
Includes bibliographical references and index.
1. United States—Religion—1960– 2. Religion and sociology—United
States. 3. United States—Social conditions—1980– 4. Economics—
Religious aspects. 5. United States—Economic conditions—1945–
I. Title.
BL2525.L45 2008
305.60973—dc22
2008017317

ISBN10: 0–415–70194–5 (hbk)
ISBN10: 0–415–68674–1 (pbk)
ISBN10: 0–203–88905–3 (ebk)

ISBN13: 978–0–415–70194–5 (hbk)
ISBN13: 978–0–415–68674–7 (pbk)
ISBN13: 978–0–203–88905–3 (ebk)

To my mother and the loving memory of my father

Contents

List of figures   xv
List of tables   xvi
Foreword   xix
Acknowledgments   xxi

Introduction   1

PART I
The role of religion in marriage and divorce   9

1 Religion as a determinant of marital stability   11

2 Religious intermarriage in the United
   States: determinants and trends   33

PART II
The role of religion in female labor supply and fertility   53

3 The effects of religion on the labor supply
   of married women   55

4 Religion as a determinant of marital fertility   79

PART III
The role of religion in education and well-being   105

5 The benefits from marriage and religion in
   the United States: a comparative analysis   107

6 Religion as a determinant of educational
attainment: an economic perspective 128

7 Religion and high school graduation:
a comparative analysis of patterns for
white and black young women 154

PART IV
A revised analytical framework, conclusions, and directions
for future research 173

8 The role of religion in union formation:
an economic perspective 175

9 Religion as a determinant of economic and
demographic behavior in the United States 198

10 Recent developments in the field and an
agenda for future research 218

Author index 231
Subject index 233

Figures

2.1 The optimal level of religious compatibility with the
    spouse   35
2.2 Factors that influence the likelihood of intermarriage   36
6.1 The supply and demand of funds for investments
    in schooling   131
6.2 The effects of differences among groups in demand
    and supply conditions   131
6.3 Comparisons between Jews (J) and mainline
    Protestants (M)   133
6.4 Comparisons between fundamentalist Protestants
    (F) and mainline Protestants (M)   136
6.5 Comparison between Catholics (C) and mainline
    Protestants (M)   137
6.6 Comparisons among Jews, mainline Protestants,
    Catholics, and fundamentalist Protestants   146
9.1 Demand and supply of funds for investments in
    schooling   206

Tables

1.1	Definition of religious groups	16
1.2	Religion variables	17
1.3	Control variables	19
1.4	The effects of the religious composition of unions on marriage dissolution	20
1.5	Comparisons among various types of homogamous marriages	22
1.6	Comparisons between intra- and interfaith unions	24
1.7	Conversion and marital stability	27
2.1	Percentage of marriages that are interfaith by respondent's affiliation	40
2.2	Definitions and means of explanatory variables	41
2.3	Logit intermarriage regressions by respondent's affiliation	43
2.4	Estimated probabilities of religious intermarriage	44
2.5	Logit intermarriage regressions by respondent's affiliation	46
3.1	Religion and gender-role attitudes	57
3.2	Employment status by period	59
3.3	Means of explanatory variables	61
3.4	Multinomial logit coefficients	63
3.5	Reestimating the model for period 2 with exclusivist Protestant wives as benchmark	65
3.6	The effects of religion on the probability of full-time work, part-time work, and non-employment	66
3.7	The effects of the control variables on the probability of full-time work, part-time work, and non-employment	68
3.8	Ordered probit estimates for period 2	71
3.9	Actual proportions vs. multinomial logit and ordered probit estimates (period 2)	72
4.1	The expected effects of out-marriage on fertility	82
4.2	Means of religion variables	85

4.3	The control variables	86
4.4	The effects of religion on family size	88
4.5	Predicted family size by wife's religion (model 1) and by type of homogamous union (model 3)	90
4.6	Predicted family size for homogamous and heterogamous unions	91
4.7	Making a distinction between naturally homogamous and conversionary unions	94
4.8	Natural vs. conversionary homogamy	95
4.9	The role of religiosity	96
4.10	Predicted family size by religiosity	97
4.11	The role of marriage cohort	98
4.12	Predicted family size by marriage cohort	99
6.1	Educational attainment by religion	130
6.2	Variable definitions and means	139
6.3	The effects of religious upbringing on years of schooling: OLS regressions	140
6.4	The effects of religious upbringing on schooling transitions: logit regressions	142
6.5	Estimated probabilities of schooling transitions	143
6.6	Wage regressions by religion	145
7.1	Descriptive statistics: religion variables	157
7.2	Descriptive statistics: means of dependent variable and control variables	158
7.3a	Religious affiliation and high school graduation: white women. Logit regressions	160
7.3b	Religious affiliation and high school graduation: black women. Logit regressions	161
7.4	Predicted probabilities of high school graduation by religious affiliation	162
7.5	Comparisons between white and black women in the religious affiliation–high school graduation relationship. Logit regressions	163
7.6	Predicted probabilities of high school completion by religious affiliation and by high vs. low religious participation	165
8.1	Definitions and means of explanatory variables	184
8.2	The effects of religious upbringing on union formation: Cox proportional hazards models	186
8.3	Predicted probabilities based on competing-risk models of Table 8.2	187

xviii *Tables*

8.4 Variations by frequency of attendance to religious
     services: Cox proportional hazards models   191
8.5 Predicted probabilities by frequency of attendance
     to religious services based on competing-risk models of
     Table 8.4   192

Foreword

The Economics of Religion is a relatively new field that applies the theoretical and empirical tools of modern economics to the study of religion (indeed the Economics of Religion has its own JEL code, Z120). Religion has many dimensions, including spirituality, community or social aspects, and, for some denominations, the "after-life" for themselves or their loved ones. Regardless of dimension, religion is clearly an economic good. People are willing to spend money on religious practice, whether it is on church membership, religious artifacts, pilgrimages to holy sites, or religious education for themselves and for their children. Religion also involves time costs, that is, time spent in formal church services, religious education, home practice, etc. People make these expenditures because they perceive that there will be benefits that are greater than the costs, hence religion is an economic good.

The primary principle of economics is that people respond to changes in incentives (relative prices). This happens in religion as well. People alter their religious practices in response to changing incentives. They can do this by changing their affiliation, by their denomination changing its doctrine, or by merely changing their own individual practice without changing their denominations.

The Economics of Religion seeks to ask and answer two fundamental questions:

1   How do economic incentives and institutions influence the style and practice of religion (denomination) and religiosity (the intensity of religious practice)?
2   How do religion and religiosity influence economic and demographic behaviors?

Evelyn Lehrer had a keen interest in labor market and demographic behavior when she was introduced to the Economics of Religion. The important effects of "control" variables for religion led her to explore more deeply the effects of religion and religiosity on marital patterns, fertility, female labor supply and investment in children's schooling. Her research has resulted in a large number of very high-quality papers in a variety of economics, demographic and social science journals. These studies have expanded the reach of the Economics of Religion and have demonstrated two important propositions. One is that religion and religiosity play an important role in determining demographic and human capital investment behavior. The other is that perhaps more important than denomination per se is religiosity, that is, the actual practice of religion.

Being a colleague of Evelyn Lehrer with overlapping interests, I have had the privilege of numerous conversations with her on research in the Economics of Religion and of reading many of her papers in draft. I have consistently been impressed with her creativity and innovative ideas, her skills in economics, demography, and econometrics, her respect and attention to the details of data, and the clarity of her writing.

The social sciences in general, and not just economics, owe a debt of gratitude to Evelyn Lehrer for her on-going research. And another debt is owed for her putting together within one set of covers an impressive collection of her papers published in diverse journals that shed much light on the role of religion and religiosity in shaping economic and demographic life.

Barry R. Chiswick
UIC Distinguished Professor
Department of Economics
University of Illinois at Chicago
and
Program Director for Migration Studies
IZA – Institute for the Study of Labor

March 2008

Acknowledgments

As this book goes to press, covering research I have conducted over the past 15 years, I would like to thank several people. Marc Nerlove, my dissertation supervisor and mentor at Northwestern University, first introduced me to Economic Demography, a field that was just getting started at the time and brimming with excitement. I was blessed with the opportunity to study and work with him. He was part of a group of economists, including Gary Becker, Theodore W. Schultz, and H. Gregg Lewis, who were pioneers in using the tools of economics to understand the interactions between economic variables and population processes and to study such decisions as marriage and childbearing. I owe an enormous intellectual debt to Marc Nerlove, both for triggering my interest in Economic Demography and for all I learned from him regarding the art and science of econometrics.

I am also deeply indebted to Barry Chiswick, my colleague at the University of Illinois at Chicago since I joined the Economics Department as an Assistant Professor. He has critically read many of the papers I have written over the course of my career, including most of those included in this volume, always giving me valuable comments which helped me improve my work. I have also been significantly influenced by his writings on human capital investments and on the Economics of Religion.

I am grateful to Laurence Iannaccone, the father of the Economics of Religion, for his encouragement as I pursued this line of research, and for an inspiring seminar he gave at the University of Illinois when he was beginning to develop his now famous 1992 *Journal of Political Economy* article on sacrifice and stigma. As I listened to his talk, the seeds were planted for my interest in this new field. In 2002, for the first annual meetings of the Association for the Study of Religion, Economics, and Culture, he invited me to participate in the Keynote session honoring Gary Becker's contributions to the Economics of Religion. In the process of preparing my presentation, I was led for the first time to put together the various pieces I had written on the role of religion in economic and demographic behavior, each one of them strongly influenced by Gary Becker's seminal works. Developing further the material in that presentation, I wrote the article that appears as Chapter 9 in this volume, and went on from there to the thought of compiling some of my articles in this field, i.e. this book.

Over the years, I have benefited from stimulating intellectual discussions with Carmel Chiswick and Linda Waite; I also thank them for agreeing to have papers we have co-authored included here – Chapters 1 and 5, respectively. Shoshana Grossbard critically read some of the articles in draft, providing helpful comments, and encouraged me to pursue the idea of putting this book together when I was beginning to consider it. I am also thankful to Houston Stokes for his helpful practical advice on how to do this. Lawrence Officer read several chapters and offered invaluable new insights and perspectives.

Lastly, I would like to express my deepest gratitude to my husband, Nelson Lehrer, and my daughters, Jocelyn and Vivian, for their unfailing support and encouragement over the course of this project, and always.

Introduction

Religion is an important aspect of life in the United States. According to a large-scale survey conducted in 2001, 75 percent of adults consider themselves to be religious or somewhat religious, 91 percent report that they believe in God, and 54 percent live in households where either they themselves or someone else belongs to a religious congregation or house of worship (Kosmin and Keysar 2006). This book is a compilation of some of the articles I have written over the past 15 years on the role that religion plays in various dimensions of the economic and demographic behavior of American individuals and families, including education, cohabitation, marriage, divorce, fertility, and female employment. My objective in each of these studies was to expand our understanding of mechanisms through which religion may affect behavior and to quantify the underlying relationships.

Although the correspondence is not exact, the order in which the articles are arranged is roughly chronological, showing the development of my thinking on these issues over time. My interest in how religion affects demographic and economic behavior was piqued by surprising results that emerged from a study I conducted on the influence of human capital investments on marital stability (Lehrer 1996). I was struck by the large magnitude of the effect associated with a dummy variable that I had included in the analyses simply as a control: religious intermarriage. Based on data from the 1982 National Survey of Family Growth (NSFG), the estimates showed that for a typical white woman in her first marriage, the probability that her union would be dissolved within five years was 0.20 if her partner shared her religious affiliation, compared to 0.37 if he did not. For black women in first marriages, the corresponding percentages were 0.20 and 0.40. The patterns for white and black women in second and higher-order marriages revealed similarly large effects.

Part 1 of the book focuses on the role of religious affiliation in union formation and dissolution. Written in collaboration with Carmel Chiswick, Chapter 1 examines in more detail the effects of marrying outside one's faith on marital stability. Rather than a simple dichotomous variable for religious intermarriage, it includes a set of dummy variables for various types of religiously homogamous and heterogamous marriages. Analyses of the first-marriage experiences of white female respondents in the 1987–88 National Survey of Families and Households (NSFH) show that for religiously homogamous couples, the probability that the union would be dissolved within five years ranges from 0.13 to 0.27. Homogamous Mormon unions have the lowest risk of divorce; there are no significant differences in stability among homogamous unions involving mainline Protestants, conservative Protestants, Catholics, and Jews. For the various types of religiously heterogamous couples, the fifth-year dissolution probability ranges from 0.24 to 0.42. Generally in line with my earlier estimates based on the 1982 NSFG, these new results underscore a point that had not received attention in the literature to date: interfaith marriage comes in various shades and forms. While unions involving members of two different ecumenical denominations are relatively stable, those involving religions that have very different theologies, or at least one that is near the exclusivist end of the ecumenical–exclusivist continuum (Kelley 1972), are highly unstable. For the case of unions in which one or both members grew up with no religious affiliation, the fifth-year dissolution probability ranges from 0.31 to 0.38, highlighting the beneficial influence of some religious involvement per se for marital stability.

Chapter 1 also addresses another question that had not been examined before: does conversion solve the problem? For Protestants and Catholics, the two large groups for which an analysis of this issue is possible, the answer that emerges is clearly affirmative. Marriages in which homogamy was achieved through conversion are found to be at least as stable as those involving spouses who were raised in the same faith, suggesting that what really matters for marital harmony is religious compatibility at the time of marriage and thereafter.

The finding that religious intermarriage can have a substantial destabilizing influence raises the question as to why it happens so often that people marry outside their faith, sometimes to partners with whom the level of religious compatibility is very low, and more generally, the question of what role religion plays in the choice of marital partner. Chapter 2 addresses these issues, also using data from the 1987–88 NSFH. This work builds on earlier research I had done in collaboration with Carmel Chiswick. Our model was based on the premise that although a high level of religious compatibility between the spouses is desirable, religion is only one among many traits that influence the quality of a match. Given this multidimensional nature of the optimal match, individuals need to consider tradeoffs between religious compatibility with the partner and other desirable traits (Chiswick and Lehrer 1991).

The empirical analyses show that men and women who live in areas where there is a low concentration of coreligionists are more likely to intermarry, as are those who are less committed to the religion in which they were raised. In addition, highly educated conservative Protestants are more likely to marry outside their faith than their counterparts with less schooling: in analyses that set the family background variables at the typical values, the probability of intermarriage is 0.68 for a college graduate, compared to 0.51 for a high school graduate. Given the relatively low mean level of schooling among conservative Protestants, this result suggests the importance of assortative mating by education: for conservative Protestants at the top of the educational distribution, it may be easier to find a same-education partner outside their faith. The estimates also reveal a substantial increase over time in the rate of intermarriage for mainline Protestants and Catholics, in contrast to remarkable stability in the case of conservative Protestants. These findings suggest a resistance to secularization among members of the latter group, and help explain its continued strength.

Part 2 examines the effects of husbands' and wives' religious affiliation on female labor supply and fertility, also relying on data from the 1987 NSFH. As point of departure, the analyses in Chapters 3 and 4 assume that variations in norms and values across religious groups may be translated into corresponding differences in patterns of division of labor within the family and in tradeoffs between the quality and quantity of children. In addition, extending Becker et al.'s (1977) pioneering research, they develop the concept of a "marital stability effect," whereby women in interfaith unions are expected to respond to their greater vulnerability to marital instability by restricting their fertility and making more investments in human capital specific to the labor market. The analyses develop also a second influence, the "bargaining effect": women married to partners with different religious beliefs may need to negotiate with them to resolve differences in desired fertility or in views pertaining to the extent of their participation in the labor market. Consideration of the bargaining effect is important, as it can reinforce or counteract the marital stability effect, depending on the particular denominations that are involved.

The results reported in Chapter 3 show that among married women in homogamous unions who have a child under age 6, the labor force participation rate (for respondents with typical family background characteristics) is lowest among conservative Protestants (45 percent) and highest among Catholics (64 percent); the difference between Catholics and mainline Protestants is not significant. As to the effects of religious intermarriage, it is found to be associated with large increases in the labor force participation rate for mainline Protestant and conservative Protestant women with a young child – 13 and 20 percentage points, respectively.

Chapter 4 shows that among homogamous unions, Mormons have by far the highest fertility, in accordance with the strongly pronatalist norms of the Mormon faith. Setting the family background variables at the typical values, the point estimate for completed family size is 3.1 for Mormons, compared to 2.4, 2.2, and 2.1, respectively, for Catholics, conservative Protestants, and mainline Protestants. Out-marriage has a pronounced negative effect on fertility for Mormons, reducing completed family size from 3.3 to 2.4–2.5, and a small effect for Catholics, from 2.4 to 2.0–2.2.

Put together, Chapters 3 and 4 show that among married couples, the religious affiliations of both spouses matter for fertility and female labor supply decisions. They also demonstrate that religious intermarriage has effects that extend beyond marital stability: it has repercussions also for family size and women's employment.

While Parts 1 and 2 of the book focus only on religious affiliation, most of the analyses in Parts 3 and 4 include consideration of religious participation, another dimension of religion. Iannaccone (1990) has developed the notion that through religious participation people can increase their stock of religious human capital, and a growing number of studies have found that such participation is associated with positive effects in numerous domains of life. Written in collaboration with Linda Waite, Chapter 5 provides a new way of thinking about religion, drawing parallels to marriage – both in the benefits associated with these two social institutions, and in the underlying causal mechanisms. In the case of religion, there is a large body of evidence linking participation in religious activities to enhanced health and well-being. For youth, the beneficial outcomes include better performance in school, delayed sexual debut, and fewer problems with substance use and other risky behaviors. Mechanisms that may explain these relationships include: (a) religious participation helps integrate people into supportive social networks; (b) the teachings of religious traditions and the norms of religious groups generally encourage healthy, constructive conduct; and (c) participation in religious activities can generate important psychological benefits. Marriage has been similarly linked to widespread benefits for health and well-being, and two of the key pathways of causality are direct counterparts to (a) and (b) above: a social capital effect, whereby marriage has an integrative influence, and a regulative effect, whereby marriage promotes healthy behaviors.

Chapter 6 builds on a human capital model developed by Becker and Chiswick (1966), Becker (1967), and Chiswick (1988) to provide an economic perspective on how membership in various religious groups may affect the educational attainment of women and men. On the supply side, religious beliefs can influence parents' willingness to supply funds for schooling; on the demand side they can affect benefits from schooling and incentives to invest in human capital. Based on data from the 1987 NSFH, after controlling for family background factors, mainline Protestants and Catholics are found to be at the center of the educational distribution; the number of years of schooling completed is about 0.3–0.4 years smaller for conservative Protestants, and approximately 1.2–1.3 years higher for Jews. A powerful feature of the model is that analyses of rates of return from investments permit determining whether supply- or demand-side influences are more important. The results show that demand-side forces dominate in explaining the high achievement of Jews; supply and demand effects of similar strength are behind the relatively low schooling level of conservative Protestants.

Although the 1987–88 NSFH, employed in the analyses in Chapter 6, includes unusually rich information on the religious affiliation of respondents and their spouses, the only information on religious participation that it contains is frequency of attendance at services at the time of the survey – a variable that is endogenous to the various economic and demographic outcomes of interest. The analyses in Chapter 7 utilize a different, more recent data set – the 1995 National Survey of Family Growth (NSFG). Addressed to women, this survey contains detailed information on their economic and demographic characteristics, along with variables on their religious affiliation and participation during adolescence.

In recent work I extended the model in Chapter 6 to consider the effects of religious participation on investments in human capital (Lehrer 2008). Children who grow up with some religious involvement are expected to have more positive educational outcomes than their counterparts raised with little or no religion for demand-side reasons: for the former, time and other resources devoted to human capital investments are likely to be more productive. Building on this work, Chapter 7 examines the role of both religious affiliation and participation on an early measure of educational attainment – graduating from high school. The relatively large number of respondents age 20 and over in the 1995 NSFG permitted analyses not only for non-Hispanic whites, as in the previous chapters, but also for black respondents.

For the non-Hispanic white sample, consistent with the patterns shown in Chapter 6 for years of schooling completed, the probability of graduating from high school is found to be 0.93 for a mainline Protestant respondent with typical family background characteristics, compared to 0.86 for her conservative Protestant counterpart; the corresponding figures for black respondents are 0.90 and 0.82. In the white sample, there is no significant difference in the likelihood of high school graduation between Catholics and mainline Protestants; in the black sample, the probability is lower for Catholics by a margin of nine percentage points. The estimates also show that in the white sample, the high school graduation probability is nine percentage points higher for mainline Protestants than for the unaffiliated, and in both samples, the probability for youth who attended religious services 1–3 times per month or more frequently at age 14 is 6–10 percentage points higher than that for their less religious counterparts. These results are consistent with the hypothesis that religious involvement has beneficial effects on children's ability to be productively engaged in schooling endeavors.

Part 4 of the book suggests a revised framework for studying how religion affects economic and demographic behavior, and presents conclusions and directions for further investigation. Chapter 8 uses data from the 1995 NSFG to examine the effects of childhood religious affiliation and participation on the timing of women's transition to first union and whether such transition takes the form of marriage or cohabitation. This piece develops for the first time an integrated theoretical framework where the faith in which a young woman is raised is viewed as affecting the perceived costs and/or benefits of many interrelated decisions made over the life cycle. Using this framework, the effects of religion on union formation – the focus of this chapter – are explained by systematically tracing the influence of religious affiliation on choices with regard to schooling, fertility, female employment, and divorce. As to religious participation, it is viewed as mattering for union formation partly because of its effects in discouraging premarital sex, and partly because the connection between the doctrines of a particular faith and behavior is expected to be stronger among those who are more committed to their religion.

For respondents with typical characteristics for the family background variables, the probability of having entered formal marriage by age 20 is found to range from a low of 0.02 for Jews and 0.05 for Catholics, to 0.17 for Mormons and conservative Protestants; individuals with no religion and mainline Protestants are at the center of the distribution, with a probability of 0.08–0.09. Mormons stand out for their low probability of entering informal unions. Among Catholics, mainline Protestants, and conservative Protestants, individuals who had a higher level of religious participation in adolescence are less likely to enter cohabiting arrangements by wide margins. The effect is particularly pronounced for the latter: the probability of having entered cohabitation by age 20 is 0.16 for conservative Protestants who attended religious services 1–3 times per month or more frequently at age 14, compared to 0.31 for their less observant counterparts.

The religious categories used in the models vary somewhat across the various chapters described above, partly because two different data sets were employed, partly because sample size considerations led to the exclusion of small groups (Jews, Mormons, the unaffiliated) in some of the analyses. Along with developments in the literature, the terminology I used to describe the Protestant groups evolved over time, with "mainline Protestants" and "conservative Protestants" being the terms employed in the latest chapters (Woodberry and Smith 1998). All of the statistical analyses control for family background factors.

Chapter 9 highlights some of the main findings in the previous chapters and critically reviews related US studies on the role of religion in economic and demographic behavior, organizing the discussion around the theoretical framework developed in Chapter 8. Chapter 10 closes the book with a review of analyses conducted in the past few years, a reinterpretation of some of the earlier findings in the literature, and an agenda for future research.

References

Becker, G. S. (1967) *Human Capital and the Personal Distribution of Income*. Woytinsky Lecture No. 1. Ann Arbor: University of Michigan Press.

Becker, G. S. and Chiswick, B. R. (1966) "Education and the Distribution of Earnings." *American Economic Review* 56:358–69.

Becker, G. S., Landes, E. M., and Michael, R. T. (1977) "An Economic Analysis of Marital Instability." *Journal of Political Economy* 85(6):1141–87.

Chiswick, B. (1988) "Differences in Education and Earnings Across Racial and Ethnic Groups: Tastes, Discrimination, and Investments in Child Quality." *Quarterly Journal of Economics* 103(3):571–97.

Chiswick, C. U. and Lehrer, E. L. (1991) "Religious Intermarriage: An Economic Perspective." *Contemporary Jewry* 12:21–34.

Iannaccone, L. R. (1990) "Religious Practice: A Human Capital Approach." *Journal for the Scientific Study of Religion* 29:297–314.

Kelley, D. M. (1972) *Why Conservative Churches Are Growing*. New York: Harper and Row.

Kosmin B. A. and Keysar, A. (2006) *Religion in a Free Market*. Ithaca, NY: Paramount Market Publishing, Inc.

Lehrer, E. (1996) "The Determinants of Marital Stability: A Comparative Analysis of First and Higher Order Marriages." Pp. 91–121 in T. P. Schultz (ed.) *Research in Population Economics*, vol. 8. Greenwich: JAI Press.

Lehrer, E. (2008) "Religious Affiliation and Participation as Determinants of Women's Educational Attainment and Wages." Forthcoming in C. Ellison and R. Hummer (eds.) *Religion, Family Life, and Health in the United States*. Rutgers University Press.

Woodberry, R. D. and Smith, C. S. (1998) "Fundamentalism et al.: Conservative Protestants in America." *Annual Review of Sociology* 24:25–56.

Part I

The role of religion in marriage and divorce

1   Religion as a determinant of marital stability *

Although a growing literature on the determinants of marital stability has accumulated over the past two decades (e.g., Becker et al. 1977; Castro-Martin and Bumpass 1989; Schultz 1991), the role of the religious affiliations of husband and wife has received little attention.[1] This issue has not been studied in depth in part because until recently, there were no large data sets containing for each partner detailed information on both religion and marital history. The National Survey of Families and Households (NSFH), conducted in 1987–88, provides a unique opportunity to quantify the effects of religion on the likelihood of marital dissolution.[2] The survey includes a main sample of 9,643 men and women of all marital statuses, representative of the US population age 19 and over. In addition to abundant socioeconomic and demographic information for the respondents and their first spouses (where applicable), the survey documents marital histories as well as the religious identification of each partner, before and after the respondent's first marriage.[3]

We use these data to analyze how the religious composition of unions influences the likelihood of marital breakup. A more refined set of religion variables is employed here than in previous studies; our specification permits quantification of differences in stability among various types of intrafaith unions, as well as of the extent to which out-marriage is a destabilizing force for members of each major religious group. In addition, whereas most previous analyses have relied on logit or probit regressions, or on simple cross-tabulations, proportional hazards models are used here.[4] Further, we exploit the richness of the information on religion in this survey to analyze an issue that, to the best of our knowledge, has not been studied empirically: the relationship between conversion and the probability of marital dissolution.

Analytical framework

The stability of a marriage depends in complex ways on a wide range of factors. The first section below analyzes the effects associated with the spouses'

* This chapter is by E. Lehrer and C. Chiswick, and is reprinted from *Demography* 30(3):385–404, 1993.

religious affiliations. The second section contains a brief overview of other influences that are known to be important.

The effects of religious composition on marital stability

Religion is a complementary marital trait for which the mating of likes is optimal (Becker 1974). This complementarity arises in part because marital companionship is enhanced when individual spirituality can be shared and is inhibited when the partners must look outside the marriage for religious intimacy. Similarity in the religious beliefs and practices of husband and wife implies that the spouses can participate jointly in religious observances both at home and in the church. Religion also influences many activities beyond the purely religious sphere, including the education and upbringing of children, the allocation of time and money, the cultivation of social relationships, the development of business and professional networks, and even the choice of place of residence. Clearly, households in which the partners differ in their preferences and objectives in this area would be characterized by reduced efficiency and potentially more conflict.

Other things being equal, the complementarity of religion as a marital trait implies that heterogamous unions would display more instability than homogamous unions. Yet compatibility between partners of different faiths may vary with the specific religions involved, depending in part on the similarity in beliefs and practices of the two religions, and in part on the mutual tolerance embodied in their respective doctrines. Following Kelley (1972), we view religious groups as ranging along an "exclusivist–ecumenical" continuum defined by the clarity with which they draw their membership boundaries. At one extreme, "exclusivist" religious groups are those with clear, strictly enforced membership criteria, frequently with proscriptions against out-marriage and sometimes even shunning of nonmembers. At the other extreme, "ecumenical" groups tend to have few membership criteria, often vaguely stated and weakly enforced, and place relatively little importance on religious group boundaries. The location of the spouses' religions along this continuum would influence the stability of an interfaith marriage: the closer to the ecumenical end of the spectrum, the less the marital stress and hence instability that can be expected.

Other dimensions of religious doctrine and ritual have implications not only for the consequences of out-marriage but also for differences in stability across various types of homogamous unions. Religions differ in the importance of family-centered ritual (as distinct from that which is either individual or church-centered), as well as in the compatibility between their practices and beliefs and the customs in the larger society. For religious groups in which such compatibility is low and the role of the family is central, intrafaith unions are expected to be highly stable, and the destabilizing effects of out-marriage particularly pronounced. In addition, relatively high costs of dissolution and correspondingly high marital stability are expected for homogamous marriages involving religions with proscriptions against divorce.

Apart from differences between religious groups, variations in preferences among individuals and couples also play a role. Couples differ in the weight they place on shared activities, including religious observance, and individuals differ in the priority they give to religion and to religious compatibility as a marital trait. These factors influence the degree to which differences in religious beliefs and practices affect stability adversely. Similarly, the extent to which religious complementarities are a stabilizing force for a homogamous marriage depends in part on the importance attached to religion by each of the spouses.

Another factor in the case of intrafaith unions is whether the marriage is "naturally homogamous" or conversionary. A priori it is not clear which of these should be more stable. At least initially, converts would have lower levels of religion-specific human capital – those skills and experiences specific to a particular religion, which include not only knowledge about beliefs and practices but also familiarity with traditions and friendships with coreligionists (Iannaccone 1990). As Schneider (1989, p. 198) observes, "a change in faith does not immediately 'recolor' all the images from a past lived under different assumptions." This imperfect transferability of religion-specific qualities – especially with regard to the emotional, social, and sometimes ethnic components of religious experience – suggests that conversionary couples would have less religious compatibility than their naturally homogamous counterparts, other things being equal. On the other hand, a change of religious affiliation in connection with marriage may signal a high priority placed on religious compatibility during the search process, by the individual or by the spouse, in which case conversionary unions should be highly stable. The importance of this effect is suggested by evidence that levels of religious observance and involvement in the religious community are often high among converts (Billette 1967; Mayer and Avgar 1987).

Other factors affecting marital stability

Age at marriage has been identified as a major determinant of marital stability in previous studies. A very young age is generally associated with short duration of search, suggesting relatively poor information about the partner's characteristics, a high likelihood of divergence from the ideal match, and a high probability of subsequent marital dissolution (Becker 1991).

Like religion, education is generally a complementary trait for which positive assortative mating is optimal.[5] Since this means that individuals with more highly valued characteristics gain more from marriage (Becker 1974), schooling should enhance stability for both men and women. In the case of husband's education, this effect is reinforced by the fact that it is highly correlated with family income. In the case of wife's education, there is a countervailing effect: holding the husband's years of schooling constant, an increase in the wife's education would reduce gains from the traditional division of labor within marriage. Several studies summarized by Michael (1979) find that husband's education and other indicators of economic status indeed have a stabilizing effect. Researchers have obtained conflicting results regarding the net impact of the wife's education (Becker et al. 1977; Michael 1979; Lehrer 1996).

The effects of a broken-home background are ambiguous a priori and may vary with the reason for the dissolution of the marriage (Bumpass and Sweet 1972; Pope and Mueller 1976; Michael 1979; McLanahan and Bumpass 1988). For example, children of divorced parents may view marriage dissolution with greater acceptance. Persons raised in one-parent homes may have more skills or more confidence for managing a household alone, thus reducing the perceived costs of divorce and increasing their readiness to end an unhappy union. On the other hand, their experience may also give them a greater sense of the difficulties of single parenthood and therefore raise such costs. Similar ambiguity is associated with the effect of growing up in a home where the mother is employed: although working mothers make fewer informal investments in certain types of human capital that may enhance the marital stability of their offspring later in life, it is unclear whether they make fewer investments in total; moreover, the effects may vary by the child's sex, the timing of employment, and other factors (Desai et al. 1989; Blau and Grossberg 1992).

Certain experiences before marriage either influence the stability of a union or tend to be associated with unobserved traits that exert such an influence. It has been suggested that transferable marriage-specific skills developed in a previous union would have stabilizing effects in the current union (Chiswick and Lehrer 1990). On the other hand, cohabitation or prior marriage with another partner may reflect a tendency for lower levels of marital commitment, suggesting reduced stability for the current union as well; furthermore, the presence of children from previous formal or informal marriages has been found to have an adverse impact on marital stability (Menken et al. 1981; Teachman 1986; Waite and Lillard 1991; Lehrer 1996).

Methods

The effects of religion on marital stability are analyzed with a proportional hazards procedure (Cox 1972). The model is specified as follows:

$$h_j(t,z) = h_{oj}(t) \exp(\beta'z), \tag{1}$$

where $h(t,z)$ is the hazard of dissolution at time t for a marriage characterized by a vector z of covariates, β is a vector of coefficients, and $h_o(t)$ is an unspecified time-dependent function. On the basis of results from preliminary runs, this function has been allowed to vary by marital cohort: j is 1, 2, or 3 depending on whether the marriage took place in the 1960s, the 1970s, or the 1980s.

The estimated coefficients and their standard errors provide information on the direction and statistical significance of the partial effect of each variable in z. The magnitudes of the influences can be assessed by examining the complement of the survival function, which represents the probability that dissolution has occurred by time t. This probability is $1 - F_j(t,z)$, where

$$F_j(t,z) = \{F_{oj}(t)\}^{\exp(\beta'z)} \tag{2}$$

and

$$F_{oj}(t) = \exp \{ - \int_0^t h_{oj} (u) \, du \}. \tag{3}$$

We use these relationships to estimate the probabilities that unions of couples with different values of z will be dissolved before the fifth anniversary.

The analysis uses data on the first-marriage experiences of respondents from the 1987–88 National Survey of Families and Households (NSFH).[6] The dates of first marriage in these data range from the 1910s to the 1980s; preliminary analyses suggested substantial changes over this long period in the nature of the effects of the explanatory variables on the probability of dissolution. Earlier studies have also documented pronounced racial and ethnic differences in the impact of economic and demographic variables on marital stability (White 1991; Lehrer 1996). Therefore, the present study is limited to a sample of non-Hispanic white respondents whose first marriages were contracted in 1960 or later. After exclusion of cases with missing or invalid codes for key variables, this sample includes 3,060 marriages.

The beginning of a union is taken to be the date of the respondent's first formal marriage; the end is defined as the date of separation, divorce, or death of spouse, as applicable. Where separation was followed by divorce, only the date of divorce is available. (Although it would have been preferable to use the date of separation, this limitation of the data is unlikely to pose a serious problem for white women, who are the focus of this study.) Intact marriages and those ending in widowhood are treated as censored at the time of the interview and at the spouse's death respectively. In the sample used here, the respondent's first marriage was intact in 1,856 cases; it had ended in separation, divorce, or widowhood in 85, 1,053, and 66 cases, respectively.

Although the NSFH documents in detail the characteristics of the respondent's first marriage, the survey treatment of respondents and their spouses was not always symmetric. Some variables are available for the former but not for the latter. In addition, if the marriage had been dissolved by the time of the survey, questions regarding the first spouse's religion and other traits were addressed to the respondent; if the union was still intact, information about the respondent's husband or wife was obtained from a questionnaire administered directly to the spouse.

As for the explanatory variable of central interest, the NSFH identifies more than 60 religious groups, most of which are Protestant denominations.

These are divided here into seven categories, as shown in Table 1.1. Protestant denominations are classified as either "ecumenical" or "exclusivist," on the basis of the continuum suggested by Kelley (1972). Mormons are placed in a separate category because they are a relatively large denomination with distinctive patterns of demographic behavior. Additional categories identify Roman Catholics, Jews, and persons with no religion, each of which is reported in the NSFH without detail on subgroups. In particular, the "no religion" group includes atheists and agnostics as well as individuals who have no religion for other reasons (e.g., being a child from an interfaith union). A residual category, "other religion," includes all other affiliations.

The NSFH records each spouse's religious preference both before and after

Table 1.1 Definition of religious groups

Religion categories employed in this study	NSFH categories included in each group[a]
Ecumenical Protestant	Church of Brethren, Community Churches, Disciples of Christ, Episcopalian, Lutheran, Methodist, Presbyterian, Reformed Church, Unitarian, United Church of Christ, all other members of reformed Presbyterian churches and other liberal churches, Protestant – no denomination given.
Exclusivist Protestant	Assembly of God, Baptist, "Born-Again Christian," Christian and Missionary Alliance, Christian Congregation, Christian Reformed, Christian Scientist, Churches of Christ, Church of God-Anderson, Church of God – Cleveland, Church of God, Church of God in Christ, Church of the Nazarene, Evangelical Covenant Church, Evangelical Free Church, Full Gospel Fellowship, International Church of the Foursquare Gospel, Jehovah's Witness, Mennonite Church, Pentecostal, Salvation Army, Seventh-Day Adventist, Wesleyan, other members of Adventist, European Free Church, Holiness, Independent Fundamentalist, Pentecostal, Pietist, and Restoration families, "Christian."
Catholic	Roman Catholic.
Jewish	Jewish.
Mormon	Mormon, Reorganized Church of Jesus Christ of Latter-Day Saints.
Other religions	Buddhist, Charismatic, Communal groups, Hindu, Islamic, New Thought Family, Orthodox churches, Personal churches, Psychic groups, Ritual Magick groups, Shinto and Taoism, other Western Catholic churches, other miscellaneous religious bodies.
No religion	No religion.

Note
a The religions listed in this column correspond exactly to the NSFH codes. For example, all of the various Baptist groups are identified simply as "Baptist" in these data.

the date of marriage, and indicates whether either spouse changed affiliation in connection with the marriage.[7] Homogamy is defined here as occurring when both spouses have the same NSFH code after the date of marriage, with the exception of Mormons; in that case, homogamous unions include all of those in which both spouses have one of the two codes shown in Table 1.1 (Mormon, Reorganized Church of Jesus Christ of Latter Day Saints). Homogamous unions are identified with a series of dummy variables corresponding to the seven categories described above. The means of these variables are reported in Table 1.2, Panel 1. In order to analyze the effects of conversion, we further subdivide the three largest groups according to whether one of the partners changed his or her religion to achieve homogamy; the means for these subcategories are reported in Table 1.7.

Panel 2 in Table 1.2 displays means of dummy variables for various types of heterogamous marriages. Unions among Protestants with different NSFH codes have been grouped according to whether they belong to the same major category (ecumenical or exclusivist). Because of sample size considerations,

Table 1.2 Religion variables

Variable	Mean
Panel 1	
Both ecumenical Protestant, same NSFH code (benchmark)	(0.153)
Both exclusivist Protestant, same NSFH code	0.152
Both Catholic	0.168
Both Jewish	0.019
Both Mormon	0.026
Both other religion, same NSFH code	0.004
Both no religion	0.035
Panel 2	
Both ecumenical Protestant, different NSFH code	0.062
Both exclusivist Protestant, different NSFH code	0.021
Ecumenical Protestant, exclusivist Protestant	0.086
Ecumenical Protestant, Catholic	0.079
Exclusivist Protestant, Catholic	0.029
Intermarriage involving Jew[a]	0.014
Intermarriage involving Mormon[a]	0.014
Intermarriage involving other religion[b]	0.015
No religion – ecumenical Protestant	0.055
No religion – exclusivist Protestant	0.033
No religion – Catholic	0.036

Notes
a The category "Intermarriage involving Mormon" includes all couples in which one of the partners is a Mormon and the other has a different religious affiliation or no religion. The category "Intermarriage involving Jew" is defined similarly. There are no Mormon–Jewish intermarriages in these data.
b The category "Intermarriage involving other religion" includes all couples in which one of the partners has an affiliation belonging to the "other religion" group, and the other partner is Protestant, is Catholic, has no religion, or has a faith in the "other religion" group with a different NSFH code.

the dummies for intermarriages involving Jews, Mormons, and groups in the residual category do not specify the other partner's religion. (As it turns out, these data contain no intermarriages between Mormons and Jews or between Mormons and members of the "other" group; the two unions between Jews and individuals with religions in the residual category are included in the group of Jewish intermarriages.) Taken together, the series of dummy variables in Table 1.2 constitute a mutually exclusive and exhaustive set. This specification permits substantial flexibility, allowing stability to vary across different types of homogamous and heterogamous unions.[8]

Definitions and means for the variables used as controls are presented in Table 1.3. These include dummies for the wife's age at marriage and for the education levels of the two partners, for whether either of them had been married previously, and for whether their families of origin were not intact because of a parent's death or for another reason. Controls available only for the respondent include premarital cohabitation with other partner(s), the presence of an out-of-wedlock child, and the mother's employment status during early childhood. We interact these variables with the respondent's gender to permit their effects to differ between men and women.

Ideally, we would have included indicators of religiosity among the controls, interacting them with the religious composition dummies. Although the NSFH includes information on the respondent's frequency of attendance at religious services, the question refers to the time of the survey rather than to the first marriage. Thus it raises the possibility of reverse causality – from the quality and stability of the marriage to religious participation. For remarried respondents, this variable is contaminated further by the subsequent marriage experience(s). For these reasons, we do not include measures of religiosity in the present analysis.[9]

Results

The first section below focuses on the impact on marital stability of religious composition measured after the date of marriage; the second presents a respecification of the model designed to study the effects of conversion.

The estimated effects of religious composition

The Cox coefficients and standard errors are presented in Table 1.4. The reference category consists of homogamous unions belonging to Protestant denominations classified as "ecumenical"; all reported t-tests for the religion variables involve comparisons with this group. Also displayed are estimated probabilities of dissolution by the fifth year, which represent the complement of the survival function evaluated at five years and at the value of the explanatory variable indicated in the stub, with all other variables at the benchmark.[10] For the sake of brevity, we report only estimates for the 1980s marriage cohort.[11]

Table 1.3 Control variables

Variable	Definition	Mean
Wife's age at marriage	= 1 if wife's age at marriage is in category indicated	
≤ 18 years		0.215
19–24 years (benchmark)		(0.596)
25–29 years		0.136
30–34 years		0.038
≥ 35 years		0.015
Wife's Education	= 1 if wife's years of schooling at date of marriage is in the category indicated	
< 12 years		0.192
12 years (benchmark)		(0.396)
13–15 years		0.257
≥16 years		0.155
Husband's education	= 1 if husband's years of schooling at date of marriage is in the category indicated	
< 12 years		0.160
12 years (benchmark)		(0.400)
13–15 years		0.233
≥ 16 years		0.207
Wife's family not intact because of:	= 1 if wife's family of origin was not intact at age 14 for the reason indicated (benchmark is intact family)	
Death of parent		0.044
Other reasons		0.142
Husband's family not intact because of:	= 1 if husband's family of origin was not intact at age 14 for the reason indicated (benchmark is intact family)	
Death of parent		0.052
Other reasons		0.118
Male	= 1 if respondent is male	0.443
Mother's employment	= 1 if respondent's mother held a paid job for 12 months or more when he/she was 5 years old or younger	0.285
Mother's employment × Male	interaction term	0.134
Wife previously married	= 1 if wife had been married before	0.054
Husband previously married	= 1 if husband had been married before	0.078
Out-of-wedlock child	= 1 if respondent had a child before the date of first marriage	0.057
Out-of-wedlock child × male	interaction term	0.022
Other partners	= 1 if respondent cohabited with other partner(s) before his/her first marriage	0.057
Other partners × male	interaction term	0.036

Table 1.4 The effects of the religious composition of unions on marriage dissolution

	Cox regression coefficients and standard errors	Estimated fifth-year dissolution probabilities[a]
Religion variables		
Panel 1		
Both ecumenical Protestant, same NSFH code (benchmark)	–	0.20
Both exclusivist Protestant, same NSFH code	–0.078 (0.120)	0.19
Both Catholic	0.021 (0.119)	0.20
Both Jewish	0.336 (0.277)	0.27
Both Mormon	–0.493 (0.266)*	0.13
Both other religion, same NSFH code	–0.443 (0.714)	0.13
Both no religion	0.714 (0.167)**	0.36
Panel 2		
Both ecumenical Protestant, different NSFH code	0.229 (0.152)#	0.24
Both exclusivist Protestant, different NSFH code	0.522 (0.210)**	0.31
Ecumenical Protestant, exclusivist Protestant	0.422 (0.128)**	0.29
Ecumenical Protestant, Catholic	0.760 (0.130)**	0.38
Exclusivist Protestant, Catholic	0.630 (0.177)**	0.34
Intermarriage involving Jew	0.901 (0.248)**	0.42
Intermarriage involving Mormon	0.832 (0.224)**	0.40
Intermarriage involving other religion	0.855 (0.232)**	0.41
No religion – ecumenical Protestant	0.510 (0.146)**	0.31
No religion – exclusivist Protestant	0.682 (0.165)**	0.35
No religion – Catholic	0.777 (0.169)**	0.38
Control variables		
Wife's age at marriage		
≤ 18 years	0.340 (0.086)**	0.27
25–29 years	–0.369 (0.116)**	0.14
30–34 years	–0.729 (0.235)**	0.10
≥ 35 years	–1.317(0.457)**	0.06
Wife's education		
< 12 years	0.107 (0.089)	0.22
13–15 years	–0.086 (0.087)	0.18
≥ 16 years	–0.354 (0.128)**	0.14
Husband's education		
< 12 years	0.061 (0.082)	0.21
13–15 years	–0.270 (0.086)**	0.16
≥ 16 years	–0.284 (0.106)**	0.15
Wife's family not intact because of		
Death of parent	0.022 (0.141)	0.20
Other reasons	0.209 (0.083)**	0.24
Husband's family not intact because of		
Death of parent	0.360 (0.121)**	0.27
Other reasons	0.202 (0.088)**	0.24

Male respondent	−0.290 (0.081)**	0.15
Mother's employment[b]		
Female respondent[c]	0.151 (0.086)*	0.23
Male respondent[c]	0.231 (0.103)**	0.19
Wife previously married	0.660 (0.150)**	0.35
Husband previously married	0.243 (0.112)**	0.25
Out-of-wedlock child		
Female respondent	0.357 (0.153)**	0.27
Male respondent	−0.072 (0.222)	0.14
Other partners		
Female respondent	0.627 (0.198)**	0.34
Male respondent	0.351 (0.180)*	0.21
Log-likelihood	−7,221.0	
χ^2(df)	450.3**(40)	

\# $p \leq 0.15$; * $p \leq 0.10$; ** $p \leq 0.05$.
N = 3,060

Notes
a The figures in this column represent the fifth-year dissolution probability for the most recent marriage cohort (1980s), evaluated for a couple with the characteristics indicated in the stub and all the other variables set at 0. For example, the first number in this column, 0.20, corresponds to a homogamous ecumenical Protestant couple with the following nonreligious characteristics: the wife's age at marriage is 19–24, both spouses had completed 12 years of schooling at the time of marriage, their families of origin were intact at age 14, neither spouse had been married before; the respondent did not have an out-of-wedlock child and did not cohabit with other partners before the first marriage, and the mother was not employed when the respondent was 5 years old or younger; the respondent is female. Similarly, the second number in this column, 0.19, corresponds to a homogamous exclusivist Protestant couple with the same nonreligious characteristics. The effects of all the control variables are evaluated for a homogamous ecumenical Protestant couple.
b The model includes a dummy variable for male respondent, a dummy for mother's employment, and an interaction term between these two variables. The coefficient for the mother's employment dummy is reported in the row labeled "female respondent." The estimates in the "male respondent" row represent the sum of the coefficients on the mother's employment dummy and the interaction term, and the corresponding standard error. Similar remarks apply to the variables for out-of-wedlock child and other partners.
c The benchmark case – both spouses ecumenical Protestant (same NSFH code), all control variables set at 0 – corresponds to a female respondent. Thus the fifth-year dissolution probability for a female respondent whose mother was employed during early childhood, 0.23, should be compared with 0.20, the probability for a female respondent whose mother was not employed in this period. In contrast, the probabilities for the case of male respondents are 0.19 (mother was employed) and 0.15 (mother was not employed). Similar remarks apply to the variables for out-of-wedlock child and other partners.

In order to provide a full picture of the relative stability of different types of homogamous marriages, additional comparisons are necessary. Whereas all the t-tests reported in Table 1.4 are conducted with reference to ecumenical Protestants as the omitted category, information on the variance–covariance matrix is used in Table 1.5 to test the statistical significance of the difference between the coefficients for each pair of intrafaith unions. These pairwise comparisons reveal no significant differences at the 0.05 or 0.10 levels in the stability of homogamous unions involving ecumenical Protestants, exclusivist

Table 1.5 Comparisons among various types of homogamous marriages: differences between estimated fifth-year dissolution probabilities[a]

Type of homogamous union	Ecumenical Protestant	Exclusivist Protestant	Catholic	Jewish	Mormon	Other religion
Exclusivist Protestant	-0.01	—	—	—	—	—
Catholic	0.00	0.01	—	—	—	—
Jewish	0.07	0.08#	0.07	—	—	—
Mormon	-0.07*	-0.06#	-0.07*	-0.14**	—	—
Other religion	-0.07	-0.06	-0.07	-0.14	0.00	—
No religion	0.16**	0.17**	0.16**	0.09	0.23**	0.23#

$p \leq 0.15$; * $p \leq 0.10$; ** $p \leq 0.05$.

Note

a This table reports pairwise differences between the fifth-year dissolution probabilities for homogamous unions as reported in Table 1.4, Panel 1, and significance tests for the differences between the corresponding coefficients. For example, the value -0.06 in the fourth row, second column was calculated by subtracting the fifth-year dissolution probability for homogamous exclusivist Protestant couples (0.19) from that for homogamous Mormon couples (0.13). A t-test for the difference between the coefficients for both Mormon (-0.493) and both exclusivist Protestant, same NSFH code (-0.078), reveals that it is significant at the 0.15 level. Other values and significance tests reported in this table were obtained in a similar way.

Protestants, Catholics, Jews, and members of the "other" category – groups which together represent 89 percent of all intrafaith marriages. Pronounced differences emerge for two small groups, however. With fifth-year dissolution probabilities of 0.13 and 0.36 respectively, homogamous Mormon marriages are the most stable and those among two persons reporting "no religion" the least stable.

The remarkable stability of Mormon marriages is consistent with the fact that this is a small group whose religious beliefs and practices differ substantially from the majority culture, and for which the role of the family is central. As Foster (1982, p. 7) observes, Mormonism "is not simply concerned with the family, as are so many other groups; the Mormon religion in the last analysis really is *about* the family." At the other extreme, the high instability of unions in which the partners have no religion underscores the importance of religion per se for marital stability. Because of the heterogeneity of the "no religion" group in this survey, it is unclear to what extent this result reflects outright rejection of religion or merely very low commitment to religious affiliation.

Most previous studies of religious group differences in marital stability focus on Catholic–Protestant comparisons. Those using data from earlier periods find Catholic unions to be generally more stable, a result attributed to the strong antidivorce position of the Catholic Church (Burchinal and Chancellor 1963; Christensen and Barber 1967; Michael 1979). Analyses of more recent data, however, suggest a convergence in Protestant and Catholic marital stability (McCarthy 1979), and it is noteworthy that no stability advantages associated with the Catholic religion are discerned here.[12] Similarly, the relatively high stability of Jewish marriages suggested by data from earlier periods is not evident in these data (Christensen and Barber 1967; Kobrin Goldscheider 1986).

Regarding the effects of intermarriage, a comparison of the fifth-year dissolution probabilities for homogamous and heterogamous unions in Table 1.4 suggests that marital instability is generally higher for the latter. A complete set of pairwise comparisons is reported in Table 1.6. This table compares the stability of unions between spouses of the same religious affiliation with various types of heterogamous marriages involving a member of that group, and thus provides information on the extent to which out-marriage is a destabilizing force for individuals with various religious affiliations.

The magnitude of the effects associated with intermarriage varies markedly with the degree of mutual compatibility between the groups involved. For example, the top portion of Table 1.6 shows that out-marriage of an ecumenical Protestant to another ecumenical Protestant of a different denomination raises the fifth-year dissolution probability by four percentage points, an effect which is significant only at the 0.15 level. This result is in accordance with expectations since the Protestant denominations classified as ecumenical are those for which membership boundaries are loosely defined and enforced. In contrast, when an ecumenical Protestant marries an exclusivist Protestant,

Table 1.6 Comparisons between intra- and interfaith unions: differences between estimated fifth-year dissolution probabilities[a]

Religious groups under comparison	Increase in instability associated with intermarriage
Both ecumenical Protestant, same NSFH code vs.	
Both ecumenical Protestant, different NSFH code	0.04#
Ecumenical Protestant – exclusivist Protestant	0.09**
Ecumenical Protestant – Catholic	0.18**
Ecumenical Protestant – no religion	0.11**
Both exclusivist Protestant, same NSFH code vs.	
Both exclusivist Protestant, different NSFH code	0.12**
Exclusivist Protestant – ecumenical Protestant	0.10**
Exclusivist Protestant – Catholic	0.15**
Exclusivist Protestant – no religion	0.16**
Both Catholic vs.	
Catholic – ecumenical Protestant	0.18**
Catholic – exclusivist Protestant	0.14**
Catholic – no religion	0.18**
Both Jewish vs.	
Intermarriage involving Jew	0.15#
Both Mormon vs.	
Intermarriage involving Mormon	0.27**
Both other religion, same NSFH code vs.	
Intermarriage involving other religion	0.28*
Both no religion vs.	
Ecumenical Protestant – no religion	−0.05
Exclusivist Protestant – no religion	−0.01
Catholic – no religion	0.02

$p \leq 0.15$; * $p \leq 0.10$; ** $p \leq 0.05$.

Note

a This table reports pairwise differences between the fifth-year dissolution probabilities for various heterogamous unions and each type of homogamous union, and the statistical significance of the difference between the corresponding coefficients. For example, the value 0.18 in the row for both Catholic vs. Catholic–ecumenical Protestant was calculated as follows: the fifth-year dissolution probability for a Catholic–ecumenical Protestant couple is 0.38; the probability for a homogamous Catholic couple is 0.20 (see Table 1.4). Thus when a Catholic marries an ecumenical Protestant rather than another Catholic, the fifth-year dissolution probability rises by 0.18. A t-test for the difference between the corresponding coefficients (0.760 vs. 0.021) reveals that it is statistically significant at the 0.05 level. Other values and significance tests in this table were obtained in a similar way.

the probability rises by nine percentage points and the difference is highly significant. Similarly, out-marriage of an exclusivist Protestant to another exclusivist Protestant of a different denomination raises the dissolution probability substantially, by 12 percentage points. The results also show that the destabilizing effects of out-marriage for Protestants tend to be higher when the partner is Catholic: in the case of ecumenical Protestants, union to a Catholic raises the probability by 18 percentage points; for exclusivist Protestants, the increase is 15 percentage points. This finding may reflect generally more pronounced differences in religious beliefs and practices between Protestants and Catholics than among the various Protestant denominations.

Out-marriage increases the fifth-year dissolution probability by 27 percentage points for Mormons and by 28 points for members of the residual category. These large effects are consistent with the facts that Mormonism and most religions in the "other" category tend to be exclusivist in nature, and that they have distinctive religious practices which are not incorporated into everyday American life. The destabilizing effect of out-marriage for Jews – an increase of 15 percentage points – is smaller and weaker in significance, perhaps because a large fraction of American Jews belong to groups near the ecumenical end of the exclusivist–ecumenical gradient. Finally, the marital stability of couples consisting of two individuals with no religious affiliation does not differ significantly from that of couples in which one member has no religion; this result holds whether the other partner is ecumenical Protestant, exclusivist Protestant, or Catholic.

The control variables generally are significant with the expected signs. Age at marriage has a pronounced effect on marital stability: the older the age, the more stable the union. With regard to schooling, men and women with college education have the lowest probability of marriage dissolution. A broken-home background is associated with an increased risk of marital instability for men. Among women who lost a parent, unions appear to be as stable as those of their counterparts raised in intact homes; those with a nonintact family of origin for other reasons have a higher likelihood of marital breakup. Maternal employment is associated with somewhat higher levels of instability, but the effect is only marginally significant in the case of women. A previous marriage is associated with a higher probability of disruption; this influence is particularly pronounced when it was the wife who entered the union with a previous marital history. Premarital cohabitation with other partners is also associated with relatively high rates of instability. Finally, the presence of an out-of-wedlock child has a destabilizing impact for female respondents, but no effect is discerned for males.

By examining the influences of these various control variables we can assess the relative magnitude of the impact of religious intermarriage. The probabilities in Table 1.4 show that among all the factors considered here, the effects associated with religious intermarriage are clearly among the largest. Excluding couples without a religious affiliation, the fifth-year dissolution probability for homogamous unions ranges between 0.13 and 0.27; for heterogamous couples, the probability ranges from 0.24 for the most stable intermarriages to 0.42 for the least stable. With the exception of age at marriage, changes in none of the other variables considered here produce such a large a variation in the probability of marital dissolution. The finding that the effect of religious intermarriage on the likelihood of marital breakup is large compared to that of other known determinants of stability is consistent with results based on a different data set and on much cruder measures of religious composition (Lehrer 1996).

An assumption that underlies the above analysis – as well as all previous studies in this literature – is that the propensity to intermarry is uncorrelated with unobserved factors. Yet this assumption may not hold in practice because of persistent differences among individuals in preferences, endowments, and constraints on their behavior. The same unobserved factors that lead an individual to enter an interfaith union may later influence the stability of the marriage. Insofar as persons who intermarry are disproportionately those with unobserved negative traits, the estimated coefficients on the intermarriage variables would overstate the adverse impact of low religious compatibility on marital stability.[13] On the other hand, tradeoffs play an important role in the marriage market (Chiswick and Lehrer 1991; Grossbard-Shechtman 1993). If awareness of the potentially large adverse effects associated with intermarriage leads people to enter an interfaith union only when the match in other dimensions is particularly good, the estimated coefficients would tend to understate the adverse consequences of low religious compatibility. The net direction of these biases is ambiguous a priori. Because of the richness of the controls included in this analysis, however, they are likely to be considerably less serious here than in previous research on the consequences of intermarriage.

Religious conversion and marital stability

In order to study the role of conversion, we now subdivide homogamous unions in the three larger categories (ecumenical Protestant, exclusivist Protestant, and Catholic) into two groups depending on whether one of the spouses changed affiliation to the religion of the other in connection with the marriage. We reestimate the basic model using as benchmark those ecumenical Protestant unions which are naturally homogamous. The means, coefficients, standard errors, and dissolution probabilities associated with these variables are displayed in Table 1.7. The results pertaining to the other religion variables and the controls remain virtually unchanged and are omitted.

For exclusivist Protestants and Catholics, there are no significant differences in the stability of naturally homogamous and conversionary marriages. However, in the case of ecumenical Protestants, we find that unions involving a convert are significantly more stable than those whose members shared the same faith before the marriage. The effect is large: the fifth-year dissolution probability for a naturally homogamous ecumenical Protestant couple is 0.24, but it is only 0.13 if one of the spouses converted at the time of marriage.[14] For this group the stabilizing influence of a commitment to religious compatibility clearly outweighs any adverse effects associated with imperfect transferability of religion-specific human capital. Such capital may matter less in the ecumenical Protestant denominations because of their high levels of

Table 1.7 Conversion and marital stability[a]

Type of homogamous union	Means	Cox regression coefficients and standard errors	t-tests for pairwise comparisons: No. Conversion vs. Conversion	Estimated fifth-year dissolution probability
Ecumenical Protestant, nonconversionary	(0.095)	benchmark		0.24
Ecumenical Protestant, conversionary	0.058	−0.648 (0.199)**	3.26**	0.13
Exclusivist Protestant, nonconversionary	0.121	−0.273 (0.137)**		0.19
Exclusivist Protestant, conversionary	0.030	−0.420 (0.215)*	0.70	0.16
Catholic, nonconversionary	0.129	−0.187 (0.139)		0.20
Catholic, conversionary	0.039	−0.265 (0.197)	0.40	0.19

\# $p \le 0.15$; * $p \le 0.10$; ** $p \le 0.05$.

Note

a The sample size for this model, $N = 3{,}033$, is slightly smaller than that for the previous regressions because we eliminated cases with missing information on whether one of the spouses converted at the time of marriage. This regression includes all the control variables, as well as all the religion dummy variables in the Table 1.4 model, except those for homogamous Catholic and exclusivist Protestant couples. The fifth-year dissolution probabilities for inter-marriages yielded by this model are virtually identical to those reported in Table 1.4, Panel 2; the same is true for the homogamous marriages involving Jews, Mormons, members of the residual category, and those with no religion.

tolerance for other religious beliefs and practices. In addition, the dominance of mainline Protestantism in the American culture may result in widespread acquisition of its religious capital even among individuals raised in other faiths.

Viewed from a different angle, the results suggest that differences between the spouses in religious background do not affect marital stability adversely if one of the partners converts in order to achieve homogamy. At least for these groups, the important factor in stability is not similarity in religious background but rather the religious compatibility between the partners at the time of marriage and thereafter. An intriguing question for future investigations is whether the same results hold for Mormonism, Judaism, and other religions that could not be studied here because of limitations in sample size.

Conclusions

This research has increased our understanding of the role played by the religious composition of unions as a determinant of marital stability in two main ways. We have used more refined measures of such composition than previous studies and we have explored reasons why the probability of breakup might differ across various types of homogamous and heterogamous unions. Analysis of the first-marriage experiences of white, non-Hispanic respondents from the 1987–88 National Survey of Families and Households reveals that religious heterogamy is generally associated with a higher likelihood of marital dissolution, consistent with the view that less efficiency and more conflict characterize households where the spouses differ in their religious preferences. Intermarriage, however, comes in different shades and degrees; the magnitude of its destabilizing effect varies considerably with the degree of dissimilarity between the religious beliefs and practices of the two groups, and with the clarity with which they define their respective boundaries. Comparisons among different types of intrafaith marriages show that stability generally does not differ significantly by religious affiliation. Exceptions are Mormon unions and those involving two partners with no religious identification, which are, respectively, the most and the least stable. Among Protestants and Catholics, couples who have achieved homogamy through conversion are found to be at least as stable as those involving two members who had the same religion before marriage, by a substantial margin in the case of ecumenical Protestants. At least for these groups, religious compatibility between the spouses at the time of marriage and therafter dominates any adverse effects of differences in religious background.

The specification of the religion variables used in this study, making distinctions between various types of intra- and interfaith marriages, has uncovered effects that had gone unnoticed in earlier research. Previous analyses of variations in divorce rates by religion, using either aggregate data or micro data but focusing only on the wife's religious affiliation, confound the dissolution rates for homogamous and heterogamous unions (McCarthy 1979; Smith 1985). The case of Mormons demonstrates particularly clearly why the distinctions made here are important. Finding relatively high Mormon divorce rates overall, Smith (1985, p. 287) observes: "Statistics on Mormon divorce rates provide a surprising contrast to the family-oriented Mormon practices of marrying early and creating large families." The present analysis suggests that in fact there is no contrast: although the probability of marital breakup is extremely high for Mormon intermarriages, homogamous Mormon unions are remarkably stable.

The strong observed effects of religious compatibility on marital stability raise additional questions for future research. For example, is religiosity a significant mediating factor in the relationship between the religious composition of unions and the probability of dissolution? Does gender matter – that is, for a given type of intermarriage, are there differentials that depend on which spouse is affiliated with which religion? How do the results reported here for non-Hispanic whites compare to those for other racial and ethnic groups? And how have the effects of religious composition changed over time? We hope that the results presented here will encourage further research on the complex relationships between religion and marital stability.

Acknowledgments

We are indebted to Avery Guest, Belton Fleisher, and three anonymous referees for many helpful comments, and to Hanying Yu for her skillful research assistance. An earlier version of this chapter was presented at the meetings of the Population Association of America, held in Denver, April 30–May 2, 1992.

Notes

1   Several studies have reported that interfaith marriage has a negative effect on marital stability (Burchinal and Chancellor 1963; Christensen and Barber 1967; Bumpass and Sweet 1972; Becker et al. 1977; Michael 1979; Lehrer 1996), but intermarriage is the central focus of the analysis only in Burchinal and Chancellor. Recently the impact of religious heterogamy on marital satisfaction and other measures of marital quality has been examined also (Glenn 1982; Heaton 1984; Heaton and Pratt 1990). Other analyses have compared divorce rates among various religious groups (McCarthy 1979; Smith 1985; Kobrin Goldscheider 1986).

2   This survey was designed at the Center for Demography and Ecology at the University of Wisconsin-Madison under the direction of Larry Bumpass and James Sweet. The fieldwork was done by the Institute for Survey Research at Temple University.

3   The religion categories employed in this survey are considerably more detailed than those available in the various cycles of the National Survey of Family Growth. The post-1984 cycles of the General Social Surveys contain still more refined categories, but lack information on the spouse's religion for unions that had been dissolved by the time of the interview.

4   Logit and probit models are necessarily arbitrary in the selection of interval lengths, and do not use information on the timing of the dissolution within the period under consideration. For an empirical comparison of the performance of logit and proportional hazards models, see Tuma and Michael (1986).

5   This is so because of complementarities in home production. In addition, Lam (1988) has suggested that joint consumption of household public goods generates a tendency for positive assortative mating on wages. Because of the association between education and wages, this effect also would imply positive assortative mating by education.

6   Ideally, separate analyses would have been conducted depending on whether the respondent's spouse had been married before, because first and higher-order marriage experiences differ in complex ways (Lehrer 1996). Unfortunately, limitations of sample size rule out this possibility.

7   Respondents were asked "What is your religious preference?" Where changes took place, further questions were asked, including "Did you change your religion in connection with your (first) marriage?", "What was your religious preference before you changed at that time?" and "What religion did you change to at that time?" Similar information was obtained about the respondent's first spouse in the

case of unions that had been dissolved by the time of the survey. For respondents whose first marriages were still intact, the survey documents the spouse's religious affiliation at the interview date and just before the change, if conversion took place in connection with the current union.

8 We also considered the alternative statistical specification of including dummy variables for the husband's and wife's religious affiliations as well as interaction terms between these variables. We decided against this approach for three main reasons. First, earlier work by Bean and Aiken (1976) found this type of model to be problematic for analyzing the effects of the religious composition of unions because of the high correlation between the spouses' affiliations. Second, the sample sizes for many of the religious groups are too small in the present data set to permit the distinctions by gender which this specification requires. Third, in the model we chose it is easier to make the types of comparisons and significance tests in which we are interested. For example, in order to compare the stability of intrafaith Mormon and Catholic marriages, all that needs to be done is to test whether the coefficient on the dummy for homogamous Mormon unions differs significantly from that for homogamous Catholic unions. This comparison is considerably more complicated in the alternative specification, which would include dummies for Mormon husband, Mormon wife, Catholic husband, Catholic wife, and interactions for all possible combinations of these.

9 Exploring the mediating role of religiosity is less problematic in an analysis of the determinants of marital satisfaction (as opposed to stability) for couples that are intact at the time of the interview. Heaton (1984) and Heaton and Pratt (1990) have estimated such models.

10 For respondents in intact first marriages at the time of the survey, the spouse's characteristics are not available if he or she failed to complete the questionnaire; 222 observations were lost on this account. To assess the extent to which the estimated probabilities of dissolution by the fifth year are affected by this limitation of the data, we respecified the model in Table 1.4 by dropping all the characteristics of the spouse and by replacing the variables for the religious composition of the union with a series of dummies for the respondent's religion (with ecumenical Protestants as the benchmark). We estimated this revised model twice, first using all the observations and then excluding the 222 cases in question. For the 1980s cohort, the fifth-year dissolution probability for the reference case in the second situation exceeds that in the first by three percentage points, providing an estimate for the upward bias in the probabilities reported in Table 1.4.

11 For the benchmark case (both partners ecumenical Protestants, all control variables set at 0), the fifth-year dissolution probability for the 1980s cohort is 0.20, as shown in Table 1.4. For the 1960s and 1970s cohorts respectively, the corresponding figures are 0.10 and 0.16. Note that although the time-dependent function has been allowed to vary by cohort, a single set of coefficients is estimated for the entire period.

12 In their analyses of recent Australian data, Bracher et al. (1993) also find that Catholics are not at lower risk of marital disruption than members of other religious groups. In addition, the present results are consistent with changes in the effects of Catholic religion on fertility in the United States; as shown by Mosher et al. (1992), among others, the pattern of high Catholic family size that formerly prevailed has ended.

13 For example, Bumpass and Sweet (1972, p. 760) observe that "intermarriages may be selective of persons less able to compete in the prescribed market." Along similar lines, Becker (1991, p. 337) notes that "some persons enter mixed marriages ... because they are inefficient at discovering suitable prospects or have other characteristics that lower their expected gains from marriage."

14 This pronounced difference raises the question as to whether it may be necessary

to qualify the earlier conclusion that all homogamous unions, except those involving Mormons and individuals with no religion, are equally stable. In the case of conversionary couples, t-tests for pairwise comparisons between ecumenical Protestant, exclusivist Protestant, and Catholic unions reveal no significant differences at the 0.05 or 0.10 levels. The corresponding comparisons in the case of natural homogamy show that ecumenical Protestant unions are less stable than exclusivist Protestant unions; the other two differences are insignificant.

References

Bean, F. and Aiken, L. (1976) "Intermarriage and Unwanted Fertility in the United States." *Journal of Marriage and the Family* 38(1):61–72.

Becker, G. S. (1974) "A Theory of Marriage." Pp. 299–344 in T. W. Schultz (ed.) *Economics of the Family*. Chicago: University of Chicago Press.

Becker, G. S. (1991) *A Treatise on the Family*. Cambridge, MA and London: Harvard University Press.

Becker, G. S., Landes, E. M., and Michael, R. T. (1977) "An Economic Analysis of Marital Instability." *Journal of Political Economy* 85(6):1141–87.

Billette, A. (1967) "Conversion and Consonance: A Sociology of White American Catholic Converts." *Review of Religious Research* 8(2):100–4.

Blau, F. D. and Grossberg A. J. (1992) "Maternal Labor Supply and Children's Cognitive Development." *Review of Economics and Statistics* 74:474–81.

Bracher, M., Santow G., and Trussell, J. (1993) "Marital Dissolution in Australia: Models and Explanations." *Population Studies* 47(3):403–25.

Bumpass, L. L. and Sweet, J. A. (1972) "Differentials in Marital Stability: 1970." *American Sociological Review* 37(6):754–66.

Burchinal, L. G. and Chancellor, L. E. (1963) "Survival Rates among Religiously Homogamous and Interreligious Marriages." *Social Forces* 41(4):353–62.

Castro-Martin, T. and Bumpass L. L. (1989) "Recent Trends in Marital Disruption." *Demography* 26(1):37–52.

Chiswick, C. U. and Lehrer, E. L. (1990) "On Marriage-Specific Human Capital: Its Role as a Determinant of Remarriage." *Journal of Population Economics* 3:193–213.

Chiswick, C. U. and Lehrer, E. L. (1991) "Religious Intermarriage: An Economic Perspective." *Contemporary Jewry* 12:21–34.

Christensen, H. T. and Barber, K. E. (1967) "Interfaith versus Intrafaith Marriage in Indiana." *Journal of Marriage and the Family* 29(3):461–9.

Cox, D. R. (1972) "Regression Models and Life Tables." *Journal of the Royal Statistical Society* B34:187–202.

Desai, S. P., Chase-Lansdale, L., and Michael, R.T. (1989) "Mother or Market? Effects of Maternal Employment on the Intellectual Ability of 4-Year Old Children." *Demography* 26(4):545–62.

Foster, L. (1982) "Between Heaven and Earth." *Sunstone* 7:7–15.

Glenn, N. D. (1982) "Interreligious Marriage in the United States: Patterns and Recent Trends." *Journal of Marriage and the Family* 44:555–66.

Grossbard-Shechtman, S. (1993) *On the Economics of Marriage: A Theory of Marriage, Labor and Divorce*. Boulder, CO: Westview.

Heaton, T. B. (1984) "Religious Homogamy and Marital Satisfaction Reconsidered." *Journal of Marriage and the Family* 46:729–33.

Heaton, T. B. and Pratt, E. L. (1990) "The Effects of Religious Homogamy on Marital Satisfaction and Stability." *Journal of Family Issues* 11(2):191–207.

Iannaccone, L. R. (1990) "Religious Practice: A Human Capital Approach." *Journal for the Scientific Study of Religion* 29(3):297–314.

Kelley, D. M. (1972) *Why Conservative Churches Are Growing*. New York: Harper and Row.

Kobrin Goldscheider, F. (1986) "Family Patterns among the US Yiddish-Mother-Tongue Subpopulation: 1970." Pp. 172–83 in S. M. Cohen and P. E. Hyman (eds) *The Jewish Family: Myths and Reality*. New York: Holmes and Meier.

Lam, D. (1988) "Marriage Markets and Assortative Mating with Household Public Goods." *Journal of Human Resources* 23(4):462–87.

Lehrer, E. L. (1996) "The Determinants of Marital Stability: A Comparative Analysis of First and Higher Order Marriages." *Research in Population Economics* 8:91–121.

Mayer, E. and Avgar, A. (1987) *Conversion Among the Intermarried: Choosing to Become Jewish*. New York: American Jewish Committee.

McCarthy, J. (1979) "Religious Commitment, Affiliation, and Marriage Dissolution." Pp. 179–97 in R. Wuthnow (ed.) *The Religious Dimension: New Directions in Quantitative Research*. New York: Academic Press.

McLanahan, S. and Bumpass, L. (1988) "Intergenerational Consequences of Family Disruption." *American Journal of Sociology* 94(1):130–52.

Menken, J., Trussell, J., Stempel, D., and Babakol, O. (1981) "Proportional Hazards Life Table Models: An Illustrative Analysis of Socio-Demographic Influences on Marriage Dissolution in the United States." *Demography* 18(2):181–200.

Michael, R. T. (1979) "Determinants of Divorce." Pp. 223–68 in L. Levy-Garboua (ed.) *Sociological Economics*. Beverly Hills: Sage.

Mosher, W. D., Williams, L. B., and Johnson, D. P. (1992) "Religion and Fertility in the United States: New Patterns." *Demography* 29(2):199–214.

Pope, H. and Mueller, C. W. (1976) "The Intergenerational Transmission of Marital Instability: Comparisons by Race and Sex." *Journal of Social Issues* 32:49–66.

Schneider, S. W. (1989) *Intermarriage – The Challenge of Living with Differences between Christians and Jews*. New York: Free Press.

Schultz, T. P. (1991) "Economic Aspects of Marriage and Fertility in the US." Presented at the annual meetings of the Population Association of America, Washington, DC.

Smith, J. E. (1985) "A Familistic Religion in a Modern Society." Pp. 273–98 in K. Davis (ed.) *Contemporary Marriage*. New York: Russell Sage Foundation.

Teachman, J. D. (1986) "First and Second Marital Dissolution: A Decomposition Exercise for Whites and Blacks." *Sociological Quarterly* 27(4):571–90.

Tuma, N. B. and Michael, R. (1986) "A Comparison of Statistical Models for Life Course Analysis with an Application to First Marriage." *Current Perspectives on Aging and the Life Cycle* 2:107–46.

Waite, L. J. and Lillard, L. A. (1991) "Children and Marital Disruption." *American Journal of Sociology* 96(4):930–53.

White, L. K. (1991) "Determinants of Divorce: A Review of Research in the Eighties." Pp. 141–9 in A. Booth (ed.) *Contemporary Families*. Minneapolis: National Council on Family Relations.

2 Religious intermarriage in the United States

Determinants and trends *

A growing body of research points to the far-reaching economic and demographic implications of religious intermarriage. Several studies find that interfaith marriages are at a higher risk of divorce than intrafaith unions. Lehrer and Chiswick (1993, p. 398) report that, depending on the specific religious group involved, the probability that a homogamous couple would see their union dissolved before their fifth anniversary:

> ranges between 0.13 and 0.27; for heterogamous couples, the probability ranges from 0.24 for the most stable intermarriages to 0.42 for the least stable. With the exception of age at marriage, changes in none of the other variables considered here produce such a large variation in the probability of marital dissolution.

Using different data sets and cruder measures of the religious composition of unions, other research also finds relatively large destabilizing effects associated with religious heterogamy (Burchinal and Chancellor 1963; Bumpass and Sweet 1972; Michael 1979; Heaton and Pratt 1990; Lehrer 1996a; Chiswick 1997).

Because of its impact on the likelihood of marital breakup, religious intermarriage may also be expected to influence patterns of investment in human capital. A *marital stability effect* predicts that insofar as interfaith couples recognize the relative instability of their unions, they have incentives to make fewer investments in spouse-specific human capital – children in particular. Similarly, this effect implies that women in religious intermarriages face increased incentives to work in the labor market and invest in on-the-job training, as insurance against the possibility of divorce. At the same time, a *bargaining effect* suggests that if husband and wife are affiliated to religions that embody different norms regarding fertility and the appropriate intra-family division of labor, they may need to negotiate and possibly arrive at some compromise in these areas. Empirically, several studies find that marrying

* This chapter is reprinted from *Social Science Research* 27:245–263, 1998.

outside the faith has an important impact on fertility and on female labor supply, and that both the marital stability and bargaining effects play a role in explaining the observed relationships (Lehrer 1995, 1996b, 1996c; see also Becker et al. 1977).

While the *consequences* of marrying outside the religion for the stability of unions, fertility, and women's employment have received considerable attention, relatively little is known about the *determinants* and *trends* of religious intermarriage. With the exception of recent studies that focus on the case of Catholics (Sander 1993, 1995) and Jews (Waite and Sheps 1994), most previous empirical studies on the factors that influence intermarriage are based on simple cross-tabulation analyses that examine one factor at a time. In addition, research on intermarriage trends has focused generally on unions between Protestants and Catholics (Bumpass 1970; Kalmijn 1991), without making a distinction between the main groups within Protestantism. Using data from the 1987–88 National Survey of Families and Households (NSFH), this study presents a multivariate analysis of the determinants and trends of religious intermarriage for the three main religious groups in the United States: exclusivist Protestants, ecumenical Protestants, and Catholics.[1]

Analytical framework[2]

Religious intermarriage is a dichotomous variable: for a given definition of religious categories, a marriage is either intra- or interfaith depending on whether or not the spouses belong to the same group. Conceptually, however, intermarriage comes in varying shades and degrees. For example, while differences in religious beliefs would be pronounced in a union between a Mormon and a Jehovah's Witness, they would be relatively minor in a marriage between a Presbyterian and an Episcopalian. Thus in understanding the determinants of religious intermarriage, Chiswick and Lehrer (1991) suggest that it is useful to think about an underlying continuous variable: religious compatibility (r), a measure of the degree of similarity between the husband's and wife's religious beliefs and practices. Although the correspondence need not be perfect, the low and high ends of this continuum may be thought of as representing, respectively, inter- and intrafaith unions.

Both economists and sociologists have advanced reasons why a high level of religious compatibility between the spouses should have a favorable effect on marital stability. Within the context of marriage, religion is a complementary trait for which the mating of likes is optimal (Becker 1974). As Chiswick and Lehrer (1991) elaborate, religion influences many activities that husband and wife perform jointly. Such activities include not only those related directly to religious observance, but also the upbringing of children, the allocation of time and money, the cultivation of friendships, the development of business and professional networks, the choice of place of residence, and numerous other aspects of everyday life. Greater efficiency and less conflict are thus expected to characterize those households in which the spouses share the same religious affiliation. Similar ideas are developed in the sociological literature. For example, Bumpass and Sweet's (1972) analysis emphasizes the importance for marital harmony of similarity between the spouses in religious beliefs and related values, priorities, and expectations.[3]

Although a high degree of religious compatibility between the spouses is desirable for the reasons suggested above, religion is only one among many traits that are important in the marriage market. The multidimensional nature of the optimal match implies that individuals are often faced with the need to consider tradeoffs between religious compatibility and other desirable characteristics. Thus if a potentially attractive partner belonging to a different religion has been identified, the individual must weigh the benefits of continuing the search in the marriage market against the costs. The benefits include the possibility of finding someone with a higher degree of religious compatibility; the costs involve the foregone gains from marriage with that partner plus any out-of-pocket and psychological costs associated with continuing the search process.

Chiswick and Lehrer (1991) develop a model that views the optimal level of religious compatibility with the spouse for a given individual as that value which equates the marginal benefit (MB) and marginal cost (MC) of search. The shape of these curves, illustrated in Figure 2.1, is as typical in economic

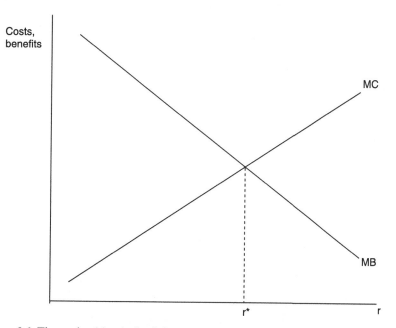

Figure 2.1 The optimal level of religious compatibility with the spouse is that which equates at the margin the benefits and the costs of search for a same-faith partner.

applications.[4] Differences across individuals in the propensity to intermarry can be understood in terms of variations in the circumstances that influence the position of the curves. Figure 2.2a illustrates that, other factors held constant, persons who face a high marginal cost of search for a same-faith partner are likely to stop searching at a relatively low level of r, i.e., they are likely to intermarry. Similarly, Figure 2.2b shows that individuals who have high marginal benefits of search for a same-faith spouse are likely to continue the search process until they reach a relatively high level of r, i.e., they are prone to marry within their religion.

Factors that primarily influence MC

A key determinant of the marginal cost of search for a same-faith partner is the availability of coreligionists in the relevant marriage market. It is clearly less costly to identify a potential partner with a high degree of religious compatibility if the pool of such individuals in the place of residence is large. Indeed, the most robust result in the literature on intermarriage is that the size of this pool has a negative impact on the probability of marrying outside the faith (Burchinal and Chancellor 1962; Rosenthal 1972; Thomas 1972; Grossbard-Shechtman 1993; Sander 1995).

A different type of factor that would also influence the costs of additional search for a same-faith partner is a premarital conception. An unplanned pregnancy during the course of dating or cohabitation would substantially raise the costs of continuing search – such costs would now include the possibility of an abortion or an out-of-wedlock birth. Given that religious compatibility with the partner appears to be less important in the context of dating or cohabitation than within marriage (Burchinal 1960; Schoen and

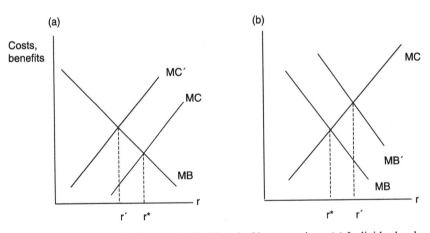

Figure 2.2 Factors that influence the likelihood of intermarriage. (a) Individuals who face a relatively high MC of search for a same-faith partner are more likely to intermarry; (b) individuals who face a relatively high MB of search for a same-faith partner are less likely to intermarry.

Weinick 1993), a premarital pregnancy is expected to be positively associated with the probability of intermarriage. An early cross-tabulation analysis by Christensen and Barber (1967) lends support to this hypothesis. The effect should be more pronounced among the more conservative religious groups, for whom the costs of an abortion or a birth outside of marriage would be perceived to be higher.

Factors that influence MC and MB

Educational attainment affects both the marginal benefits and the marginal costs of search, having an ambiguous impact on the probability of intermarriage. Individuals who possess the attractive trait of a high level of schooling generate marriage offers more easily and thus have lower costs of search for a marital partner; this effect implies that they have a lower probability of intermarriage. At the same time, greater educational attainment implies wider intellectual horizons as well as higher levels of socioeconomic achievement – additional dimensions of compatibility that may be traded off against religious compatibility. In this sense, higher education may reduce the marginal benefits of search for a same-faith partner and increase the probability of intermarriage. The net effect is ambiguous a priori and may vary across religious groups.

Factors that primarily influence MB

Several factors influence the benefits of additional search for a same-faith partner. In the tradeoff between religious compatibility and other desirable traits, individuals who have higher levels of religiosity would be expected to place more priority on the former. Several studies confirm that an increased salience of religion is indeed associated with a lower probability of intermarriage (Heiss 1960; Rosenthal 1963; Waite and Sheps 1994). The benefits of additional search for a same-faith partner also vary with the degree of commitment the individual has to the religion in which he or she was raised. Such commitment, in turn, has been found to be a function of the level of harmony experienced in the family of origin: it is lower among people who report dissatisfaction with their early child–parent relationships or strifeful family interactions during childhood (Heiss 1960).

It has been suggested that gender may also influence the benefits of continuing search for a same-faith partner, insofar as the ability to control the religious socialization of children differs between men and women (Glenn 1982). This issue has not received much attention. Early studies report that among Catholics and Protestants, the probability of entering an interfaith union is lower for men (see Salisbury [1964] for a review of this literature). The opposite pattern has been found for Jews, at least until recently (Lazerwitz 1971; Waite and Sheps 1994).

Over the past decades, two factors may have affected the perceived benefits of continuing search for a coreligionist: possible changes over time in the overall importance attached to religion in society and variations in the socio-economic and cultural distance among groups. With regard to the first issue, the prevailing view until recently was that the process of modernization – with the accompanying increases in standards of living, the progress of science and technology, and universal education – should lead to a decline in the role of religion in society (e.g., Wilson 1976). This secularization thesis has been challenged by a growing body of empirical research documenting that the observed patterns of religious beliefs and practices in the United States are inconsistent with its predictions (Greeley 1972, 1989; Hout and Greeley 1987). More recently, rational choice theory has led to the formulation of an alternative thesis – the view that in the highly pluralistic religious market of the American society, the expected condition of religion is one of vitality and vibrancy rather than decline (Iannaccone 1991, 1998; Finke and Stark 1992; Warner 1993).

This debate over general trends in the salience of religious belief and practice in the United States is likely to continue in the years ahead. However, there is less controversy regarding changes in a specific aspect of religion that is particularly relevant for its role in marriage decisions: the socioeconomic and cultural distance between religious groups. Several scholars have noted that the behavior of Catholics in the United States has become considerably less distinct over this century in such areas as educational attainment and occupational composition (Bumpass 1970; Mueller 1971; Greeley 1976), fertility (Mosher et al. 1992; Lehrer 1996b), childrearing (Alwin 1984), separation and divorce (Thornton 1985a; Lehrer and Chiswick 1993), gender roles (Brinkerhoff and MacKie 1984, 1988), female employment (Lehrer 1995), and other dimensions of family life (D'Antonio and Cavanaugh 1983). These transformations have effectively decreased the socioeconomic and cultural boundaries between Catholics and Protestants, reducing the relative benefits of a continued search for a same-faith partner. Indeed several studies report that the prevalence of intermarriage for members of these faiths has increased over the past decades, suggesting a trend towards secularization in the institution of marriage (Bumpass 1970; Johnson 1980; Glenn 1982; Kalmijn 1991; Sander 1993).

At the same time, however, Thornton (1985b, p. 386) observes that a group within Protestantism has become more distinct:

> During the last two decades – when there were important trends toward more egalitarian sex role attitudes, more acceptance of divorce, more acceptance of childlessness, and a desire for smaller families – fundamentalist Protestants changed along with the rest of the American population, but the extent of their change was smaller. The result is that they are now generally more traditional than other Americans on many aspects of family life . . . This group of Protestants also continues to have somewhat higher fertility than others . . .

In addition, the average socioeconomic status of many of the exclusivist Protestant groups continues to be comparatively low (Roof and McKinney 1987), and their patterns of maternal employment during the childrearing years also remain distinct (Lehrer 1995, 1999). Furthermore, the very nature of exclusivist religious practices and beliefs implies sharp boundaries separating them from other groups. Overall, these observations suggest that the declining role of religion in marriage decisions and the increased prevalence of interfaith marriage documented in earlier studies may not apply to members of exclusivist Protestant denominations.

Methods

The 1987–88 NSFH was addressed to a main sample of 9,643 male and female respondents, representative of the US population ages 19 and over.[5] The survey is rich in economic and demographic variables and includes the religious affiliation of the respondents and their first spouses (where applicable), both before and after the marriage.[6] An important feature of the data is that information is available on all first unions, whether or not they were still intact at the time of the interview.[7] The study is restricted to the first marriages of white, non-Hispanic respondents who resided in the United States at age 16. Even though African-Americans and Hispanics were oversampled, the number of observations available for ever-married respondents in these groups is not sufficient to permit separate analyses; similarly, the number of respondents born and raised in foreign countries is relatively small.[8] The sample is further limited to individuals born in 1960 or earlier, as some of the younger respondents had not yet married by the interview date and this relationship may vary systematically with the propensity to eventually intermarry.

Separate analyses are conducted for the first marriages of respondents belonging to three main religious groups: exclusivist Protestant, ecumenical Protestant, and Catholic. The classification of Protestants into these two categories follows that employed earlier by Lehrer and Chiswick (1993) for the NSFH data. The exclusivist group includes Baptists, Jehovah's Witnesses, Seventh-Day Adventists, Christian Scientists, and a large number of other fundamentalist denominations.[9] Episcopalians, Methodists, Presbyterians, Lutherans, Unitarians, and several other mainline Protestant bodies are classified in the ecumenical group. The sample sizes are 1,311, 1,952, and 1,204 for exclusivist Protestants, ecumenical Protestants, and Catholics, respectively.

As suggested in the previous section, the underlying concept of religious compatibility between the spouses corresponds to a continuous variable. The operational definition of religious intermarriage used here is that it occurs when a Protestant marries a Catholic, and in the case of interdenominational unions involving Protestants, when at least one of the spouses is affiliated to an exclusivist group. Unions involving members of two ecumenical Protestant denominations are treated as homogamous. Thus, for example, a marriage between a Christian Scientist and a Jehovah's Witness would be coded as interfaith, as would a marriage between a Seventh-Day Adventist and a Unitarian; a union between a Presbyterian and an Episcopalian would be considered intrafaith. This approach is based on the notion that the distinguishing feature of ecumenical denominations is a loose definition of the boundaries that separate groups. Indeed, interdenominational marriages involving ecumenical Protestants have been found to be virtually as stable as unions in which both spouses have the identical affiliation (Lehrer and Chiswick 1993).

Because the objective of this study is to understand the factors that influence individuals' decisions on whether to marry within or outside the religion in which they were raised, the analysis focuses primarily on affiliation measured before the marriage (for both the respondent and the spouse). For the stability of unions, however, there is evidence that homogamy in terms of current religious affiliation is the more important concept (Lehrer and Chiswick 1993). Thus the sensitivity of the results to measuring religion after marriage is also explored. Table 2.1 shows the percentage of unions in the sample that are interfaith by the respondent's affiliation for the two ways of measuring religion.

Table 2.2 presents definitions and means for the explanatory variables used in the analysis. Information in the NSFH on the state where each respondent lived at age 16 is used to construct a variable representing the percentage of coreligionists in the respondent's region of residence. This variable measures the size of the pool of same-faith partners, a key determinant of the position of the MC curve. The dummy for premarital pregnancy captures another factor that influences the marginal cost of search. Next in the table is the respondent's educational level, a variable that affects both the costs and benefits of additional search for a coreligionist.

The remaining variables primarily influence the marginal benefits of search. The NSFH unfortunately does not document the level of religious participation in the respondents' families of origin, nor does it contain direct measures of the level of harmony in such families. Rough indicators are available, however. For Catholics and to a lesser extent for exclusivist Protestants, the size of the family of origin may be used as a proxy, albeit imperfect, of religiosity. Evidence that exclusivist Protestant theologies favor the traditional division of labor within the household, especially when young children are present

Table 2.1 Percentage of marriages that are interfaith by respondent's affiliation

	Religion measured before marriage (%)	Religion measured after marriage (%)
Respondent's religion		
Exclusivist Protestant	51	37
Ecumenical Protestant	42	31
Catholic	44	25

Table 2.2 Definitions and means of explanatory variables

	Exclusivist Protestant	Ecumenical Protestant	Catholic
Percentage of coreligionists			
For the region where respondent lived at age 16, percentage of respondents in the sample who resided there at age 16 and had the same religious affiliation[a]	25.48	39.66	34.54
Premarital pregnancy			
1 if there was a birth within 7 months of marriage	0.07	0.07	0.07
Education			
1 if respondent's years of schooling at date of marriage is in category indicated			
< 12 years	0.43	0.23	0.22
12 years (benchmark)	(0.35)	(0.36)	(0.40)
13–15	0.15	0.26	0.25
≥ 16	0.07	0.15	0.13
Size of family of origin			
Number of siblings in respondent's family	3.55	2.94	3.52
Mother's employment			
1 if respondent's mother held a paid job for 12 months or more when he/she was 5 years old or younger	0.20	0.18	0.20
Nonintact family of origin			
1 if parents were separated or divorced when respondent was 14 years old	0.12	0.11	0.11
Male			
1 if respondent is male	0.37	0.40	0.40
Marriage cohort			
1 if date of respondent's first marriage is in category indicated			
Before 1950	0.36	0.34	0.26
1950–1959	0.16	0.14	0.12
1960–1969	0.20	0.19	0.19
1970–1979 (benchmark)	(0.22)	(0.24)	(0.30)
1980–1988	0.06	0.09	0.13
N	1,311	1,952	1,204

Note

a For exclusivist Protestants, "same religious affiliation" means a denomination identical to that of the respondent. For ecumenical Protestants, "same religious affiliation" means any ecumenical Protestant denomination. The following regions are considered: New England, Middle Atlantic, East North Central, West North Central, South Atlantic, East South Central, West South Central, Mountain, and Pacific.

(McMurry 1978; Brinkerhoff and MacKie 1984; Lehrer 1995, 1999), suggests that a dummy for maternal employment may also capture variations in religiosity for this group. In addition, a variable for dissolution of the family of origin through separation or divorce is included. A broken-family background is likely to be associated with the strifeful family interactions that have been linked to lessened commitment to the parental religion. Given the strong anti-divorce position of the Catholic Church, the dummy for marriage dissolution is also likely to capture an aspect of religiosity for this group: Catholic respondents who grew up in nonintact families come disproportionately from families with a relatively weak adherence to the tenets of the Church. The table also includes a variable for gender[10] as well as a series of dummies for marriage cohort to capture possible changes over time.

Finally, it is worth noting that the various characteristics of the spouse do not appear in Table 2.2. These variables are determined jointly with the religious nature of the match as individuals make tradeoffs in the process of selecting a spouse. Controlling for these traits in the regressions would thus introduce simultaneous equations biases. Similarly, age at marriage is excluded because the duration of search is also determined jointly with the characteristics of the partner. For example, individuals who are pessimistic about their marital prospects may end the search process at an early stage, settling for a spouse whose religious and other characteristics represent a far from optimal match. The models discussed below are reduced-form equations that provide estimates of the total effect of each explanatory variable on the probability of intermarriage.

Results

Table 2.3 presents maximum-likelihood estimates of logit equations, with the dichotomous intermarriage variable regressed on the explanatory factors described in the previous section. Separate equations are reported for the first marriages of respondents whose religion before marriage is exclusivist Protestant, ecumenical Protestant, and Catholic. This table provides information on the direction and statistical significance of each influence. The magnitude and importance of the various effects can be assessed more easily by turning to Table 2.4, which displays predicted probabilities of religious intermarriage for selected values of the covariates.

The availability of same-faith partners has the expected negative influence on the likelihood of interfaith marriage for the three religious groups. The effect is pronounced in each case: as the percentage of coreligionists in the area where the respondent lived at age 16 increases from 10 to 50 percent, the probability of intermarriage falls from 0.63 to 0.32 for exclusivist Protestants, from 0.70 to 0.44 for ecumenical Protestants, and from 0.62 to 0.41 for Catholics. To the extent that there is interregional mobility for some respondents after age 16, the variable used to indicate the size of the pool of coreligionists is measured with some error. The true effects are thus even larger in

Table 2.3 Logit intermarriage regressions by respondent's affiliation (religion measured before marriage)[a]

	Exclusivist Protestant	Ecumenical Protestant	Catholic
Percentage of coreligionists	−0.032 (0.003)**	− 0.027 (0.006)**	−0.021 (0.004)**
Premarital pregnancy	0.672 (0.238)**	0.035 (0.185)	−0.161 (0.230)
Education			
< 12 years	−0.229 (0.142)	0.164 (0.131)	0.021 (0.170)
13–15 years	0.153 (0.182)	−0.123 (0.123)	−0.049 (0.155)
≥ 16 years	0.737 (0.257)**	0.057 (0.149)	0.0004 (0.199)
Size of family of origin	−0.003 (0.021)	−0.021 (0.021)	−0.044 (0.024)*
Mother's employment	0.323 (0.161)**	0.067 (0.127)	0.113 (0.153)
Nonintact family of origin	0.058 (0.192)	0.262 (0.154)*	0.509 (0.202)**
Male	−0.393 (0.125)**	−0.244 (0.097)**	0.142 (0.124)
Marriage cohort			
Before 1950	0.027 (0.175)	−0.675 (0.138)**	−0.843 (0.178)**
1950–9	0.293 (0.200)	−0.478 (0.159)**	−0.424 (0.206)**
1960–9	−0.040 (0.186)	−0.173 (0.142)	−0.148 (0.174)
1980–8	−0.022 (0.273)	0.438 (0.185)**	−0.010 (0.200)
Constant	0.870 (0.193)**	1.165 (0.286)**	0.824 (0.237)**
Log-likelihood	−821.971	−1,286.295	−786.145
N	1,311	1,952	1,204

* $p < 0.10$, ** $p < 0.05$.

Note
a Standard errors in parentheses.

absolute magnitude than suggested by the estimates reported here. The relative abundance of same-faith partners clearly plays a major role as a determinant of the likelihood of marrying within the religion.

A premarital pregnancy is found to have a significant positive effect on the probability of religious intermarriage for exclusivist Protestants, the group that is most traditional and for whom the costs of an out-of-wedlock birth or abortion would presumably be highest. The magnitude of the effect is sizable: a premarital pregnancy is associated with an increase in the probability of interfaith marriage from 0.51 to 0.67. Although a positive influence was anticipated for Catholics also, no significant effect can be discerned for this group.

As noted earlier, the impact of education on intermarriage is ambiguous a priori: higher levels of schooling decrease the costs of additional search for a same-faith partner, but also may reduce the marginal benefits of search. For ecumenical Protestants and Catholics, the opposing influences appear to cancel each other out as the probability of outmarriage is found not to vary with education.

The second effect dominates for exclusivist Protestants. The likelihood of marrying outside the faith is greater, by a wide margin, among those with the highest schooling levels: the probability of intermarriage is 0.51 for a high

Table 2.4 Estimated probabilities of religious intermarriage (religion measured before marriage)

	Exclusivist Protestant	Ecumenical Protestant	Catholic
Reference person[a]	0.51	0.51	0.49
Selected characteristics[b]			
Percentage of coreligionists			
10	0.63	0.70	0.62
25	0.51	0.60	0.54
50	0.32	0.44	0.41
Premarital pregnancy	0.67	(0.52)[c]	(0.45)
Education			
< 12 years	(0.45)	(0.55)	(0.49)
13–15 years	(0.55)	(0.48)	(0.48)
≥ 16 years	0.68	(0.49)	(0.49)
Size of family of origin			
1	(0.51)	(0.52)	0.51
4	(0.51)	(0.50)	0.48
Mother employed	0.59	(0.52)	(0.52)
Nonintact family of origin	(0.52)	0.57	0.61
Male	0.41	0.45	(0.52)
Marriage cohort			
Before 1950	(0.52)	0.34	0.29
1950–9	(0.58)	0.39	0.38
1960–9	(0.50)	(0.46)	(0.45)
1980–8	(0.50)	0.61	(0.49)

Notes

a The reference person has the following characteristics. The percentage of coreligionists is equal to the mean value for the sample (25.48, 39.66, and 34.54 for exclusivist Protestants, ecumenical Protestants, and Catholics, respectively). The size of the family of origin is three; the mother was not employed during the respondent's early childhood, the parents were not divorced or separated when the respondent was 14 years of age. The respondent's years of schooling at the time of marriage is 12, there is no premarital pregnancy, the respondent is female, and the marriage took place in the period 1970–79.

b All characteristics are identical to those of the reference person, except as indicated in the stub.

c Figures shown in parentheses correspond to coefficients that are not significant at the 0.10 level.

school graduate compared to 0.68 for a college graduate. As Table 2.2 shows, the schooling level of exclusivist Protestants in the sample is substantially lower than that of the other religious groups. While only 7 percent of exclusivist Protestants has 16 years of schooling or more, the corresponding percentages are about double for ecumenical Protestants and Catholics: 15 and 13 percent, respectively. Among the most highly educated exclusivist Protestants, the more elevated levels of intellectual development and socioeconomic achievement associated with greater schooling – which may be found more easily in a partner outside the religion – appear to represent an important aspect of compatibility that is traded off against religious homogamy. This result is consistent with evidence in the literature that one reason for religious switching (which frequently accompanies marriage to a partner raised in a different faith) is the desire to move to a more compatible socioeconomic membership (Newport 1979).

This finding is also consistent with research that emphasizes the import-ance of assortative mating by education in the marriage market (Kalmijn 1991; Mare 1991). Because of the comparatively low average schooling level of exclusivist Protestants, the most highly educated members of this group face a more acute tradeoff between religious compatibility with the spouse and assortative mating by education than do their ecumenical Pro-testant and Catholic counterparts. The pronounced effect of a college educa-tion on the probability of intermarriage for exclusivist Protestants suggests that in this tradeoff, the desire for a partner with a similar schooling level often dominates.

The size of the family of origin has a significant negative coefficient in the Catholic sample, the group for which this variable is expected to proxy most closely for religiosity. However, the magnitude of the effect is small: as family size increases from 1 to 4, the probability of intermarriage falls only slightly, from 0.51 to 0.48. At the same time, the maternal employment variable, which is expected to capture the salience of religion for exclusivist Protestants, attains significance for this group and the direction of the effect is as predicted. The size of the influence is modest: the mother's employment is associated with an increase in the probability of intermarriage, from 0.51 to 0.59. The coefficients on the nonintact family of origin variable are positive as antici-pated, but attain significance only for ecumenical Protestants and Catholics. For the former, a broken-family background increases the probability of inter-marriage from 0.51 to 0.57. As anticipated, the increase is more pronounced for the latter, from 0.49 to 0.61.

The coefficients on male respondents are negative for the two groups of Protestants, consistent with results from previous analyses; the coefficient is insignificant for Catholics. If this pattern by gender is confirmed by subsequent studies, it would be useful to explore further whether interfaith marriages involving a Protestant husband display a greater tendency than other types of heterogamous unions for the wife to control the religious upbringing of the children.

The marriage cohort coefficients provide information on changes in the prevalence of intermarriage over time for the various religious groups. The results show that the probability of interfaith marriage has increased substan-tially over the past decades for ecumenical Protestants and Catholics. The changes over time follow somewhat different trajectories for the two groups. In the case of ecumenical Protestants, the probability of intermarriage is 0.34 and 0.39, respectively, for the pre-1950 and 1950s marriage cohorts; it increases to the 0.46–0.51 range for the 1960s and 1970s cohorts, rising further to 0.61 for the 1980s cohort. In the case of Catholics, most of the increase occurred earlier: from 0.29 for the pre-1950 cohort to 0.38 for the 1950s cohort, stabilizing at the 0.45–0.49 level thereafter.

In sharp contrast, the marriage cohort coefficients are insignificant in the exclusivist Protestant sample: the prevalence of intermarriage has not changed significantly for this group over the past decades. This remarkable stability is consistent with the observation made earlier that the gap between exclusivist Protestants and other groups of society remains large and that the boundaries that separate them continue to be sharp.

Finally, Table 2.5 reports results of the logit regressions reestimated with religion measured *after* marriage. The interpretation of the coefficients in this table is less straightforward than that in the previous specification, as intra-faith unions in this context include not only those in which both spouses were raised in the same religion but also those in which either the respondent or the spouse converted to achieve homogamy. Thus, while most effects remain similar in the new regressions, it is not surprising to observe some changes. Notably, the strong effect of a college education for exclusivist Protestants found in Table 2.3 is not detected in Table 2.5. This result reflects the fact that highly educated exclusivist Protestants who switch religious affiliations at the time of marriage are classified here as homogamously married. It is also worth noting that intermarriage trends under both specifications are similar, showing stability over the period for exclusivist Protestants but significant increases for the other two groups.

Table 2.5 Logit intermarriage regressions by respondent's affiliation (religion measured after marriage)[a]

	Exclusivist Protestant	Ecumenical Protestant	Catholic
Percentage of coreligionists	−0.017 (0.003)**	−0.013 (0.004)**	−0.010 (0.005)**
Premarital pregnancy	0.806 (0.219)**	0.190 (0.195)	−0.062 (0.266)
Education			
< 12 years	−0.211 (0.142)	0.238 (0.141)*	0.140 (0.204)
13–15 years	−0.253 (0.185)	−0.071 (0.132)	−0.163 (0.187)
≥ 16 years	0.323 (0.250)	−0.215 (0.164)	−0.127 (0.237)
Size of family of origin	0.025 (0.022)	−0.037 (0.023)	−0.018 (0.029)
Mother's employment	0.212 (0.162)	0.168 (0.132)	0.244 (0.174)
Nonintact family	−0.040 (0.187)	0.350 (0.164)**	0.547 (0.229)**
Male	−0.244 (0.125)**	−0.341 (0.107)**	0.020 (0.149)
Marriage cohort			
Before 1950	−0.078 (0.175)	−0.640 (0.147)**	−1.146 (0.223)**
1950–9	0.213 (0.198)	−0.336 (0.168)**	−0.432 (0.240)*
1960–9	−0.061 (0.182)	−0.148 (0.155)	−0.455 (0.208)**
1980–8	0.136 (0.257)	0.592 (0.193)**	0.330 (0.224)
Constant	−0.068 (0.192)	0.079 (0.223)	−0.416 (0.273)
Log-likelihood	−818.151	−1,141.378	−591.573
N	1,287	1,914	1,107

* $p < 0.10$, ** $p < 0.05$.

Note

a Standard errors in parentheses.

Conclusions

A growing literature documents that religious intermarriage has important effects on the economic and demographic behavior of families. Yet few empirical studies have examined the determinants of this phenomenon for the main religious groups in the United States within the context of a multivariate framework. The present study has attempted to fill this gap in the literature.

The analysis is based on a model that views religious compatibility with the spouse as a desirable marital trait, but one that may have to be traded off against other attractive characteristics in the marriage market. In this framework, the optimal level of religious compatibility with the spouse is a function of the benefits and costs associated with additional search for a same-faith partner. Several hypotheses derived from this model are tested with data on exclusivist Protestant, ecumenical Protestant, and Catholic respondents in the 1987–88 National Survey of Families and Households.

The main determinant of the costs of finding a same-faith spouse is the proportion of individuals with the same religious affiliation in the relevant marriage market. The results strongly support the hypothesis that the greater such proportion, the lower the probability of marrying outside the religion. A different type of factor that influences the costs of continued search for a same-faith partner is the occurrence of pregnancy in the course of dating or cohabitation. Such an event is found to increase the probability of interfaith marriage by a substantial amount, but only for exclusivist Protestants – a group for which the costs of an abortion or an out-of-wedlock child are relatively high.

Educational attainment has an ambiguous effect on the probability of intermarriage, as higher levels of schooling decrease the marginal costs of search for a same-faith partner and may also reduce the marginal benefits of such a search. For ecumenical Protestants and Catholics, education is found to have no effect on the likelihood of intermarriage, suggesting that the countervailing forces are offsetting each other. The second effect dominates for exclusivist Protestants: in this group, those with the highest levels of schooling are most likely to marry outside the religion. Because positive assortative mating by education within the religion is relatively difficult for exclusivist Protestants who have college degrees, this finding is suggestive of the relative strength and importance of educational homogamy.

Those who are more religious and more committed to the faith in which they were raised are predicted to have a lower probability of intermarriage. Only imperfect proxies for these factors are available in these data, and their coefficients are not always significant; however, the results are generally supportive of this hypothesis. The estimates also uncover an asymmetry by gender in the probability of intermarriage for ecumenical and exclusivist Protestants, possibly reflecting a corresponding asymmetry in the ability to control the religious socialization and education of the children.

Overall, the results on the determinants of religious intermarriage are generally consistent with the hypotheses derived from the theoretical model.

Based on an assessment of the benefits and costs of search for a same-faith partner at the margin, the model provides a cohesive structure for understanding how various factors influence the likelihood of marrying outside the religion and avoids the ad hoc explanations for one variable at a time often found in earlier studies.

With regard to long-run trends, an important finding of this research is that the past decades have witnessed a significant increase in the rate of intermarriage for Catholics and ecumenical Protestants; at the same time, the pattern has been one of notable stability in the case of exclusivist Protestants. For the dimension of religion considered in this study – the salience of religious factors in marriage decisions – this result may be interpreted as a confirmation of secularizing trends among ecumenical Protestants and Catholics and an indication of a resistance to secularization among exclusivist Protestants.

The conclusion that barriers to interfaith marriage remain unchanged for exclusivist Protestants is consistent with evidence that this group continues to display distinctive patterns of economic and demographic behavior. Several researchers have studied and documented the relative strength of exclusivist Protestant denominations (Kelley 1972; Roof and McKinney 1987; Iannaccone 1992, 1994). An intriguing topic for future investigation is the extent to which their stable intermarriage patterns, documented here, have contributed to such strength.

Recent research suggests that the theoretical framework that has been found useful for analyzing the demographic consequences of interfaith marriage may be applied, with some modification, to understanding the demographic implications of other types of intermarriages. Berg and Pullum (1996) find that the marital stability and bargaining effects described in the introduction help explain the observed effects of interethnic and interracial marriage on fertility behavior. Along similar lines, extension of the analysis presented in this article may shed additional light on the determinants of racial and ethnic heterogamy in the marriage market.

Acknowledgments

I am indebted to Carmel Chiswick, Shoshana Grossbard-Shechtman, and anonymous referees for helpful comments on earlier drafts of this paper.

Notes

1 This terminology follows Kelley (1972), who classifies religious groups along an ecumenical–exclusivist gradient depending on the clarity with which membership boundaries are drawn.
2 This section builds on the model of intermarriage developed by Chiswick and Lehrer (1991).
3 For a different theoretical perspective, which views religious heterogamy as a positive marital trait under special circumstances, see Grossbard-Shechtman (1993).
4 The MC curve slopes upward, reflecting the fact that if a partner with a very low

r has been identified, it is relatively easy (inexpensive) to improve on that dimension; once a partner with a high *r* has been found, further improvements in this aspect become very costly. Similarly, the downward slope of the MB curve reflects the notion that the benefits of further increases in *r* vary inversely with the level of compatibility with the partner who has already been identified.

5 This survey was designed at the Center for Demography and Ecology at the University of Wisconsin-Madison under the direction of Larry Bumpass and James Sweet. The field work was done by the Institute for Survey Research at Temple University.

6 Respondents were asked "What is your religious preference?" Where changes took place, there were further questions, including "Did you change your religion in connection with your (first) marriage?," "What was your religious preference before you changed at that time?," and "What religion did you change to at that time?" Similar information was obtained about the respondent's first spouse in the case of unions that had been dissolved by the time of the survey. For respondents whose first marriages were still intact, the survey documents the spouse's religious affiliation at the time of the interview and just before the change if conversion took place in connection with the marriage.

7 Earlier analyses of trends in religious intermarriage by Bumpass (1970) and Glenn (1982) are based on samples of unions that were still intact at the interview date. As Bumpass (1970) discusses in detail, this limitation of the data creates problems of selective sample attrition because interfaith marriages have a higher probability of dissolution.

8 It would be inappropriate to lump all respondents together and simply include dummy variables for race/ethnicity and country of birth, because the determinants of intermarriage are likely to differ across groups.

9 The NSFH does not make a distinction among the various Baptist denominations. Also, although it would have been desirable to use separate categories for Baptists and the smaller exclusivist denominations, sample size limitations do not permit this refinement.

10 Male and female respondents were pooled due to limitations of sample size. It is worth noting, however, that in preliminary analyses the null hypothesis that the structures are the same for men and women could not be rejected at the 0.05 or 0.10 levels for any of the religious groups.

References

Alwin, D. F. (1984) "Trends in Parental Socialization Values: Detroit, 1958–1983." *American Journal of Sociology* 90(2):359–82.

Becker, G. S. (1974) "A Theory of Marriage." Pp. 299–344 in T. P. Schultz (ed.) *Economics of the Family*. Chicago: University of Chicago Press.

Becker, G. S., Landes, E. M., and Michael, R. T. (1977) "An Economic Analysis of Marital Instability." *Journal of Political Economy* 85(6):1141–87.

Berg, R. R. and Pullum, T. W. (1996) "Low Fertility among Intermarried Mexican Americans: An Assessment of Three Hypotheses." Presented at the annual meetings of the Population Association of America, New Orleans.

Brinkerhoff, M. B. and MacKie, M. M. (1984) "Religious Denominations' Impact Upon Gender Attitudes: Some Methodological Implications." *Review of Religious Research* 25(4):365–78.

Brinkerhoff, M. B. and MacKie, M. M. (1988) "Religious Sources of Gender Traditionalism." Pp. 232–57 in D. Thomas (ed.) *The Religion and Family Connection*. Religious Studies Center, Salt Lake City: Brigham Young University.

Bumpass, L. (1970) "The Trend of Interfaith Marriage in the United States." *Social Biology* 17:253–9.

Bumpass, L. L. and Sweet, J. A. (1972) "Differentials in Marital Stability: 1970." *American Sociological Review* 37(6):754–66.

Burchinal, L. G. (1960) "Membership Groups and Attitudes toward Cross-Religious Dating and Marriage." *Marriage and Family Living* 22(3):248–53.

Burchinal, L. G. and Chancellor, L. E. (1962) "Proportions of Catholics, Urbanism, and Mixed-Catholic Marriage Rates Among Iowa Counties." *Social Problems* 9:359–65.

Burchinal, L. G. and Chancellor, L. E. (1963) "Survival Rates among Religiously Homogamous and Interreligious Marriages." *Social Forces* 41:353–62.

Chiswick, C. U. (1997) "Determinants of Religious Intermarriage: Are Jews Really Different?" Pp. 247–57 in *Papers in Jewish Demography 1993, in Memory of U. O. Schmelz*, Proceedings of the Demographic Sessions held at the 11th World Congress of Jewish Studies, Jerusalem, June 1993.

Chiswick, C. U., and Lehrer, E. L. (1991) "Religious Intermarriage: An Economic Perspective." *Contemporary Jewry* 12:21–34.

Christensen, H. T. and Barber, K. E. (1967) "Interfaith versus Intrafaith Marriage in Indiana." *Journal of Marriage and the Family* 29(3):461–9.

D'Antonio, W. V. and Cavanaugh, M. J. (1983) "Roman Catholicism and the Family." Pp. 141–62 in W. V. D'Antonio and J. Aldous (eds) *Families and Religions: Conflict and Change in Modern Society*. Beverly Hills, CA: Sage.

Finke, R. and Stark, R. (1992) *The Churching of America, 1776–1990: Winners and Losers in Our Religious Economy*. New Brunswick, NJ: Rutgers University Press.

Glenn, N. D. (1982) "Interreligious Marriage in the United States: Patterns and Recent Trends." *Journal of Marriage and the Family* 44:555–66.

Greeley, A. M. (1972) *Unsecular Man: The Persistence of Religion*. New York: Schocken Books.

Greeley, A. M. (1976) *Ethnicity, Denomination, and Inequality*. Beverly Hills, CA: Sage.

Greeley, A. M. (1989) *Religious Change in America*. Cambridge, MA: Harvard University Press.

Grossbard-Shechtman, S. (1993) *On the Economics of Marriage: A Theory of Marriage, Labor, and Divorce*. Boulder, CO: Westview Press.

Heaton, T. B. and Pratt, E. L. (1990) "The Effects of Religious Homogamy on Marital Satisfaction and Stability." *Journal of Family Issues* 11(2):191–207.

Heiss, J. S. (1960) "Premarital Characteristics of the Religiously Intermarried in an Urban Area." *American Sociological Review* 25(1):47–55.

Hout, M. and Greeley, A. M. (1987) "The Center Doesn't Hold: Church Attendance in the United States." *American Sociological Review* 52:325–45.

Iannaccone, L. R. (1991) "The Consequences of Religious Market Structure." *Rationality and Society* 3:156–77.

Iannaccone, L. R. (1992) "Sacrifice and Stigma: Reducing Free-Riding in Cults, Communes, and Other Collectives." *Journal of Political Economy* 100(2):271–91.

Iannaccone, L. R. (1994) "Why Strict Churches are Strong." *American Journal of Sociology* 99(5):1180–211.

Iannaccone, L. R. (1998) "Introduction to the Economics of Religion." *Journal of Economic Literature* 36:1465–96.

Johnson, R. A. (1980) *Religious Assortative Marriage in the United States*. New York: Academic Press.

Jones, E. F. and Westoff, C. E. (1979) "The End of 'Catholic' Fertility." *Demography* 16(2):209–18.

Kalmijn, M. (1991) "Shifting Boundaries: Trends in Religious and Educational Homogamy." *American Sociological Review* 56:786–80.

Kelley, D. M. (1972) *Why Conservative Churches Are Growing*. New York: Harper and Row.

Lazerwitz, B. (1971) "Intermarriage and Conversion: A Guide for Future Research." *Jewish Journal of Sociology* 13(1):41–63.

Lehrer, E. L. (1995) "The Effects of Religion on the Labor Supply of Married Women." *Social Science Research* 24:281–301. (Chapter 3 this volume.)

Lehrer, E. L. (1996a) "The Determinants of Marital Stability: A Comparative Analysis of First and Higher Order Marriages." pp. 91–121 in T. P. Schultz (ed.) *Research in Population Economics*, vol. 8. Greenwich: JAI Press.

Lehrer, E. L. (1996b) "Religion as a Determinant of Marital Fertility." *Journal of Population Economics* 9:173–96. (Chapter 4 this volume.)

Lehrer, E. L. (1996c) "The Role of the Husband's Religious Affiliation in the Economic and Demographic Behavior of Families." *Journal for the Scientific Study of Religion* 35(2):145–55.

Lehrer, E. L. (1999) "Married Women's Labor Supply Behavior in the 1990s: Determinants and Implications for Family Income Distribution." *Social Science Quarterly* 80(3):574–90.

Lehrer, E. L. and Chiswick, C. (1993) "Religion as a Determinant of Marital Stability." *Demography* 30(3):385–404. (Chapter 1 this volume.)

Mare, R. D. (1991) "Five Decades of Educational Assortative Mating." *American Sociological Review* 56:15–32.

McMurry, M. (1978) "Religion and Women's Sex Role Traditionalism." *Sociological Focus* 11(2):81–95.

Michael, R. (1979) "Determinants of Divorce." Pp. 223–54 in L. Levy-Garboua (ed.) *Sociological Economics*. Beverly Hills, CA: Sage.

Mosher, W. D., Williams, L. B., and Johnson, D. P. (1992) "Religion and Fertility in the United States: New Patterns." *Demography* 29(2):199–214.

Mueller, S. A. (1971) "The New Triple Melting Pot: Herberg Revisited." *Review of Religious Research* 13:18–33.

Newport. F. (1979) "The Religious Switcher in the United States." *American Sociological Review* 44(4):528–52.

Roof, W. C. and McKinney, W. (1987) *American Mainline Religion: Its Changing Shape and Future*. New Brunswick, NJ: Rutgers University Press.

Rosenthal, E. (1963) "Studies of Jewish Intermarriage in the United States." *American Jewish Yearbook* 64:3–53.

Rosenthal, E. (1972) "Jewish Intermarriage in Indiana." Pp. 222–42 in M. L. Barron (ed.) *The Blending American: Patterns of Intermarriage*. Chicago: Quadrangle Books.

Salisbury, W. S. (1964) *Religion in American Culture*. Homewood, IL: Dorsey Press.

Sander, W. (1993) "Catholicism and Intermarriage in the United States." *Journal of Marriage and the Family* 55:1037–41.

Sander, W. (1995) *The Catholic Family: Marriage, Children, and Human Capital*. Boulder, CO: Westview Press.

Schoen, R. and Weinick, R. M. (1993) "Partner Choice in Marriages and Cohabitations." *Journal of Marriage and the Family* 55:408–14.

Thomas, J. L. (1972) "The Factor of Religion in the Selection of Marriage Mates." Pp. 172–80 in M. L. Barron (ed.) *The Blending American: Patterns of Intermarriage.* Chicago: Quadrangle Books.

Thornton, A. (1985a) "Changing Attitudes Toward Separation and Divorce: Causes and Consequences." *American Journal of Sociology* 90(4):856–72.

Thornton, A. (1985b) "Reciprocal Influences of Family and Religion in a Changing World." *Journal of Marriage and the Family* May:381–94.

Waite, L. and Sheps, J. (1994) "The Impact of Religious Upbringing and Marriage Markets on Jewish Intermarriage." Presented at the annual meetings of the Population Association of America, Miami, FL.

Warner, R. S. (1993) "Work in Progress Toward a New Paradigm in the Sociology of Religion." *American Journal of Sociology* 98:1044–93.

Wilson, B. (1976) *Contemporary Transformations of Religion.* New York: Oxford University Press.

Part II

The role of religion in female labor supply and fertility

3 The effects of religion on the labor supply of married women *

There is a growing literature on the role of religion in economic and demographic behavior. Research has focused on the effects of religious affiliation on the process of marital search and choice of spouse (Chiswick and Lehrer 1991; Grossbard-Shechtman 1993; Waite and Sheps 1994), on the stability of marriages (Becker et al. 1977; Heaton and Pratt 1990; Lehrer and Chiswick 1993), and on the number and timing of children (Heckert and Teachman 1985; Williams and Zimmer 1990; Mosher et al. 1992). Very little is known, however, about how religion affects women's decisions regarding the allocation of time between home and market. Drawing from both economic and sociological theories, the present study examines channels through which religion may affect such decisions, focusing on the special case of married women.

A rich data set, the 1987–88 National Survey of Families and Households (NSFH) is used in the empirical analysis.[1] This survey was addressed to a main sample of 9,643 men and women of all marital statuses, representative of the US population age 19 and over. It includes detailed socioeconomic and demographic variables for the respondents and their current husbands or wives (where applicable), as well as their employment status and religious affiliation. Information on currently married respondents is used to quantify differences in labor supply among women in various types of intrafaith unions, and to estimate the effects of out-marriage on the wife's commitment to the labor market for members of each major religious group.

Analytical framework

The sociological literature suggests that one channel through which religion may influence female employment decisions is through differences across religious groups in attitudes toward gender roles and the appropriate division of labor within the family. A linkage between religion and such attitudes has indeed been documented in many studies. Exclusivist Protestant groups tend to be least egalitarian in their definitions of the male and female roles,

* Reprinted from *Social Sciences Research* 24:281–301, 1995.

individuals with no religious affiliation are most egalitarian, with ecumenical Protestant groups falling somewhere in between (McMurry 1978; Brinkerhoff and MacKie 1985).[2] The placement of Roman Catholics along this continuum appears to have changed substantially over time. While early studies found that Catholics made a sharp distinction between appropriate male and female roles (Campbell 1966; Meir 1972; McMurry 1978), recent analyses suggest that Catholics have become more egalitarian (Brinkerhoff and MacKie 1984) and indeed less traditional in this respect than either group of Protestants (Brinkerhoff and MacKie 1988). The direction of this change is consistent with transformations that have taken place in the attitudes and behavior of Catholics in issues related to childrearing (Alwin 1984); separation and divorce (Thornton 1985; Lehrer and Chiswick 1993); fertility (Mosher et al. 1992; Lehrer 1996a), and other areas of family life (D'Antonio and Cavanaugh 1983).

As Table 3.1 shows, data from the survey used in the present study confirm the finding in the literature that gender role attitudes vary systematically by religion, with exclusivist Protestants at the least egalitarian end of the continuum and individuals who have no religion at the other end. While the difference between the two extremes is very pronounced, that between the groups in the middle, ecumenical Protestants and Catholics, is minor.[3]

In a recent study, Heaton and Cornwall (1989) made a first attempt to examine whether the differentials by religion in gender role attitudes described above are translated into differentials in actual female labor force behavior. Using data on labor force participation rates from the 1971 and 1981 Canadian censuses, ratios of male to female employment are calculated for various religious groups. The results suggest that men's and women's labor supply patterns are most similar among those with no religious affiliation and least similar for members of exclusivist Protestant groups; ecumenical Protestants and Catholics fall in between. While the findings are suggestive of an impact of religion on women's labor supply decisions, the analysis is intended to be descriptive and does not control for other economic and demographic variables that influence female time allocation decisions. Since religion is known to be correlated with such variables, the question of whether there is an effect of religion per se on labor supply behavior remains open.

The present study focuses on the labor supply of married women, and as such it is appropriate to consider possible effects of the husband's faith as well. The fact that his religious beliefs may differ from the wife's raises the possibility of conflict. Recent studies have analyzed the resolution of marital conflict within the framework of bargaining models (Manser and Brown 1980; McElroy and Horney 1981; Lundberg and Pollak 1993). This perspective suggests that in comparing a union whose members are both affiliated to an egalitarian religious group and who therefore do not need to compromise in the area of female employment, with another in which only one member belongs to such group, the wife's commitment to the labor market should be stronger in the former. Similarly, in comparing a union whose members are

Table 3.1 Religion and gender-role attitudes[a]

	Exclusivist Protestant	Ecumenical Protestant	Catholic	No religion
"It is much better for everyone if the man earns the main living and the woman takes care of the home and family." (Strength of agreement or disagreement with this statement)				
1 (strongly agree)	24.6	13.7	11.9	8.3
2	26.6	23.1	19.0	14.6
3	30.4	33.1	36.2	36.8
4	12.4	18.9	22.7	21.5
5 (strongly disagree)	6.0	11.2	10.2	18.8
Total	100.0%	100.0%	100.0%	100.0%
N	549	776	538	144
$\chi^2 = 91.8**$ (12 df)				
"Mothers who work full time when their youngest child is under age 5." (Strength of approval or disapproval with this behavior)				
1 (strongly approve)	7.4	8.1	8.9	11.1
2	7.1	9.7	9.8	10.4
3	9.1	9.6	11.7	11.8
4	31.5	31.5	27.3	41.7
5	14.0	15.0	15.0	12.5
6	13.2	11.1	12.1	6.3
7 (strongly disapprove)	17.8	15.1	15.2	6.3
Total	100.0%	100.0%	100.0%	100.0%
N	552	775	539	144
$\chi^2 = 31.6**$ (18 df)				

** $p < 0.05$.

Note

a This analysis is based on responses by all wives in the sample of Table 3.2, omitting cases with missing information on the attitudinal variables. The criteria for inclusion in the sample are discussed at length in the section on methods in the text.

both affiliated to a religious group that emphasizes distinctive roles for men and women with another in which only one member is affiliated to such religion, the level of the wife's labor supply should be higher in the latter. This mechanism, which will be referred to as the "bargaining effect," suggests that out-marriage may lead to an increase or a decrease in the wife's labor supply, depending on the placement of her husband's faith along the least egalitarian–most egalitarian continuum.[4]

The economic literature suggests another channel through which the religious composition of unions may affect female labor supply behavior, namely, through the effect of religious intermarriage on incentives to invest in various forms of human capital. Becker et al. (1977) note that insofar as interfaith couples recognize the relative instability of their unions, they have an incentive to make fewer investments in spouse-specific capital, primarily children, because such investments would decline in value following the dissolution of the marriage – a hypothesis that has been supported by empirical research.[5] Extension of this reasoning suggests that women in interfaith unions would face incentives to invest in labor market experience and on-the-job training, as these forms of human capital would retain their value and become, indeed, particularly useful in the event of a divorce. This "marital stability effect" therefore implies that women in interreligious unions should display higher levels of labor supply than their counterparts in homogamous marriages, other factors held constant. The importance of this effect is suggested by research documenting that the impact of the religious composition of unions on marital stability is large in magnitude (Michael 1979; Lehrer and Chiswick 1993; Lehrer 1996b; Chiswick 1997) and that the expected probability of divorce has a substantial influence on the labor supply behavior of married women (Greene and Quester 1982; Johnson and Skinner 1986).

The theoretical considerations outlined above suggest some testable hypotheses regarding the effect of the religious composition of unions on female labor supply behavior for the four groups considered in this study: ecumenical Protestant, exclusivist Protestant, Catholic, and no religion. Focusing first on comparisons among women in various types of intrafaith unions, the ranking of religious groups along the most egalitarian–least egalitarian continuum implies that attachment to the labor force should be highest for women who have no religious affiliation, lowest for exclusivist Protestant women, with Catholic and ecumenical Protestant women occupying positions in between these two extremes.

Turning to the impact of out-marriage, labor supply is predicted to be unambiguously higher for exclusivist Protestant women in interfaith marriages than for their counterparts in homogamous unions, because in this case the bargaining effect reinforces the intermarriage effect. As discussed above, the intermarriage effect always implies that marrying outside the religion leads to increased female employment. For exclusivist Protestant women, the bargaining effect operates in the same direction as this group is at the least egalitarian end of the continuum, and marriage to a member of any other group would therefore tend to increase female attachment to the labor force. The influences of out-marriage on female labor supply for ecumenical Protestant, Catholic, and unaffiliated women are more complex, since in these cases the bargaining effect may operate in a direction opposite to the intermarriage effect, depending on the particular religious group to which the husband belongs.

Because the emphasis placed on the domestic role for women by some religions is likely to be connected closely with the presence of children, young children especially, the impact of religion on married women's labor supply is expected to vary systematically over the life cycle. In particular, any differences in the intra-family division of labor among the various types of homogamous unions should be most pronounced when young children are present in the home. In addition, the intermarriage effect is also expected to be largest in magnitude at this stage of the life cycle, as the adverse effect of interfaith marriage on marital stability is likely to be particularly acute when decisions must be made regarding the religious education and socialization of children (Chiswick and Lehrer 1991). Put together, these two arguments suggest that the influence of the religious composition of unions on the wife's labor supply should be relatively weak initially, when there are no children in the household, becoming stronger when young children arrive. After all children have reached school age, the measured effect of religious composition is expected to decline, partly because religion should matter less, partly because those interfaith unions that have remained intact until that stage of the life cycle represent a select group for whom religious complementarities are relatively unimportant.

Methods

Following Lehrer and Nerlove (1984), three groups of currently married respondents from the 1987–88 NSFH are analyzed separately depending on life-cycle stage: period 1, in which there are no children yet in the household (N = 312);[6] period 2, in which children are present and the youngest is under 6 years of age (N = 806); and period 3, which begins when the youngest child reaches age 6 and ends when all the children have left the household (N = 926). These samples are restricted to non-Hispanic white wives, because even though African-Americans and Hispanics were oversampled, the number of observations available for currently married respondents in periods 1, 2, and 3 is too small to permit separate analyses.[7] And the alternative strategy of lumping all groups together with controls for race/ethnicity is inappropriate in light of the large body of research documenting systematic differences in the determinants of female labor supply behavior across groups (e.g., see Carliner 1981; Cooney and Ortiz 1983; Lehrer and Nerlove 1984; Reimers 1985; Lehrer 1992).

For periods 2 and 3, a multinomial logit framework is used to analyze wives' decisions of whether to work in the labor market full time, part time, or not at all, as a function of a common set of variables.[8] For period 1, only the dichotomous choice – in or out of the labor force, can be meaningfully studied due to limitations of sample size. Table 3.2 presents descriptive statistics for employment status, based on hours worked the week before the survey,

Table 3.2 Employment status by period

	Full-time work	*Part-time work*	*Non-employment*	*Total*
Period 1	235 (75.3%)	45 (14.4%)	32 (10.3%)	312 (100%)
Period 2	270 (33.5%)	209 (25.9%)	327 (40.6%)	806 (100%)
Period 3	412 (44.5%)	238 (25.7%)	276 (29.8%)	926 (100%)

or the usual hours worked per week if the one preceding the interview was not typical (e.g., because of temporary illness or vacation). Full-time status is defined as 35 hours or more. As expected, Table 3.2 shows very marked variations in female labor supply behavior over the three life cycle stages. The fraction of women working on a full-time basis drops from fully 75 percent in period 1 to only 34 percent in period 2, increasing to 45 percent in period 3; at the same time, the part-time participation rate rises from 14 percent in period 1 to 26 percent in periods 2 and 3.

The explanatory variable of central interest is religion. The empirical analysis focuses on the spouses' current affiliations, as opposed to the faiths they were raised in, for three reasons. First, the quality of the current religion variable in these data is superior.[9] Second, when the religion in which the individual was raised is used, couples who have achieved homogamy through conversion are classified as "interfaith" marriages. Yet in terms of both levels of religious compatibility between the spouses and marital stability patterns, such unions are more similar to naturally homogamous couples than to those involving individuals who came into the marriage with different religions, choosing to keep them unchanged (Lehrer and Chiswick 1993). In this sense, using current affiliations results in a better classification system. And third, the gender role attitudes associated with the husband's and wife's current faiths are likely to be more relevant to decisions regarding the division of labor during married life than those of any religion either of them may have been affiliated to in an earlier period. On the other hand, the religion in which the individual was raised has the advantage of being truly exogenous, uncontaminated by some of the biases that may affect affiliation at the time of the interview. The implications of using this alternative measure are therefore discussed later in the text.

Over 60 religious groups are identified in the NSFH, most of them Protestant denominations. Protestants are divided into two groups, ecumenical and exclusivist, following the classification used earlier for these data by Lehrer and Chiswick (1993).[10] Additional categories identify Roman Catholics and individuals who have no affiliation. Because of sample size considerations, the analysis excludes Mormon and Jewish women, as well as members of other small religious groups. Means for variables representing the wife's religious affiliation are reported in the first four lines of Table 3.3.

The dummy variable "husband different religion," shown next in the table, takes the value one to indicate that the union is heterogamous, i.e., the husband's faith differs from the wife's, or one spouse has some religious affiliation and the other does not.[11] While marriages composed of members of different exclusivist Protestant groups are considered heterogamous, those involving individuals from different ecumenical denominations are classified as homogamous, as the distinguishing feature of such denominations is a loose definition of the boundaries that separate groups. This approach follows earlier research that has shown that interdenominational marriages involving ecumenical Protestants are virtually as stable as unions in which both spouses have the identical denomination (Lehrer and Chiswick 1993). The implications of treating all interdenominational marriages as heterogamous are considered later in the text. Table 3.3 also shows interaction terms between the wife's and the husband's religious affiliations. These variables are included in the model because the effect of out-marriage on female labor supply is expected to vary with the wife's faith.

The second part of Table 3.3 reports means for variables other than religion that are known to influence female labor supply behavior. Since the wage rate and previous experience are endogenous and adequate instruments are not available in these data, reduced-form equations are estimated by including their exogenous determinants: education, age, the square of age, and the

Table 3.3 Means of explanatory variables

	Period 1	Period 2	Period 3
Religion variables			
Wife ecumenical Protestant (benchmark)	(0.36)	(0.38)	(0.41)
Wife exclusivist Protestant	0.25	0.27	0.28
Wife Catholic	0.30	0.27	0.25
Wife no religion	0.09	0.08	0.06
Husband different religion	0.44	0.37	0.29
Wife exclusivist Protestant*			
Husband different Religion	0.11	0.11	0.10
Wife Catholic*			
Husband different religion	0.12	0.08	0.06
Wife no religion*			
Husband different religion	0.05	0.05	0.03
Control variables			
Wife's education			
<12 years	0.05	0.09	0.13
12 years (benchmark)	(0.33)	(0.39)	(0.49)
13–15 years	0.30	0.28	0.21
≥16 years	0.32	0.24	0.17
Wife's age	28.60	30.45	41.24
Wife's age squared	845.67	954.49	1,765.15
Number of children in household	–	2.08	1.83
Log of other family income	9.70	9.92	9.90
Husband married before	0.19	0.16	0.22
Wife married before	0.14	0.16	0.19
Husband older than wife by six years or more	0.16	0.14	0.18
Metropolitan area – core (benchmark)	(0.51)	(0.45)	(0.45)
Metropolitan area – fringe	0.22	0.19	0.19
Non-metropolitan area – adjacent to			
metropolitan area	0.16	0.23	0.22
Non-metropolitan area – not adjacent to			
metropolitan area	0.11	0.13	0.14
South	0.38	0.29	0.33
N	312	806	926

number of children, a proxy for interruptions in labor market activity. The children variable also captures current productivity in the home. A variable representing the husband's earnings plus any income from investments is included to control for sources of income available to the household aside from the wife's contribution. Additional income effects may be captured by a dummy indicating that the husband had been married before, as a previous marriage may be associated with the responsibility to contribute to the support of another household. In the case of the wife, a dummy indicating a previous divorce may capture an effect of expected marital stability on labor supply, if women in second or higher-order marriages perceive a higher probability of marital breakup. Like religion, age is a complementary trait in home production, and a pronounced difference in this characteristic between the spouses may also affect expected stability; a dummy indicating that the husband is older than the wife by six years or more is therefore included. Finally, a set of place of residence variables controls for geographical variations that may have an impact on female employment.

Results

Table 3.4 reports results of the dichotomous logit model for period 1 and the multinomial logit model for periods 2 and 3. For the latter model, it should be noted that given two coefficients (e.g., for full-time work vs. nonemployment, and part-time work vs. nonemployment), the third is automatically determined; however, the standard error for this third coefficient cannot be computed on the basis of the other two standard errors. Therefore, all coefficients and standard errors are shown. Two statistical tests are reported: t-tests for the individual coefficients and χ^2 tests for each set of coefficients.

The first section below focuses on the estimated impact of religion on female labor supply behavior; the second section briefly discusses the control variables, and the third section explores the sensitivity of the results to changes in the econometric specification and in the definitions of the religion variables.

The effects of religion

Ecumenical Protestant wives and the case of homogamy are used as the benchmark categories in the model of Table 3.4, and all the reported tests therefore reflect comparisons against these groups. Inspection of the estimates for the religion variables (focusing on t-tests for period 1 and χ^2 tests for periods 2 and 3) suggests that there are some significant effects in the second period but not in the first and third. However, a full picture of the role of religion on labor supply requires additional pairwise comparisons between the various types of homogamous marriages, as well as between each type of intra- and interfaith union. Such comparisons may be performed by using

Table 3.4 Multinomial logit coefficients[a]

	Period 1		Period 2				Period 3		
	FT or PT vs. NE[b]	x^2 2 df	FT vs. NE	PT vs. NE	FT vs. PT	x^2 2 df	FT vs. NE	PT vs. NE	FT vs. PT
Religion variables									
Wife exclusivist Protestant	0.605 (0.818)	3.23	−0.452 (0.299)	−0.462 (0.324)	0.009 (0.357)	3.42	0.242 (0.256)	−0.244 (0.292)	0.486* (0.267)
Wife Catholic	−0.200 (0.695)	1.81	0.367 (0.276)	0.224 (0.282)	0.144 (0.288)	2.47	0.377 (0.254)	0.118 (0.271)	0.259 (0.242)
Wife no religion	−1.180 (0.980)	0.73	0.450 (0.539)	0.308 (0.569)	0.142 (0.553)	1.25	−0.185 (0.509)	−0.659 (0.619)	0.474 (0.564)
Husband different religion	0.958 (0.825)	5.44*	0.716** (0.312)	0.462 (0.332)	0.254 (0.316)	2.01	0.306 (0.296)	−0.079 (0.337)	0.385 (0.301)
Wife exclusivist Protestant* Husband different religion	−0.992 (1.301)	1.07	−0.022 (0.465)	0.450 (0.495)	−0.473 (0.512)	1.62	−0.110 (0.442)	0.460 (0.507)	−0.570 (0.455)
Wife Catholic* Husband different religion	−0.384 (1.166)	2.51	−0.767 (0.484)	−0.427 (0.506)	−0.340 (0.488)	3.47	−0.865* (0.495)	−0.244 (0.545)	−0.621 (0.493)
Wife no religion* Husband different religion	−0.199 (1.381)	1.11	−0.562 (0.707)	−0.778 (0.782)	0.216 (0.746)	0.43	0.489 (0.756)	0.256 (0.954)	0.232 (0.843)
Control variables									
Wife's education									
<12 years	−1.543** (0.732)	5.38*	−0.862** (0.383)	−0.289 (0.400)	−0.573 (0.470)	10.08**	−0.733** (0.254)	−0.706** (0.299)	−0.0267 (0.309)
13–15 years	1.316** (0.644)	4.39	0.445** (0.220)	0.323 (0.238)	0.122 (0.241)	3.05	0.368* (0.218)	0.147 (0.247)	0.220 (0.218)
≥16 years	0.294 (0.569)	8.39**	0.491* (0.253)	0.733** (0.262)	−0.242 (0.261)	14.14**	0.917** (0.266)	0.860** (0.285)	0.057 (0.226)
Wife's age	0.705* (0.409)	10.71**	0.506** (0.173)	0.405** (0.182)	0.102 (0.204)	9.93**	0.279** (0.091)	0.181* (0.100)	0.098 (0.101)
Wife's age squared	−0.012* (0.007)	10.07**	−0.008** (0.003)	−0.006** (0.003)	−0.002 (0.003)	14.43**	−0.004** (0.001)	−0.003** (0.001)	−0.001 (0.001)

(Continued Overleaf)

Table 3.4 Continued

	Period 1		Period 2				Period 3		
	FT or PT vs. NE[b]	x^2 2 df	FT vs. NE	PT vs. NE	FT vs. PT	x^2 2 df	FT vs. NE	PT vs. NE	FT vs. PT
Number of children in household	—	35.07**	-0.538** (0.099)	-0.329** (0.099)	-0.209* (0.110)	13.19**	-0.371** (0.104)	-0.254** (0.113)	-0.117 (0.108)
Log of other family income	0.148 (0.113)	8.84**	-0.179** (0.072)	0.025 (0.091)	-0.204** (0.088)	1.98	-0.025 (0.050)	-0.057 (0.064)	-0.082 (0.060)
Husband married before	0.621 (0.672)	2.79	0.399 (0.271)	0.0006 (0.305)	0.399 (0.296)	11.85**	0.480* (0.253)	-0.426 (0.307)	0.907** (0.278)
Wife married before	-0.658 (0.622)	0.15	-0.080 (0.268)	0.0237 (0.284)	-0.104 (0.290)	0.13	0.083 (0.247)	0.085 (0.289)	-0.002 (0.258)
Husband older than wife by six years or more	-1.542** (0.609)	2.19	-0.188 (0.270)	-0.450 (0.309)	0.262 (0.314)	5.64*	-0.554** (0.234)	-0.269 (0.267)	-0.285 (0.257)
Metropolitan area – fringe	-0.483 (0.520)	2.25	-0.366 (0.245)	-0.162 (0.249)	-0.205 (0.264)	2.77	-0.218 (0.232)	0.158 (0.249)	-0.376* (0.230)
Non-metropolitan area – adjacent to metropolitan area	0.557 (0.732)	0.84	0.077 (0.227)	-0.155 (0.250)	0.232 (0.256)	0.83	0.062 (0.221)	0.215 (0.246)	-0.153 (0.217)
Non-metropolitan area – not adjacent to metropolitan Area	-0.302 (0.708)	5.59*	0.594** (0.292)	0.607** (0.301)	-0.013 (0.291)	0.28	-0.035 (0.255)	-0.151 (0.300)	0.117 (0.273)
South	0.857 (0.525)	12.43**	0.212 (0.209)	-0.604** (0.237)	0.816** (0.241)	2.13	-0.099 (0.192)	-0.311 (0.218)	0.212 (0.200)
Constant	-9.724 (5.853)		-5.773** (2.657)	-6.483** (2.866)	0.710 (3.162)		-3.674 (1.927)	-2.908 (2.140)	-0.766 (2.124)
Log-likelihood	-84.025		-799.928				-924.028		

* $p < 0.10$, ** $p < 0.05$.

Notes

a Standard errors are in parentheses.

b FT, full-time work; PT, part-time work; NE, non-employment.

information on the variance–covariance matrix, or more easily by reestimating the model with different benchmark categories. For the case of periods 1 and 3, these additional computations revealed no significant effects, suggesting that religion does not play a role in female labor supply decisions at these stages of the life cycle. In contrast, additional significant effects were uncovered for period 2, involving comparisons against exclusivist Protestants. These results are shown in Table 3.5. While Tables 3.4 and 3.5 provide information on the direction and significance of the various influences, the magnitudes of the effects can be more easily assessed by examining Table 3.6, which displays the estimated probabilities of nonemployment, part-time, and full-time work for women in unions with different religious compositions. Together, Tables 3.4, 3.5, and 3.6 provide a complete description of the effects of religion on female employment in period 2.

Focusing first on comparisons between the various types of intrafaith unions, Table 3.5 shows that the odds of participating in the labor force on a full-time or part-time basis as opposed to being nonemployed are significantly higher for Catholic women in homogamous unions than for their exclusivist Protestant counterparts. Table 3.6 indicates that while the probabilities of full-time and part-time work for the latter are only 0.21 and 0.24, respectively, the corresponding figures for the former are 0.32 and 0.32 – sizable effects. Table 3.6 also shows that the differences in probabilities between exclusivist Protestant unions and couples in which the two partners are

Table 3.5 Reestimating the model for period 2 with exclusivist Protestant wives as benchmark[a]

	χ^2 *(2 df)*	*Full-time work vs. non-employment*	*Part-time work vs. non-employment*	*Full-time work vs. part-time work*
Wife ecumenical Protestant	3.23	0.452 (0.299)	0.462 (0.324)	−0.009 (0.357)
Wife Catholic	7.66**	0.820** (0.327)	0.685** (0.346)	0.134 (0.377)
Wife no religion	3.06	0.903 (0.559)	0.770 (0.597)	0.132 (0.600)
Husband different religion	7.51**	0.694** (0.350)	0.912** (0.373)	−0.219 (0.408)

* p < 0.10, ** p < 0.05.

Note

a The model also includes interaction terms between "Husband different religion" and "Wife ecumenical Protestant," "Wife Catholic," and "Wife no religion." All the control variables are also included, and have, of course, coefficients that are identical to those shown in Table 3.4. Note that in this specification, the coefficients on the variable "Wife ecumenical Protestant" provide information on the difference between homogamous unions in which the spouses are ecumenical Protestant and those in which they are exclusivist Protestant. The coefficients on the second and third variables in this table have a similar interpretation; those on the fourth variable provide information on the effects of out-marriage for exclusivist Protestant women.

Table 3.6 The effects of religion on the probability of full-time work, part-time work, and non-employment – period 2[a]

	χ^2 2 df	Full-time work	Part-time work	Non-employment
(A) Differences by type of hornogamous union				
Homogamous ecumenical Protestant union vs.		0.26	0.30	0.43
Homogamous exclusivist Protestant union	3.23	(0.21)	(0.24)	(0.55)
Homogamous Catholic union	1.81	(0.32)	(0.32)	(0.36)
Husband and wife unaffiliated	0.73	(0.33)	(0.33)	(0.34)
Homogamous exclusivist Protestant union vs.		0.21	0.24	0.55
Homogamous Catholic union	7.66**	0.32	0.32	0.36
Husband and wife unaffiliated	3.06	(0.33)	(0.33)	(0.34)
Homogamous Catholic union vs.		0.32	0.32	0.36
Husband and wife unaffiliated	0.03	(0.33)	(0.33)	(0.34)
(B) The effects of out-marriage				
Homogamous ecumenical Protestant union vs.		0.26	0.30	0.43
Wife ecumenical Protestant, husband other	5.44*	0.37	0.33	0.30
Homogamous exclusivist Protestant union vs.		0.21	0.24	0.55
Wife exclusivist Protestant, husband other	7.51**	0.27	0.38	0.35
Homogamous Catholic union vs.		0.32	0.32	0.36
Wife Catholic, husband other	0.05	(0.31)	(0.33)	(0.36)
Husband and wife unaffiliated vs.		0.33	0.33	0.34
Wife unaffiliated, husband some religion	0.49	(0.40)	(0.25)	(0.36)

* p < 0.10, ** p < 0.05.

Note

a These probabilities are based on the model of Table 3.4, setting the number of children at two, the wife's age and other family income at the means for period 2, and the categorical variables at the benchmark (which in each case represents the modal group). The probabilities shown in parentheses reflect effects that are insignificant at the 0.10 level, as indicated by the χ^2 tests.

unaffiliated are very similar in magnitude; however, the number of unions in which neither spouse has a religion is small and these differences do not attain significance at conventional levels. The point estimates also suggest that labor supply is lower among women in exclusivist Protestant unions than among those in ecumenical Protestant unions, but significance again is weak. The direction of all these effects, however, is as expected.

Turning now to the impact of out-marriage on female employment, the results support the hypothesis that labor supply is higher among exclusivist Protestant women in interfaith marriages than among their counterparts in homogamous unions. The estimates for the "husband different religion" variable in Table 3.5 show that out-marriage significantly increases the odds that exclusivist Protestant women will work on a full- or part-time basis, as opposed to being out of the labor force. As Table 3.6 indicates, out-marriage is associated with a large increase in the probability of working part time, from 0.24 to 0.38, and with a modest increase in the probability of working full time, from 0.21 to 0.27.

The nature of the effect of out-marriage for the other religious groups is ambiguous a priori, as discussed in the theoretical section. Empirically, the estimates for the "husband different religion" variable in Table 3.4 indicate that out-marriage is also associated with stronger attachment to the labor force for ecumenical Protestants, specifically, with an increase in the odds of working full-time as opposed to not at all; as Table 3.6 shows, the probability of full-time employment rises from 0.26 to 0.37. No significant effects of out-marriage, however, are discerned for Catholic or unaffiliated women.

Overall, the findings for period 2 that, among homogamous unions, the level of employment is lowest for exclusivist Protestant women, and that out-marriage significantly increases labor market activity for such women, are both consistent with expectations based on the theoretical model. It had been hypothesized also that the religious composition of unions should matter most when young children are present in the household. The empirical results show that in fact it matters only in this stage of the life cycle. The absence of significant effects of religion in period 1 is offered tentatively, however, because of the small sample size for this group.

The control variables

The influences of the variables that are included as controls in the model are generally as expected, as shown in Tables 3.4 and 3.7. Female attachment to the labor force increases with education and with age, and the effects of age follow the non-linear pattern that is commonly found. Additional children significantly depress labor supply, an effect that is particularly large in magnitude in period 2. The variable for other family income is significant in period 2 but not in periods 1 and 3, suggesting that other sources of income represent an important factor in the wife's labor supply decisions only when young children are present in the home. Research based on data from the 1970s had found that such income had an insignificant role in period 1 (Lehrer and Nerlove 1984); the lack of significance in period 3 also appears to be a new development of the 1980s. No difference can be discerned between the labor supply of women in first versus higher-order marriages, but a previous union of the husband does affect female employment in the expected direction after all children have reached school age. Women whose husbands are considerably older than they tend to work less in the market than their counterparts married to men of more similar ages, suggesting that contrary to the case of religion, complementarities in home activities are not very important in the case of age. Grossbard-Shechtman (1993, p. 133) finds a similar result, interpreting an older age as a negative trait within the context of marriage:

> a husband with traits that are relatively undesirable in comparison with his wife's traits has to compensate her materially by letting her have a larger proportion of his income. When such compensating differentials occur, married women are less likely to need work as a source of income and, therefore, less likely to participate in the labor force.

Table 3.7 The effects of the control variables on the probability of full-time work, part-time work, and non-employment[a]

	Period 1		Period 2			Period 3		
	Full- or part-time work	Non-employment	Full-time work	Part-time work	Non-employment	Full-time work	Part-time work	Non-employment
Reference case[b]	0.92	0.08	0.26	0.30	0.43	0.38	0.34	0.28
Wife's education								
<12 years	0.70	0.30	0.15	0.29	0.56	0.29	0.27	0.44
13–15 years	0.98	0.02	(0.33)	(0.33)	(0.34)	(0.45)	(0.32)	(0.23)
≥16 years	(0.94)	(0.06)	0.29	0.42	0.29	0.47	0.39	0.14
Wife's age								
25	0.89	0.11	0.21	0.27	0.52	0.30	0.36	0.34
30	0.92	0.08	0.26	0.30	0.44	0.36	0.36	0.28
40	0.78	0.22	0.22	0.26	0.52	0.39	0.34	0.27
Number of children in household								
1	–	–	0.35	0.32	0.33	0.44	0.34	0.22
3	–	–	0.19	0.27	0.54	0.33	0.33	0.34
Other family income								
$15,000	(0.91)	(0.09)	0.29	0.29	0.42	(0.40)	(0.32)	(0.28)
$30,000	(0.92)	(0.08)	0.27	0.30	0.43	(0.39)	(0.34)	(0.28)
$45,000	(0.92)	(0.08)	0.25	0.31	0.44	(0.38)	(0.34)	(0.28)
$60,000	(0.92)	(0.08)	0.24	0.31	0.44	(0.38)	(0.35)	(0.28)
Husband married before	(0.95)	(0.05)	(0.35)	(0.27)	(0.38)	0.55	0.20	0.25
Wife married before	(0.85)	(0.15)	(0.25)	(0.31)	(0.44)	(0.39)	(0.35)	(0.26)
Husband older than wife by six years or more	0.70	0.30	(0.26)	(0.23)	(0.51)	0.29	0.34	0.37
Metropolitan area – Fringe	(0.87)	(0.13)	(0.21)	(0.29)	(0.50)	(0.31)	(0.40)	(0.28)

Non-metropolitan area – adjacent to metropolitan area	(0.95)	(0.05)	(0.29)	(0.26)	(0.44)	(0.37)	(0.38)	(0.25)
Non-metropolitan area – not adjacent to metropolitan area	(0.89)	(0.11)	0.33	0.38	0.30	(0.40)	(0.31)	(0.29)
South	(0.96)	(0.04)	0.35	0.18	0.47	(0.40)	(0.28)	(0.32)

Notes

a Estimates shown in parentheses correspond to effects that are insignificant at the 0.10 level (based on t-test for period 1, χ^2 test for periods 2 and 3).

b The reference case corresponds to a couple with two children (for periods 2 and 3); the wife's age and other family income are set at the means (for the entire sample), and all categorical variables are set at the benchmark.

There are some significant variations across regions in period 2. Labor supply is highest in non-metropolitan areas that are not adjacent to metropolitan areas, probably reflecting the fact that mother's employment and childrearing activities are most compatible in such places. In addition, living in the South strongly encourages either full-time participation in the labor force or nonemployment, as opposed to part-time work – the option in the middle. As Table 3.7 shows, Southern residence increases the probability of full-time work from 0.26 to 0.35, and the probability of nonemployment from 0.43 to 0.47; at the same time that of part-time work falls from 0.30 to only 0.18. This finding suggests that the fixed costs of employment for women with children under six may be particularly high in the South, consistent with results from the literature on childcare arrangements which show that reliance on the formal, more expensive types of childcare is more frequent in the South than in other regions of the country (Lehrer and Kawasaki 1985; Leibowitz et al. 1988; Lehrer 1989).

The estimated effects of the control variables provide a way of assessing the relative importance of religion as a determinant of female employment. As Table 3.6 shows, while the probability of nonemployment for exclusivist Protestant women in homogamous unions is 0.55, the probability for their Catholic counterparts is only 0.36, and that for exclusivist Protestant women in interfaith marriages is only 0.35 – differences of about 20 percentage points in each case. Inspection of Table 3.7 suggests that only the wife's education, the number of children, and residence in the South have effects of comparable orders of magnitude. It is clear, therefore, that religion plays a much more important role in decisions regarding female employment than had been recognized in the literature until now.

Sensitivity analysis

Examining first how the results are affected by using a different econometric specification, Table 3.8 presents the model for period 2 reestimated using ordered probit. This procedure has the advantage that it utilizes the information on the ordering of the three states – nonemployment, part-time, and full-time work – and therefore should be expected to yield more precise estimates. On the other hand, the ordered probit model assumes that the entire range of labor supply responses can be described by one vector of parameters, thus ruling out a priori the existence of non-linearities such as those illustrated in Tables 3.4 and 3.7 for the case of residence in the South.

The results regarding the effects of religion obtained from this alternative specification support the conclusions from the multinomial logit model and in fact strengthen them. The ordered probit estimates confirm the earlier findings that out-marriage has a significant positive impact on the labor supply of ecumenical and exclusivist Protestant women. In addition, for the case of comparisons among intrafaith unions, these estimates show that the labor supply of exclusivist Protestant women is significantly lower not only than

Table 3.8 Ordered probit estimates for period 2[a,b]

Religion variables	
Wife exclusivist Protestant	−0.265 (0.142)*
Wife Catholic	0.159 (0.127)
Wife no religion	0.159 (0.247)
Husband different religion	0.315 (0.143)**
Wife exclusivist Protestant* husband different religion	0.060 (0.216)
Wife Catholic* husband different religion	−0.345 (0.222)
Wife no religion* husband different religion	−0.176 (0.330)
Control variables	
Wife's education	
<12 years	−0.404 (0.174)**
13–15 years	0.220 (0.105)**
≥16 years	0.219 (0.116)*
Wife's age	0.251 (0.080)**
Wife's age squared	−0.004 (0.001)**
Number of children in household	−0.259 (0.045)**
Log of other family income	−0.090 (0.035)**
Husband married before	0.185 (0.129)
Wife married before	−0.036 (0.125)
Husband older than wife by six years or more	−0.103 (0.131)
Metropolitan area – fringe	−0.164 (0.113)
Non-metropolitan area – adjacent to metropolitan area	0.025 (0.108)
Non-metropolitan area – not adjacent to metropolitan area	0.269 (0.132)**
South	0.098 (0.100)
Constant	−2.488 (1.240)**
Log-likelihood	−818.245

* p < 0.10, ** p < 0.05.

Notes

a Standard errors are in parentheses.

b The tests reported in this table reflect comparisons against homogamous ecumenical Protestant unions. Reestimation of the model with exclusivist Protestants as benchmark reveals that the labor supply of women in homogamous exclusivist Protestant unions is lower than that of their counterparts in homogamous Catholic marriages (0.05 level) or in unions in which both partners are unaffiliated (0.10 level); in addition, the effect of out-marriage on labor supply for exclusivist Protestant women is significantly positive (0.05 level).

that of their Catholic counterparts, but also than that of ecumenical Protestant and unaffiliated women. These results are consistent with the view that the greater amount of information about the nature of the dependent variable used by the ordered probit model produces more precise estimates. However, there is little difference in how well the two models predict female labor supply behavior for couples with different religious compositions, as Table 3.9 suggests.[12] It is also worth noting that in the ordered probit model, the coefficient on the South dummy variable is insignificant, masking the pronounced non-linearities uncovered in the multinomial logit specification.

Turning now to the measurement of religion, it was noted earlier that if the husband's and wife's religious affiliations are measured before the marriage, the group of "interfaith" unions would include couples who have

Table 3.9 Actual proportions vs. multinomial logit and ordered probit estimates (period 2)

	Full-time work			Part-time work			Non-employment		
	Actual	Logit	Probit	Actual	Logit	Probit	Actual	Logit	Probit
Homogamous ecumenical Protestant union[a]	0.33	0.30	0.29	0.28	0.26	0.28	0.40	0.44	0.43
Homogamous exclusivist Protestant union	0.24	0.24	0.21	0.16	0.20	0.26	0.59	0.56	0.53
Homogamous Catholic union	0.33	0.36	0.35	0.29	0.27	0.28	0.38	0.37	0.37
Husband and wife unaffiliated	0.35	0.37	0.35	0.27	0.28	0.28	0.38	0.35	0.37
Wife ecumenical Protestant, Husband other	0.43	0.42	0.41	0.28	0.28	0.28	0.29	0.30	0.31
Wife exclusivist Protestant, Husband other	0.30	0.31	0.33	0.27	0.33	0.28	0.42	0.36	0.39
Wife Catholic, husband other	0.37	0.35	0.34	0.31	0.28	0.28	0.32	0.37	0.38
Wife unaffiliated, husband other	0.46	0.44	0.40	0.21	0.20	0.28	0.33	0.36	0.32
R^2 for regression of actual on predicted values		0.91	0.81		0.60	0.66		0.83	0.87

Note

a The interpretation of the first three values in this row is as follows. In the sample of homogamous ecumenical Protestant unions, the fraction of wives who work full time is 0.33. With all the control variables set at the means, "Wife ecumenical Protestant" set at 1, and "Husband other religion" set at 0, the multinomial logit model predicts that the probability of full-time work is 0.30; a similar calculation with the ordered probit model yields 0.29.

achieved homogamy through conversion and whose unions are highly stable; the measured intermarriage effect should therefore be considerably weaker. Consistent with this reasoning, when the period 2 model in Table 3.4 was reestimated using religion before marriage, the estimated effects of out-marriage for both ecumenical and exclusivist Protestant women became insignificant at all conventional levels. However, the conclusions regarding differences across various types of homogamous unions remained largely unchanged (results not shown).

Finally, the model of Table 3.4 was reestimated one more time treating all inter-denominational unions as heterogamous, including those composed of members of two different ecumenical Protestant groups. Once again in this alternative definition of heterogamy, the "interfaith" group includes couples that actually have relatively high levels of religious compatibility. The distinction between homogamous and heterogamous marriages is thus blurred, and not surprisingly, no significant effect of out-marriage on female labor supply could be discerned for ecumenical Protestant women when this alternative specification was employed. The other results were substantially unaffected.

Conclusions

Two mechanisms through which religious affiliation may influence the labor supply behavior of married women have been explored. One avenue is through differences among religions in views regarding the appropriate division of labor within the family, and the need to resolve conflict between husband and wife if the attitudes embodied in their respective religions differ. The second avenue is through the effect of religious intermarriage on the probability of marital breakup, and the impact in turn of such probability on female attachment to the labor force. Comparison of employment patterns for women in various types of intra- and interfaith marriages, using data from the 1987–88 National Survey of Families and Households, reveals a significant influence of religion when young children are present in the home. Among women in homogamous unions, those affiliated to exclusivist Protestant denominations display the lowest levels of attachment to the labor force. In addition, out-marriage has a significant positive impact on labor supply for both ecumenical and exclusivist Protestant women. These effects are large in magnitude, suggesting that religion plays an important role in female time allocation decisions.

While the results suggest that life cycle stage affects the strength of the religion–female labor supply linkage, it is important to emphasize that the present analyses are "life cycle" in a narrow sense only – a cross-section of families has been divided into three groups depending on the presence and ages of children. Reexamination of the effects of husband's and wife's religion on female employment using longitudinal data would be a fruitful area for further research.

Several questions that could not be addressed here due to limitations of sample size warrant investigation with larger data sets. It would be useful to study possible interactions between religion and various levels of husband's and wife's religiosity as determinants of female labor supply behavior. It would also be interesting to extend the analysis to include Jews and Mormons, important religious minorities that are known to have distinctive patterns of demographic and economic behavior.

The results presented in this study provide an interpretation for findings in the literature on differences in economic success across religious groups, and also suggest directions for further research in this area. While the earliest studies used family income as the dependent variable, yielding conflicting rankings of economic status by religion (Featherman 1971; Greeley 1976, 1981; Roof 1979, 1981), more recent analyses based on the framework of human capital theory and focusing on female earnings in particular, suggest that Catholic women earn more than their Protestant counterparts (Tomes 1985; Steen and Dubbink 1994). The present study, which finds a pronounced difference in the labor supply behavior of Catholic women and an important group of Protestant women, namely, those affiliated to exclusivist Protestant denominations, provides a possible explanation in terms of differences in the amount, intensity, and continuity of labor market experience. More generally, the finding in this study that the extent of the intra-family division of labor and specialization varies across religious groups suggests that the earnings rankings by religion may well differ for men and women. This possibility, first recognized by Tomes (1985), deserves systematic investigation in future research.

Acknowledgments

I am indebted to Carmel Chiswick and anonymous referees for many helpful comments on earlier drafts of this paper.

Notes

1   This survey was designed at the Center for Demography and Ecology at the University of Wisconsin-Madison under the direction of Larry Bumpass and James Sweet. The fieldwork was done by the Institute for Survey Research at Temple University.
2   This terminology, classifying Protestant groups into "ecumenical" and "exclusivist," is based on Kelley's (1972) work. See also Lehrer and Chiswick (1993).
3   The NSFH contains several other questions on gender role attitudes, the responses to all of which reveal similar patterns (results not shown).
4   The literature reviewed in the text emphasizes a possible role of the husband's and wife's affiliations on time allocation decisions through differences among groups in gender role attitudes. Chiswick (1986) has suggested another mechanism, namely, differences between religious groups in patterns of investments in child quality. Specifically, he advances the hypothesis that the success of Jews in the labor market may reflect relatively high levels of investments by mothers in their

young children and correspondingly low levels of female labor supply during the childrearing years. This mechanism is not pursued here, because previous studies have produced conflicting rankings in terms of economic success for the religions considered in this study (Featherman 1971; Greeley 1976, 1981; Roof 1979, 1981; Tomes 1984, 1985; Steen and Dubbink 1994).

5 Investments in children "decline in value" following marriage dissolution for several reasons discussed at length by Becker et al. (1977), Chiswick and Lehrer (1990), and Lehrer (1996b). These include the fact that the father generally has less contact with the children after divorce (e.g., see Furstenberg et al. 1983). In addition, from the mother's perspective, the presence of children from a previous union decreases the probability of remarriage and raises the risk of divorce in a subsequent marriage (Becker et al. 1977; Chiswick and Lehrer 1990; Lehrer 1996b). Empirically, a growing body of research suggests that couples who perceive that their unions are unstable (because of religious incompatibility or other reasons) respond by restricting their fertility. Becker et al. (1977) and Lehrer (1996a) find that differences between husband and wife in religious beliefs are associated with smaller family size, ceteris paribus. Along similar lines, Lillard and Waite's (1993) simultaneous equations model of divorce and childbearing shows that the hazard of marital disruption has a negative effect on the probability of conception. For additional discussion of these issues and a recent debate on rational choice theories of fertility, see Friedman et al. (1994) and Lehrer et al. (1996).

6 Since period 1 is intended to cover the initial years of marriage, before the arrival of the first child, the few childless couples in which the wife was 40 years of age or older are excluded.

7 The sample sizes for African-American wives in periods 1, 2, and 3, respectively, are only 30, 128, and 194; for Hispanic women, the corresponding figures are even smaller: 18, 64, and 58.

8 Unemployed women are excluded because their number is too small to permit a separate category, and it would be inappropriate to lump these cases with the full- or part-time workers or with those out of the labor force. Women enrolled in an educational program are also excluded from this analysis.

9 In addition to the wife's and husband's current affiliations, the survey documents the religion in which the respondent was raised as well as the spouse's faith just prior to the present marriage, if different from the current affiliation. The latter can safely be assumed to represent the religion in which the husband or wife was raised for most, but not all cases.

10 The ecumenical denominations include Episcopalians, Lutherans, Methodists, Presbyterians, as well as other mainline Protestant bodies. The exclusivist denominations include Baptists, Jehovah's Witnesses, Seventh-Day Adventists, Christian Scientists, and a large number of other fundamentalist groups. For details, see Lehrer and Chiswick (1993).

11 Ideally, more detailed categories would have been used for the husband's religion, but sample size limitations unfortunately precluded this possibility.

12 The approach used in Table 3.9 follows similar procedures employed by Nakamura et al. (1979) and Lehrer (1992).

References

Alwin, D. F. (1984) "Trends in Parental Socialization Values: Detroit, 1958–1983." *American Journal of Sociology* 90(2):359–82.

Becker, G. S., Landes, E. M., and Michael, R. T. (1977) "An Economic Analysis of Marital Instability." *Journal of Political Economy* 85(6):1141–87.

Brinkerhoff, M. B. and MacKie, M. M. (1984) "Religious Denominations' Impact Upon Gender Attitudes: Some Methodological Implications." *Review of Religious Research* 25(4):365–78.

Brinkerhoff, M. B., and MacKie, M. M. (1988) "Religious Sources of Gender Traditionalism." Pp. 232–57 in D. Thomas (ed.) *The Religion and Family Connection.* Religious Studies Center, Salt Lake City: Brigham Young University.

Campbell, D. F. (1966) "Religion and Values Among Nova Scotian College Students." *Sociological Analysis* 27:80–93.

Carliner, G. (1981) "Female Labor Force Participation Rates for Nine Ethnic Groups." *Journal of Human Resources* 16(2):286–93.

Chiswick, B. (1986) "Labor Supply and Investments in Child Quality: A Study of Jewish and non-Jewish Women." *The Review of Economics and Statistics* 68(4):700–3.

Chiswick, C. (1997) "Determinants of Religious Intermarriage: Are Jews Really Different?" Pp. 247–57 in S. DellaPergola and J. Even (eds) *Papers in Jewish Demography 1993, in Memory of U. O. Schmelz.* Proceedings of the Demographic Sessions held at the 11th World Congress of Jewish Studies, Jerusalem, June 1993.

Chiswick, C. and Lehrer, E. (1990) "On Marriage-Specific Capital: Its Role as a Determinant of Remarriage." *Journal of Population Economics* 3:193–213.

Chiswick, C., and Lehrer, E. (1991) "Religious Intermarriage: An Economic Perspective." *Contemporary Jewry* 12:21–34.

Cooney, R. S. and Ortiz, V. (1983) "Nativity, National Origin, and Hispanic Female Participation in the Labor Force." *Social Science Quarterly* 64(3):511–23.

D'Antonio, W. V. and Cavanaugh, M. J. (1983) "Roman Catholicism and the Family." Pp. 141–62 in W. V. D'Antonio and J. Aldous (eds) *Families and Religions: Conflict and Change in Modern Society.* Beverly Hills: Sage.

Featherman, D. L. (1971) "The Socioeconomic Achievement of White Religio-Ethnic Subgroups: Social and Psychological Explanations." *American Sociological Review* 36:207–22.

Friedman, D., Hechter, M., and Kanazawa, S. (1994) "A Theory of the Value of Children." *Demography* 31(3):375–401.

Furstenberg, F. F., Jr., Nord, W., Peterson, J. L., and Zill, N. (1983) "The Life Course of Children and Divorce: Marital Disruption and Parental Contact." *American Sociological Review* 48(10):656–68.

Greeley, A. M. (1976) *Ethnicity, Denomination and Inequality.* Beverly Hills: Sage.

Greeley, A. M. (1981) "Catholics and the Upper Middle Class: A Comment on Roof." *Social Forces* 59(3):824–30.

Greene, W. H. and Quester, A. O. (1982) "Divorce Risk and Wives' Labor Supply Behavior." *Social Science Quarterly* 63(1):16–27.

Grossbard-Shechtman, S. (1993) *On the Economics of Marriage: A Theory of Marriage, Labor, and Divorce.* Boulder, CO: Westview Press.

Heaton, T. and Cornwall, M. (1989) "Religious Group Variation in the Socioeconomic Status and Family Behavior of Women." *Journal for the Scientific Study of Religion* 28(3):283–99.

Heaton, T. B. and Pratt, E. L. (1990) "The Effects of Religious Homogamy on Marital Satisfaction and Stability." *Journal of Family Issues* 11(2):191–207.

Heckert, A. and Teachman, J. D. (1985) "Religious Factors in the Timing of Second Births." *Journal of Marriage and the Family* 47(2):361–7.

Johnson, W. R. and Skinner, J. (1986) "Labor Supply and Marital Separation." *American Economic Review* 76(3):455–69.

Kelley, D. M. (1972) *Why Conservative Churches are Growing*. New York: Harper and Row.

Lehrer, E. (1989) "Preschoolers with Working Mothers: An Analysis of the Determinants of Child Care Arrangements." *Journal of Population Economics* 1:251–68.

Lehrer, E. (1992) "The Impact of Children on Married Women's Labor Supply: Black–White Differentials Revisited." *Journal of Human Resources* 27(3):422–444.

Lehrer, E. (1996a) "The Role of the Husband's Religion on the Economic and Demographic Behavior of Families." *Journal for the Scientific Study of Religion* 35(2):145–55.

Lehrer, E. (1996b) "The Determinants of Marital Stability: A Comparative Analysis of First and Higher Order Marriages." *Research in Population Economic* 8:91–121.

Lehrer, E. and Chiswick, C. (1993) "Religion as a Determinant of Marital Stability." *Demography* 30(3):385–404. (Chapter 1 this volume.)

Lehrer, E., Grossbard-Shechtman, S., and Leasure, W. (1996) "Comment on 'A Theory of the Value of Children'." *Demography* 33(1):133–6.

Lehrer, E. and Kawasaki, S. (1985) "Child Care Arrangements and Fertility: An Analysis of Two-Earner Households." *Demography* 22(4):499–513.

Lehrer, E. and Nerlove, M. (1984) "A Life-Cycle Analysis of Family Income Distribution." *Economic Inquiry* 22(3):360–74.

Leibowitz, A., Waite, L., and Witsberger, C. (1988) "Child Care for Preschoolers: Differences by Child's Age." *Demography* 25(2):205–20.

Lillard, L. and Waite, L. (1993) "A Joint Model of Marital Childbearing and Marital Disruption." *Demography* 30(4):653–82.

Lundberg, S., and Pollak, R. A. (1993) "Separate Spheres Bargaining and the Marriage Market." *Journal of Political Economy* 10(6):988–1010.

Manser, M. and Brown, M. (1980) "Marriage and Household Decision-Making: A Bargaining Analysis." *International Economic Review* 21:31–44.

McElroy, M. B. and Horney, M. J. (1981) "Nash-Bargained Household Decisions: Toward a Generalization of the Theory of Demand." *International Economic Review* 22:333–49.

McMurry, M. (1978) "Religion and Women's Sex Role Traditionalism." *Sociological Focus* 11(2): 81–95.

Meir, H. C. (1972) "Mother-Centeredness and College Youths' Attitudes Toward Social Equality for Women: Some Empirical Findings." *Journal of Marriage and the Family* 34:115–21.

Michael, R. (1979) "Determinants of Divorce." Pp. 223–54 in L. Levy-Garboua (ed.) *Sociological Economics*. Beverly Hills: Sage.

Mosher, W. D., Williams, L. B., and Johnson, D. P. (1992) "Religion and Fertility in the United States: New Patterns." *Demography* 29(2):199–214.

Nakamura, M., Nakamura, A., and Cullen, D. (1979) "Job Opportunities, the Offered Wage, and the Labor Supply of Married Women." *American Economic Review* 69(5):787–805.

Reimers, C. (1985) "A Comparative Analysis of the Wages of Hispanics, Blacks and Non-Hispanic Whites." Pp. 27–75 in G. Borjas and M. Tienda (eds) *Hispanics in the U.S. Economy*. New York: Academic Press.

Roof, W. C. (1979) "Socioeconomic Differentials Among White Socioreligious Groups in the United States." *Social Forces* 58: 280–289.

Roof, W. C. (1981) "Unresolved Issues in the Study of Religion and the National Elite: Response to Greeley." *Social Forces* 59(3): 831–6.

Steen, T. P. and Dubbink, K. S. (1994) "The Impact of Religion on the Earnings and Human Capital of Women." Presented at the meetings of the Midwest Economics Association, March 24–26, Chicago, IL.

Thornton, A. (1985) "Changing Attitudes Toward Separation and Divorce: Causes and Consequences." *American Journal of Sociology* 90(4):856–72.

Tomes, N. (1984) "The Effects of Religion and Denomination on Earnings and the Return to Human Capital." *Journal of Human Resources* 19:472–88.

Tomes, N. (1985) "Human Capital and Culture: The Analysis of Variations in Labor Market Performance." *American Economics Association, Papers and Proceedings* 75(2):245–50.

Waite, L. and Sheps, J. (1994) "The Impact of Religious Upbringing and Marriage Markets on Jewish Intermarriage." Presented at the meetings of the Population Association of America, May 5–7, Miami, Florida.

Williams, L. and Zimmer, B. (1990) "The Changing Influence of Religion on U.S. Fertility: Evidence from Rhode Island." *Demography* 27(3):475–81.

4 Religion as a determinant of marital fertility *

There is an extensive literature on the role of religion in fertility behavior in the United States. Research focuses on Catholic–Protestant differentials and how they have changed over time (Jones and Westoff 1979; Mosher and Hendershot 1984a; Mosher et al. 1992); the distinctive fertility behavior of other groups including Mormons, Jews, and persons who have no religious affiliation (Thornton 1979; Della Pergola 1980; Mosher et al. 1992) and the role of differences in religiosity within the various groups (Heaton 1986; Williams and Zimmer 1990; Goldscheider and Mosher 1991).

While some studies explore the influence of religion on the timing and extent of marriage (Mosher et al. 1986; Mosher et al. 1992; Sander 1993), most analyze its effects on marital fertility. In this context, attention is focused almost exclusively on the wife's religious affiliation. Yet a growing body of literature on fertility behavior emphasizes that both husbands and wives participate in the decision-making process and that their interests may be conflicting (Lehrer and Nerlove 1984; Schultz 1990). This study explores channels through which the husband's religion may play a role, and develops hypotheses regarding the effects of the religious composition of unions on fertility. The hypotheses are based on two central ideas. First, religious groups differ in their fertility norms and related tradeoffs between the quality and quantity of children (Becker 1991). The spouses in religious inter-marriages therefore face the possibility of conflict in their fertility decisions, which may be resolved through bargaining. Second, within the context of marriage, religion is a complementary trait for which the mating of likes is optimal; interfaith couples thus have an elevated risk of divorce (Lehrer and Chiswick 1993). In turn, the relative instability of such couples reduces their incentives to make investments in spouse-specific human capital, children in particular.

The hypotheses that are developed from these two ideas are tested with data from the 1987–88 National Survey of Families and Households, a source rich in information on both fertility and religion. The analysis focuses on

---

* Reprinted from *Journal of Population Economics* 9:173–196, 1996.

five major religious groups: ecumenical Protestant, exclusivist Protestant, Catholic, Mormon, and no religion.[1]

Analytical framework

A central focus in the literature on fertility differentials by wife's religion is the extent to which such differentials reflect an effect of religion per se, as opposed to merely being an artifact of socioeconomic and demographic differences across religious groups. It has been suggested that an important avenue through which religion itself may influence fertility behavior is through differences among groups in norms regarding marriage, contraceptive practice, abortion, desired family size, divorce, and gender roles (Thornton 1979; Mosher et al. 1992). Both the Mormon and Catholic faiths embody important pronatalist ideologies. In the United States, adherence to the teachings of the religion in this area remains strong among Mormons (Thornton 1985; Heaton 1986); in the case of Catholics, however, it has been declining substantially over time (Jones and Westoff 1979; Mosher et al. 1992; Greeley 1994). To a lesser extent, some exclusivist Protestant denominations also contain pronatalist elements (Marcum 1981; Goldscheider and Mosher 1991). In the economics literature, these differences across religious groups are viewed as influencing fertility by affecting the relative prices of the quantity and quality of children (Tomes 1983; Becker 1991).[2]

The husband's religion would be expected to have an impact on fertility for similar reasons. The fact that his religious beliefs may differ from the wife's, however, raises the possibility of conflict. Recent studies have analyzed the resolution of marital conflict within the framework of bargaining models (Manser and Brown 1980; McElroy and Horney 1981; Lundberg and Pollak 1993). This perspective suggests that (other factors held constant) a union whose members are both affiliated to the same pronatalist religious group – and who therefore do not need to compromise in the areas of desired family size or contraceptive practice – should have higher fertility than another involving only one member of such group. Similarly, a union composed of spouses who share a faith that does not promote large family sizes should have lower fertility than one involving a member of this group and another affiliated to a religion with a pronatalist ideology. This mechanism, which will be referred to as the "bargaining effect," suggests that when a woman outmarries the impact on fertility may be negative or positive; the outcome depends on the presence and strength of pronatalist elements in the theology of her husband's religion.

Another channel through which the husband's religious affiliation may affect marital fertility was suggested many years ago by Becker et al. (1977), but has received little attention in the literature. The authors advance the hypothesis that insofar as interfaith couples recognize the relative instability of their unions, they have an incentive to make fewer investments in spouse-specific human capital because such investments would decline in value following the dissolution of the marriage. Thus they predict that intermarriages should be characterized by relatively low fertility, since children represent the main type of investment in spouse-specific capital. The importance of the linkage between religion and fertility advanced by Becker et al. (1977) is suggested by subsequent research showing that the impact of the religious composition of unions on marital stability is large in magnitude (Michael 1979; Lehrer and Chiswick 1993; Lehrer 1996a; Chiswick 1997).

The high risk of divorce that characterizes interfaith couples implies that their fertility will be low simply because of the relatively short duration of their marriages. Becker et al.'s (1977) hypothesis, however, suggests that the religious composition of unions should influence marital fertility beyond this mechanical connection. If heterogamous couples are aware of the large dissolution probabilities they face, they would tend to restrict fertility *even while their unions are still intact*. This "marital stability effect" therefore implies that women in interfaith unions should have lower fertility than those in intrafaith unions, the duration of the marriage and other factors held constant.

The theoretical considerations outlined above suggest several hypotheses regarding the effects of marrying outside the religion for women with the various affiliations considered in this study. First, in comparing homogamous Catholic marriages with unions of a Catholic woman to a Protestant or to an individual who has no religious affiliation, fertility should be lower for the intermarriages; a similar result should hold for the comparison between homogamous Mormon unions and intermarriages involving a Mormon. These predictions are based on the fact that the pronatalist theologies that characterize Catholicism and Mormonism imply that in both cases the bargaining effect should work in the same direction as the marital stability effect, reinforcing it.

Second, marriage of an ecumenical or exclusivist Protestant woman to a Catholic, as opposed to another Protestant, has an ambiguous effect on fertility. In this case the bargaining effect implies an increase in fertility, counteracting the marital stability effect which operates in the opposite direction. If the countervailing influences are of similar magnitude, the net impact should be small. Third, out-marriage of an ecumenical Protestant woman to an individual who has no religious affiliation should have a negative impact on fertility. In this case, the bargaining effect is neutral and only the marital stability effect operates to produce a negative influence. The total impact should thus be weaker than in the case of out-marriage of a Catholic woman to an individual who has no religion, where the bargaining effect reinforces the marital stability mechanism. These and other hypotheses regarding the signs of the effects of out-marriage on fertility for the various religious groups are summarized in Table 4.1.

While the column for the marital stability effect in Table 4.1 indicates that out-marriage is associated uniformly with a reduction in fertility, the magnitude of this influence may vary. Empirically, Lehrer and Chiswick (1993) find that marrying outside the religion has a significant and fairly large adverse influence on marital stability for Catholics and Protestants; the effect is especially pronounced for Mormons. At the other extreme, there is no significant difference in the probability of marriage dissolution between couples consisting of two individuals who have no religion and others in which only one member is unaffiliated. Corresponding variations in the size of the marital stability effect are expected across the various cases shown in Table 4.1.

An additional issue in the case of intrafaith marriages is whether the homogamy is "natural" (i.e., the two partners were raised in the same religion) or whether it was achieved through conversion of one spouse to the faith of the other. Several opposing influences are at work here, making the nature of the

Table 4.1 The expected effects of out-marriage on fertility

Religious composition of union	Marital stability effect	Bargaining effect	Total effect
Wife and husband Catholic vs.			
Wife Catholic and husband			
Ecumenical Protestant	negative	negative	negative
Exclusivist Protestant	negative	negative	negative
Mormon	negative	neutral	negative
No religion	negative	negative	negative
Wife and husband ecumenical Protestant vs.			
Wife ecumenical Protestant and husband			
Catholic	negative	positive	ambiguous
Exclusivist Protestant	negative	positive	ambiguous
Mormon	negative	positive	ambiguous
No religion	negative	neutral	negative
Wife and husband exclusivist Protestant (same denomination) vs.			
Wife exclusivist Protestant and husband			
Exclusivist Protestant, different denomination	negative	neutral	negative
Ecumenical Protestant	negative	negative	negative
Catholic	negative	positive	ambiguous
Mormon	negative	positive	ambiguous
No religion	negative	negative	negative
Wife and husband Mormon vs.			
Wife Mormon and husband			
Ecumenical Protestant	negative	negative	negative
Exclusivist Protestant	negative	negative	negative
Catholic	negative	neutral	negative
No religion	negative	negative	negative
Wife and husband "no religion" vs.			
Wife no religion and husband			
Ecumenical Protestant	negative	neutral	negative
Exclusivist Protestant	negative	positive	ambiguous
Catholic	negative	positive	ambiguous
Mormon	negative	positive	ambiguous

relationship between conversion and fertility ambiguous a priori. Individuals raised in a faith with a strong pronatalist orientation, having generally higher levels of its religion-specific human capital, should be influenced by its theology and norms more strongly than those who have adopted such faith later in life.[3] Counteracting this effect may be a process of selectivity, whereby persons who find the ideology of a particular religion appealing – including possibly a pronatalist component – are those most likely to convert to it (Sander 1992, 1993).[4] Perhaps more importantly, levels of religious observance among converts tend to be high (Billette 1967; Mayer and Avgar 1987), suggesting that this group would follow the teachings of the church more closely. Furthermore, as Lehrer and Chiswick (1993) discuss in detail, additional opposing effects make it ambiguous a priori whether marital stability – and hence fertility – should be higher for naturally homogamous or conversionary unions.[5] The comparison between the probability of marital breakup for conversionary homogamous unions and for interfaith marriages (where husband and wife choose to remain affiliated to their respective religions) is clearer: the latter are characterized by lower levels of religious compatibility between the partners and a higher rate of divorce (Lehrer and Chiswick 1993); the marital stability mechanism therefore predicts that their fertility should be lower. As always, the direction of the bargaining effect depends on the specific pair of religions involved.

Finally, the salience of religion is known to be an important mediating factor in the relationship between religious affiliation and fertility. Thus the elevated fertility displayed by intrafaith unions involving pronatalist religions is expected to be most apparent among couples who adhere closely to the tenets of the church. In addition, the magnitude of the marital stability effect is expected to vary directly with the level of religiosity. If the intensity of commitment to religion is high for one or both spouses in a heterogamous union, the negative impact on marital stability and hence on fertility should be pronounced. On the other hand, if neither spouse places a high priority on religion, even marked differences between the beliefs and practices associated with their faiths are unlikely to have much influence on the probability of dissolution or fertility.

Methods

The 1987–88 National Survey of Families and Households (NSFH) was addressed to a main sample of 9,643 men and women representative of the United States population aged 19 and over.[6] It includes socio-economic and demographic information for the respondents and their first spouses (where applicable), as well as marital and fertility histories. Very importantly, the survey documents the religious affiliation of the respondent and his or her first spouse, both before and after the marriage.[7] The marriages in this data set range from the 1910s to the 1980s. Because fertility behavior has changed considerably over this long period of time, and varies also by race and ethnicity, the analysis is restricted to non-Hispanic white respondents and to marriages that took place in 1960 or afterwards.[8] In addition, since virtually all previous studies that have examined the effect of religion on marital fertility focus on women's first marriage experiences, the same is done here in order to facilitate comparisons. After eliminating cases with missing codes for key variables as well as those corresponding to marriages contracted less than nine months before the survey, the sample contains approximately 2,600 observations.

The measure of fertility used is the number of children born to the couple; any children born before the date of the marriage or after its dissolution, if applicable, are excluded. Using ordinary least squares, the number of children is regressed on a vector of religion variables as well as several control factors described below.

The explanatory variable of central interest is religion. The main models are estimated in two ways, using pre- and post-marriage religion, because each measure has its own advantages and limitations. On the one hand, pre-marriage affiliation is uncontaminated by some of the biases that may affect religion measured after marriage (e.g., ceteris paribus, the propensity to convert may be higher among those who have a stronger commitment to their partners or a weaker attachment to the religion in which they were raised). On the other hand, when religion is measured before marriage, couples who have achieved homogamy through conversion are classified as "interfaith" marriages. Yet in terms of both levels of religious compatibility between the spouses and marital stability patterns, such unions are more similar to naturally homogamous couples than to those involving individuals who came into the marriage with different religions and chose to keep them unchanged (Lehrer and Chiswick 1993). In this sense, using post-marriage affiliations is a more appropriate classification system. This reasoning suggests that in comparing estimates based on pre- and post-marriage religion, the former should reflect a weaker marital stability effect; in this case the "interfaith" group includes couples whose members have very similar religious beliefs and practices, and who therefore face relatively low dissolution probabilities.

Although the faith in which a woman was raised is clearly not a choice variable from her perspective, the same cannot be said about the religion in which *her husband* was raised. The latter is an aspect of the marital match, determined in the marriage market. The empirical analysis is based on the working assumption that the religious dimension of the match (including the possibility of conversion by one of the spouses) is uncorrelated with those unobserved variables which affect the couple's subsequent fertility decisions. The implications of this assumption are discussed later in the text.

Over 60 religious groups are identified in the NSFH, most of them Protestant denominations. Protestants are divided into two groups, ecumenical and exclusivist. Additional categories identify Roman Catholics, Mormons, and individuals who have no religious affiliation. The few cases corresponding to husbands or wives with other religious affiliations are excluded. Means for dummy variables representing the wife's religious affiliation are displayed in the first part of Table 4.2. The second part reports means for a set of dummy variables indicating the husband's religion: same as the wife's, different religion, and no religion.[9] (Ideally, more detailed categories would have been used for the husband's affiliation; unfortunately sample size limitations precluded this possibility.) Finally, the third part of the table shows interaction terms between the wife's and husband's religion categories.

Three versions of the number of children equation are estimated. The first is the conventional model based on the wife's religious affiliation only; the second includes the husband's religion variables, and the third adds the interaction terms. In the context of the third model, five types of homogamous unions are considered: the spouses are both ecumenical Protestant, exclusivist Protestant, Catholic, Mormon, or unaffiliated. Nine types of heterogamous unions are distinguished. Four of them correspond to cases in which the wife is either ecumenical Protestant, exclusivist Protestant, Catholic, or Mormon, and the husband has a different affiliation; another four to cases in which the wife is either ecumenical Protestant, exclusivist Protestant, Catholic, or Mormon, and the husband has no religion; and in the last case, the husband has a religious affiliation but the wife does not. This specification of the

Table 4.2 Means of religion variables

Variable	Religion after marriage	Religion before marriage
Wife's religion		
Catholic (benchmark)	(0.269)	(0.286)
Ecumenical Protestant	0.363	0.365
Exclusivist Protestant	0.258	0.255
Mormon	0.037	0.036
No religion	0.074	0.059
Husband's religion[a]		
Same as wife's (benchmark)	(0.618)	(0.488)
Different religion	0.291	0.418
No religion	0.091	0.094
Interaction terms		
Wife ecumenical Protestant * husband different religion	0.090	0.129
Wife exclusivist Protestant * husband different religion	0.102	0.135
Wife Mormon * husband different religion	0.004	0.008
Wife no religion * husband different religion	0.039	0.040
Wife ecumenical Protestant * husband no religion	0.042	0.041
Wife exclusivist Protestant * husband no religion	0.023	0.024
Wife Mormon * husband no religion	0.002	0.003
N	2,568	2,573

Note

a The category "same as wife's" includes cases in which both spouses are unaffiliated. The "different religion" group includes cases in which the husband's religion differs from the wife's, as well as those in which he has some affiliation and she does not.

religion variables is flexible, allowing fertility to vary across different types of intra- and interfaith unions.

Table 4.3 reports means for the variables employed as controls in the analyses. These include the husband's and wife's years of schooling at the time of marriage, a dummy variable for whether the husband had been married before, dummies for the duration of the union,[10] and dummies for the respondent's region of residence at age 16.[11]

Table 4.3 The control variables

Variable[b]	Mean[a]
Wife's years of schooling	
< 12	0.182
(12)	(0.405)
13–15	0.264
≥ 16	0.149
Husband's years of schooling	
< 12	0.156
(12)	(0.407)
13–15	0.240
≥ 16	0.197
Husband's marital history	
Previously married	0.080
(not previously married)	(0.920)
Duration of marriage (in years)	
1–2	0.107
3–4	0.142
5–6	0.121
7–8	0.098
9–10	0.089
11–12	0.073
13–14	0.070
(15 or more)	(0.300)
Respondent's region of residence at age 16	
New England	0.061
Middle Atlantic	0.141
South Atlantic	0.144
East South Central	0.050
West South Central	0.085
East North Central	0.250
West North Central	0.097
Mountain	0.067
(Pacific)	(0.088)
Foreign country	0.017

Notes

a The means reported in this table correspond to the sample used in the models with religion measured after marriage; the values for the sample based on pre-marriage religion are virtually the same.

b The benchmark categories are reported in parentheses.

The coefficients on these control variables are not reported in the tables for the sake of brevity. The estimates show that higher levels of male and female education are associated with lower fertility, a previous marital history for the husband depresses the number of children, marriage duration has the expected positive influence, and there are some significant differences across geographical regions reflecting in part varying levels of urbanization.

Finally, it is worth commenting briefly on some variables that do not appear in Table 4.3. The survey includes complete fertility histories for each respondent, and it is thus possible to ascertain whether there was a birth prior to the first marriage. Preliminary regressions included controls for the presence of an out-of-wedlock child, the sex of the respondent, and the interaction between the two. This set of variables turned out to be insignificant in all models and was therefore dropped in the final specification.

In addition, the models reported here do not control for the wife's age at marriage. Earlier analyses of the determinants of fertility behavior differ in whether or not they include this factor (e.g., see Heckert and Teachman 1985; Nerlove and Razin 1981). On the one hand, excluding it may lead to omitted variables biases; on the other hand, to the extent that decisions regarding entry into marriage and family size are made jointly, inclusion of this control would introduce simultaneous equations biases. Preliminary regressions suggested that the results of central interest here are not very sensitive to the treatment of this variable. Adding a series of dummies for the wife's age at marriage to the equations made the Catholic–Protestant fertility differentials more pronounced and attenuated the high Mormon fertility effect. The direction of these changes is in accordance with the fact that entry into marriage is earliest for Mormon women and latest for their Catholic counterparts (Heaton and Goodman 1985; Castleton and Goldscheider 1989). These differences were very small in magnitude, however, and the qualitative conclusions reported in the text below remained unchanged.

Results

The effects of husband's and wife's religion on fertility

Table 4.4 displays estimates for the three number of children equations, with religion measured after the marriage (columns 1–3) and before (columns 4–6). The Catholic religion and the case of homogamy (for models 2 and 3) are used arbitrarily as benchmarks, and all the reported t-tests are based on comparisons with these groups. A full picture of the effects of religion on fertility behavior requires additional comparisons. Using information on the variance–covariance matrix, Tables 4.5 and 4.6 report results of t-tests for the significance of each of the differences of interest. Specifically, Table 4.5 presents comparisons by wife's religion (model 1) and by type of homogamous union (model 3); the latter provide information on whether there are significant variations in fertility across the different kinds of intrafaith unions.

Table 4.4 The effects of religion on family size[a]

Variable	Religion after marriage			Religion before marriage		
	Model 1	Model 2	Model 3	Model 1	Model 2	Model 3
Wife's religion						
Catholic (benchmark)	–			–		
Ecumenical Protestant	−0.254 (0.053)**	−0.250 (0.053)**	−0.333 (0.064)**	−0.201 (0.052)**	−0.198 (0.052)**	−0.307 (0.071)**
Exclusivist Protestant	−0.155 (0.062)**	−0.152 (0.062)**	−0.262 (0.076)**	−0.125 (0.062)**	−0.127 (0.062)**	−0.242 (0.087)**
Mormon	0.755 (0.128)**	0.751 (0.128)**	0.830 (0.143)**	0.797 (0.134)**	0.801 (0.135)**	0.939 (0.161)**
No religion	−0.160 (0.086)*	−0.168 (0.087)*	−0.353 (0.120)**	−0.130 (0.094)	−0.146 (0.095)#	−0.230 (0.161)#
Husband's religion						
Same as wife's (benchmark)	–			–		
Different religion		−0.015 (0.046)	−0.220 (0.098)**		0.019 (0.043)	−0.127 (0.082)#
No religion		−0.120 (0.072)*	−0.427 (0.142)**		−0.100 (0.071)#	−0.229 (0.136)*
Interaction terms						
Wife ecumenical Protestant * husband different religion			0.227 (0.126)*			0.241 (0.110)**
Wife exclusivist Protestant * husband different religion			0.256 (0.132)*			0.211 (0.119)*
Wife Mormon * husband different religion			−0.637 (0.345)*			−0.562 (0.277)**
Wife no religion * husband different religion			0.418 (0.179)**			0.170 (0.200)

Wife ecumenical Protestant * husband no religion			0.362 (0.177)**			0.179 (0.175)
Wife exclusivist Protestant * husband no religion			0.492 (0.207)**			0.191 (0.199)
Wife Mormon * husband no religion			−0.323 (0.460)			−0.350 (0.414)
Constant	2.376 (0.091)**	2.393 (0.092)**	2.458 (0.094)**	2.352 (0.091)**	2.359 (0.093)**	2.436 (0.100)**
Adjusted R^2	0.362	0.362	0.365	0.356	0.357	0.358
F-test for husband's religion variables	1.433				1.157	
Degrees of freedom	2/2,538				2/2,543	
F-test for husband's religion variables and interaction terms			2.656**			1.818*
Degrees of freedom			9/2,531			9/2,536
N	2,568	2,568	2,568	2,573	2,573	2,573

# $p < 0.15$; * $p < 0.10$; ** $p < 0.05$.

Note

a The regressions include all the control variables in Table 4.3. Standard errors are reported in parentheses.

Table 4.5 Predicted family size by wife's religion (model 1) and by type of homogamous union (model 3)[a]

	Religion after marriage	Religion before marriage
Wife's religion (based on model 1)		
Catholic vs.	2.376	2.352
Ecumenical Protestant	2.122**	2.151**
Exclusivist Protestant	2.221**	2.228**
Mormon	3.132**	3.149**
No religion	2.216*	2.222
Wife's and husband's religion (based on model 3)		
Both Catholic vs.	2.458	2.436
Both ecumenical Protestant	2.125**	2.129**
Both exclusivist Protestant	2.195**	2.194**
Both Mormon	3.288**	3.375**
Both no religion	2.105**	2.205#

\# $p < 0.15$; * $p < 0.10$; ** $p < 0.05$.

Note

a Predicted family size is calculated by setting the control variables at the benchmark and the religion variables at the categories indicated in the stub. The significance tests refer to t-tests on the relevant coefficients. For example, the two stars on the value in the first column, second row, indicate that the fertility of ecumenical Protestant wives is significantly lower than that of Catholic wives. All the tests reported in the table reflect comparisons against Catholic wives (model 1) or homogamous Catholic unions (model 3). Pairwise comparisons of other coefficients reveal that the Mormon category is significantly different from all others at the 0.05 level, for both models 1 and 3, and for the case of religion measured before as well as after marriage; in addition, the exclusivist Protestant category is significantly different at the 0.10 level from the ecumenical Protestant category in model 1 with post-marriage religion. No other differences are discerned at the 0.15 level.

Table 4.6 focuses on comparisons between unions composed of two individuals with the same religion and intermarriages in which the wife belongs to that group, and thus provides information on whether marrying outside the religion affects fertility significantly for women in each major religious category. The results based on post-marriage religion are described first, followed by a discussion of how the picture changes when affiliation before marriage is used instead.

The regression in the first column of Table 4.4, which includes the wife's religious affiliation only, replicates results from earlier studies covering a similar time period. Other factors held constant, the fertility of Mormon women is significantly higher than that of all other women, and the fertility of Catholic women is significantly higher than that of their ecumenical and exclusivist Protestant counterparts; there is also a marginally significant gap between the fertility of exclusivist and ecumenical Protestant women. Table 4.5 shows that for marriages with a duration of 15 years or more (and for which

Table 4.6 Predicted family size for homogamous and heterogamous unions

Type of union	Religion after marriage	Religion before marriage
Homogamous Catholic union vs.	2.458	2.436
Wife Catholic, husband different religion	2.237**	2.309#
Wife Catholic, husband no religion	2.031**	2.207*
Homogamous ecumenical Protestant union vs.	2.125	2.129
Wife ecumenical Protestant, husband different religion	2.131	2.243#
Wife ecumenical Protestant, husband no religion	2.060	2.079
Homogamous exclusivist Protestant union vs.	2.195	2.194
Wife exclusivist Protestant, husband different religion	2.231	2.278
Wife exclusivist Protestant, husband no religion	2.261	2.156
Homogamous Mormon union vs.	3.288	3.375
Wife Mormon, husband different religion	(2.431)**	(2.686)**
Wife Mormon, husband no religion	(2.538)*	(2.796)#
Wife no religion, husband no religion vs.	2.105	2.205
Wife no religion, husband has some religious affiliation	2.096	2.249

# $p < 0.15$; * $p < 0.10$; ** $p < 0.05$.

Note

a All the control variables are set at the benchmark. The significance tests reported in this table reflect t-tests on the relevant coefficients. Estimates in parentheses correspond to cases with 20 observations or less.

fertility can be presumed to be complete in most cases) the point estimates of family size for Mormon, Catholic, exclusivist Protestant, and ecumenical Protestant women are, respectively, 3.1, 2.4, 2.2, and 2.1. These values are similar to those reported by Heaton and Goodman (1985): 3.3 for Mormons, 2.4 for Catholics, and between 2.3 and 2.0 for Protestants depending on whether they belong to exclusivist or ecumenical denominations.

Women who have no religious affiliation have lower fertility than Catholics, but the difference between the fertility of unaffiliated women and Protestants is insignificant. While some previous studies have found that women who report no affiliation have fewer children than Protestants (Mosher and Hendershot 1984b; Mosher et al. 1992), others find no significant differences (Heaton and Goodman 1985). The "no religion" category is heterogeneous, including atheists, agnostics, and individuals with no affiliation for other reasons (e.g., being a child of an interfaith couple); variations across samples in the composition of this group may account for the different findings.

In the second model of Table 4.4, which includes the husband's religion, the coefficients on the variables indicating that he is unaffiliated or that he has a religion which differs from the wife's are jointly insignificant at all conventional levels. In contrast, when interaction terms are added allowing the effects of the husband's affiliation to differ depending on the wife's, the husband's religion and the interaction terms are jointly significant. As discussed in more detail below, the estimates of this third model imply that the effects of out-marriage on fertility vary across the different affiliations. Model 2, which omits the interaction terms, yields average effects that conceal such variations.

Model 3 permits a full analysis of how the religious composition of unions affects fertility. Focusing first on comparisons among the various types of intrafaith marriages shown in Table 4.5, homogamous Mormon unions are found to have significantly higher fertility than all other types of intrafaith marriages. In addition, the fertility of homogamous Catholic couples is high compared to that of homogamous Protestant couples and to that of unions in which both partners are unaffiliated. In the first model, based on the wife's religion only, the Catholic–ecumenical Protestant differential is 11.3 percent and the Mormon–ecumenical Protestant differential is 38.4 percent. When fertility is compared among the corresponding homogamous unions in the third model, wider gaps are found – 14.5 percent and 43.0 percent, respectively. Similar patterns hold for the Catholic–exclusivist Protestant and Mormon–exclusivist Protestant differentials.

Turning to the comparisons in Table 4.6 between unions composed of two members of the same religious group with others in which only the wife is a member of that group, out-marriage is found to decrease fertility for Catholic and Mormon women significantly and by sizable amounts. Specifically, the fertility of "Wife Catholic–husband different religion" and "Wife Catholic–husband no religion" unions is lower than that of intrafaith Catholic couples by 9.4 percent and 19.0 percent, respectively, and the fertility of Mormon intermarriages is lower than that of homogamous Mormon unions by over 25 percent. The direction of these effects is in accordance with expectations, as is the finding that marrying outside the religion has a particularly pronounced impact on fertility for Mormon women. The results for this group, however, are offered only tentatively because of the small number of observations available in the sample.

The theoretical model yields an ambiguous prediction regarding the influence of out-marriage on fertility for ecumenical and exclusivist Protestant women, as the bargaining effect may operate in a direction opposite to the marital stability effect (see Table 4.1); empirically, the net impact is statistically insignificant. In addition, no significant difference is observed between the fertility of homogamous Protestant unions (ecumenical or exclusivist) and that of intermarriages in which the wife is Protestant and the husband has no religion. While the negative influence on fertility of marrying an unaffiliated partner was expected to be weaker for Protestants than for Catholics, zero effects were not anticipated. Finally, Table 4.6 shows that there is no significant difference between the fertility of couples in which both spouses are unaffiliated and that of unions in which only the wife has no religion. This result is consistent with the hypothesis that the bargaining effect is neutral in this case (for the most common type of intermarriage, namely "wife no religion–husband ecumenical Protestant"), and with the finding noted earlier that the marital stability of individuals who have no affiliation does not vary significantly with whether or not the spouse has a religion.

As noted earlier, the magnitudes of both the Catholic–Protestant and Mormon–Protestant differentials are lower when analyzing fertility behavior by wife's affiliation than when making comparisons among the corresponding homogamous unions. The finding that out-marriage depresses fertility for Catholic and Mormon women but has no effect for Protestant women can explain this result. In the present sample, 31.7 percent of Catholic women and 18.3 percent of Mormon women are married to men of different affiliations (based on post-marriage religion). The fertility of such women is lower than that of their Catholic and Mormon counterparts in homogamous unions; thus the fact that model 1 includes them in the group of Catholic and Mormon wives, respectively, tends to decrease the estimated Catholic–Protestant and Mormon–Protestant fertility gaps.

These results demonstrate the difficulties in interpreting the coefficients of the conventional specification based on the wife's religion only. Such coefficients capture a mixture of (a) the effects on fertility of the wife's affiliation with a particular religion, (b) the propensity of women with various faiths to intermarry with each of the other religious groups, and (c) the fertility patterns for these different types of heterogamous unions. The model that adds variables for the husband's affiliation and interactions with the wife's religion provides clean measures of the fertility behavior for each kind of intrafaith marriage, and of the effects of out-marriage on family size for each major religious group.

Whether pre- or post-marriage religion is used has relatively little influence on the comparisons by wife's religious affiliation (model 1) or by type of homogamous union (model 3) reported in Table 4.5. An exception is the Catholic–no religion gap, which decreases in both magnitude and significance when pre-marriage religion is employed. A reduction in the Catholic–Protestant differential is also observed, consistent with results reported by Sander (1992), but the magnitude of the change is small.

More pronounced differences emerge in Table 4.6. For Catholic and Mormon women, the estimated negative effect of out-marriage on fertility decreases when religion is measured before marriage. In addition, while the model based on religion after marriage indicates that marrying someone with a different affiliation has no effect on fertility for ecumenical Protestant women, a weak positive influence emerges when pre-marriage religion is used. Both of these changes may be interpreted as reflecting the fact noted earlier that, in the case of religion measured before marriage, "interfaith unions" include couples who have achieved a high degree of religious compatibility through conversion; for such couples, the negative influence on stability and fertility associated with marrying outside the religion (the marital stability mechanism) is not operative. For Catholic and Mormon women, both the marital stability and bargaining effects imply a negative impact of out-marriage on fertility; the smaller marital stability effect in the model with pre-marriage religion accounts for the weaker negative influence that out-marriage is observed to have on fertility. For ecumenical Protestant women, the marital stability and bargaining effects operate in opposite directions; the smaller marital stability effect in the model with pre-marriage religion allows the bargaining effect to dominate in this case.

Extensions of the model

Using the post-marriage affiliations of husband and wife as well as information on whether one of them converted in connection with the marriage, the model reported in Table 4.7 explores further the relationship between fertility behavior and conversion. Because of sample size limitations, only the largest religious groups are considered. The basic model of Table 4.4, column 3, was revised by eliminating all cases in which either the husband or wife is Mormon or unaffiliated, and by including all Protestants in one category. This procedure leaves two groups for the wife's religion – Catholic and Protestant, and two for the husband's religion – same as the wife's and different. For this simplified model and reduced sample, the category "husband's religion same as wife's" is subdivided into two groups depending on whether the homogamy is natural or conversionary. The first case is used as benchmark and a dummy variable for the second is included in the regression. An interaction term between conversionary unions and Protestant wife is also included to allow the effects of conversion on fertility to differ for Catholic

Table 4.7 Making a distinction between naturally homogamous and conversionary unions[a] (religion measured after marriage)

Variable	Coefficient (standard error)
Wife's religion	
Catholic (benchmark)	–
Protestant	−0.343 (0.067)**
Husband's religion	
Same as wife's – no conversion (benchmark)	–
Same as wife's – conversion	−0.044 (0.110)
Different religion	−0.262 (0.103)**
Interaction terms	
Wife Protestant * husband same religion, conversion	0.143 (0.128)
Wife Protestant * husband different religion	0.260 (0.139)*
Constant	2.507 (0.112)**
Adjusted R^2	0.343

* $p < 0.10$; ** $p < 0.05$.
N = 2,041

Notes
a All the control variables are included in the regression.
b The means of the husband's religion variables are 0.65, 0.21, and 0.14 for same as wife's – no conversion, same as wife's – conversion, and different religion, respectively.

and Protestant women. Statistical tests for the differences of central interest are reported in Table 4.8.

As discussed in the theoretical section, several opposing influences are associated with the process of conversion; some suggest elevated fertility for conversionary unions relative to their naturally homogamous counterparts, others point in the opposite direction. Empirically, these countervailing forces appear to cancel each other out in the case of Catholics, as no significant difference is discerned between the fertility of naturally homogamous Catholic unions and those that achieved homogamy through conversion. In the case of Protestants, naturally homogamous unions have slightly lower fertility, a difference that is significant at the 0.15 level. The direction of this effect is consistent with Lehrer and Chiswick's (1993) finding that for ecumenical Protestants (who constitute the majority of Protestants), couples whose members shared the same faith before marriage have a higher probability of divorce than those that include a convert.

Both the bargaining and marital stability mechanisms imply that the fertility of interfaith unions involving a Catholic wife should be lower than that of Catholic couples who have achieved homogamy through conversion; empirically, Table 4.8 shows that the difference in fertility has the expected sign and is statistically significant. In the corresponding comparison for Protestants, the two effects operate in opposite directions and no significant difference is found.

The remainder of this section uses post-marriage religion and the simplified version of model 3 (with the largest religious groups only) to study the role of religiosity in fertility behavior, as well as changes over time in the linkages between religion and fertility.

With regard to religiosity, the NSFH contains information on frequency of attendance to services by the respondent and his or her current spouse (if any), measured at the time of the survey. In the context of the present study,

Table 4.8 Natural vs. conversionary homogamy

Type of union	Predicted family size[a]
Homogamous Catholic union, conversion vs.	2.464
Homogamous Catholic union, nonconversion	2.507
Wife Catholic, husband Protestant	2.245 *
Homogamous Protestant union, conversion vs.	2.264
Homogamous Protestant union, nonconversion	2.164#
Wife Protestant, husband Catholic	2.162

\# p < 0.15; * p < 0.10; ** p < 0.05.

Note

a The control variables are set at the benchmark. Additional t-tests reveal that the difference between the categories "homogamous Catholic union, non conversion" and "wife Catholic, husband Protestant" is significant at the 0.05 level. The difference between "homogamous Protestant union, non conversion" and "wife Protestant, husband Catholic" is insignificant.

this variable is of little value for those respondents whose first unions had ended by the date of the interview: it does not refer to the first marriage experience, and is contaminated by the implications of divorce and also remarriage in many cases. For the purposes of exploring differentials by religiosity, the sample is thus limited to respondents whose first unions were still intact at the interview date. Because this group tends to be selective of the more stable marriages, the results must be interpreted with some caution. Even in this restricted sample, the contemporaneous nature of the religious participation measure makes it difficult to disentangle the two channels of causality – from fertility behavior to religiosity and vice versa (e.g., see Marcum 1981, 1988; Mott and Abma 1992). The analysis that follows is thus offered as descriptive only.

Table 4.9, column 1 shows estimates for the basic model augmented by a dummy variable indicating that the wife attends religious services nearly once a week or more often, as well as interaction terms between this "high religiosity" dummy and each of the religion variables. The interaction terms allow the effects of religiosity to vary with the religious composition of the union. The model in the second column of Table 4.9 repeats this procedure, using

Table 4.9 The role of religiosity[a] (religion measured after marriage)

Variable	Wife's religiosity	Husband's religiosity
Wife's religion		
Catholic (benchmark)	–	–
Protestant	−0.195 (0.107)*	−0.228 (0.099)**
Husband's religion		
Same as wife's (benchmark)	–	–
Different religion	−0.306 (0.181)*	−0.233 (0.157)[#]
Interaction term		
Wife Protestant * husband different religion	0.199 (0.240)	0.246 (0.218)
Religiosity variables		
High religiosity[b]	0.329 (0.121)*	0.404 (0.119)**
Wife Protestant * high religiosity	−0.217 (0.141)#	−0.188 (0.140)
Husband different religion * high religiosity	−0.111 (0.300)	−0.371 (0.466)
Wife Protestant * husband different religion * high religiosity	0.142 (0.432)	0.119 (0.578)
Constant	2.328 (0.150)**	2.334 (0.144)**
Adjusted R^2	0.300	0.305
F-test for religiosity variables	2.569**	5.012**
Degrees of freedom	4/1,233	4/1,233

# $p < 0.15$; * $p < 0.10$; ** $p < 0.05$.
N = 1,264

Notes
a All the control variables are included in the regressions. Standard errors are reported in parentheses.
b The means for the "high religiosity" variables are 0.49 and 0.40 in columns 1 and 2, respectively.

information on the husband's frequency of attendance to services instead. In both cases, F-tests indicate that the religious participation variables are significant at the 0.05 level. Significance tests for various comparisons of interest are reported in Table 4.10.

The relationship between fertility and religion is generally found to be mediated by religiosity in the directions predicted by the theoretical framework. The gap between the fertility of homogamous Catholic and Protestant unions is larger and stronger in significance among those with high levels of religious participation, consistent with expectations. For the high religiosity group, the gap is 16.9 percent or 16.4 percent, depending on whether the wife's or the husband's frequency of attendance at services is used; the corresponding figures are only 8.7 percent and 10.3 percent for the case of low religiosity. For Catholic women, the differentials by religiosity in the effects of out-marriage on fertility are also as predicted. Among those with high levels of religious participation, the fertility gap between homogamous Catholic unions and out-marriages involving a Catholic woman is 17.0 percent if the analysis is based on the wife's frequency of attendance and 24.8 percent if it is based on the husband's; in the case of low religiosity, the corresponding differentials are only 14.1 percent and 10.5 percent. These patterns are consistent with the prediction that the size of the marital stability effect should vary directly with religious participation. For Protestant women, the net impact of out-marriage on fertility is ambiguous a priori and empirically it is found to be zero for all levels of religiosity.

Finally, in order to explore how the relationships between fertility and religion have changed over time, the basic model was re-estimated one more time by adding a dummy variable for marriage cohort ($1970^+ = 1$ if the marriage took place in 1970 or after) as well as interaction terms between this dummy and the religion variables. As Table 4.11 shows, the cohort variables

Table 4.10 Predicted family size by religiosity[a]

Type of union	Wife's religiosity		Husband's religiosity	
	High	Low	High	Low
Homogamous Catholic union vs.	2.657	2.328	2.738	2.334
Homogamous Protestant union	2.244**	2.133*	2.322**	2.106**
Wife Catholic, husband Protestant	2.240*	2.022*	2.134#	2.101#

# $p < 0.15$; * $p < 0.10$; ** $p < 0.05$.

Note

a All the control variables are set at the benchmark. The significance tests reported in this table reflect comparisons against the first row. For example, the two stars on the value in the first column, second row indicate that, among wives with high religiosity, the fertility of homogamous Protestant unions is significantly lower than that of homogamous Catholic unions. Additional t-tests reveal that the differences between the fertility of homogamous Protestant unions and intermarriages involving a Protestant wife are insignificant in all cases.

Table 4.11 The role of marriage cohort (religion measured after marriage)

Variable	Coefficient (standard error)
Wife's religion	
Catholic (benchmark)	–
Protestant	–0.544 (0.096)**
Husband's religion	
Same as wife's (benchmark)	–
Different religion	–0.577 (0.185)**
Interaction term	
Wife Protestant * husband different religion	0.702 (0.243)**
Cohort variables[b]	
1970[+]	–0.379 (0.106)**
Wife Protestant * 1970[+]	0.351 (0.115)**
Husband different religion * 1970[+]	0.433 (0.214)**
Wife Protestant * husband different religion * 1970[+]	–0.615 (0.285)**
Constant	2.673 (0.119)**
Adjusted R^2	0.347
F-test for cohort variables	3.521**
Degrees of freedom	4/2,050

* $p < 0.10$; ** $p < 0.05$.
N = 2,081

Notes
a All the control variables are included in the regressions.
b The mean of the variable "1970[+]" is 0.67.

are jointly significant at the 0.05 level. Additional results for this model, reported in Table 4.12, reveal a pronounced decrease in the Catholic–Protestant fertility gap: from 22.6 percent for marriages contracted before 1970 to only 8.7 percent for unions initiated later. Furthermore, while the effect of out-marriage for Catholic women is significant and large in magnitude for the pre-1970 cohort, it is small and insignificant at conventional levels for unions of the later period. In general, the results confirm the weakening influence of religion on fertility over time documented in earlier investigations (e.g., Mosher and Hendershot 1984a, 1984b; Mosher et al. 1992).

Limitations of the analysis

In interpreting the results described above, an important qualification must be kept in mind. As noted in the previous section, the analyses assume that the religious composition of unions can be treated as determined exogenously. This assumption is problematic if there are persistent, unobserved differences among individuals in preferences, endowments, or constraints on their behavior which affect the marriage decision (whether to enter a union that is interfaith, naturally homogamous, or homogamous through

Table 4.12 Predicted family size by marriage cohort[a]

Type of union	Before 1970	1970 and after
Homogamous Catholic union vs.	2.673	2.294
Homogamous Protestant union	2.130**	2.102**
Wife Catholic, husband Protestant	2.096 **	2.150

** p < 0.05.

Note

a The control variables are set at the benchmark. The significance tests in this table reflect comparisons against the first row. For example, the two stars on the value in the first column, third row indicate that among marriages contracted in the pre-1970 period, the fertility of intermarriages involving a Catholic wife is significantly lower than that of homogamous Catholic unions. Additional tests show that the differences between homogamous Protestant unions and intermarriages involving a Protestant wife are insignificant for both cohorts.

conversion) and also subsequent fertility behavior. To the extent that this is the case, the results would be subject to simultaneous equations bias. Ideally the marriage and fertility decisions would be modeled as jointly determined, but data limitations unfortunately preclude this refinement in the present study for two reasons. First, there are no variables in the data set employed here that could plausibly be hypothesized to influence fertility but not the marriage decision and vice versa. And variables on place of residence at the time of the marriage and fertility decisions, which would permit supplementing the survey data with other information, are unavailable. Second, a larger sample size would be needed. Exploratory analyses with these data found structural differences in the intermarriage/conversion decision among the various religious groups, suggesting that separate analyses by wife's affiliation would be required. As richer data sets become available, extending the present work to address this limitation would be a fruitful avenue for further research.

Conclusions

This study suggests two avenues through which the husband's and wife's affiliations may influence fertility: the bargaining and marital stability effects. The first emphasizes the importance of the quality–quantity tradeoffs embodied in the religions of each spouse and the possibility of conflict if the two differ. The second is based on the influence of the religious compatibility between the spouses on the probability of divorce, and on the impact in turn of expected marital instability on fertility. Empirically, these effects were examined by comparing the number of children for various types of religiously homogamous and heterogamous unions using data on non-Hispanic, white respondents from the 1987–88 National Survey of Families and Households.

The results demonstrate the importance of using information on the husband's religious affiliation in analyses of fertility. There are significant differences in family size across various types of homogamous unions, and calculations based on the wife's religious affiliation only do not provide accurate estimates of such differences. Comparing intra- and interfaith unions, results based on post-marriage affiliations reveal that marrying outside the religion has a substantial depressing effect on the number of children for Catholic and Mormon women; this finding is consistent with the hypothesis that the bargaining and marital stability mechanisms operate in the same direction in these two cases, reinforcing each other. In contrast, no effect of out-marriage on fertility can be discerned in the case of ecumenical and exclusivist Protestant women, for whom the bargaining effect may offset the marital stability influence. Additional models explored the implications of pre- versus post-marriage measurement of religious affiliation, conversion, and differentials by religiosity. The results also show that, although the influence of religion on fertility has generally declined substantially over time, a small Catholic–Protestant differential persists. Further analyses of the NSFH data focusing on the intended fertility of couples in childrearing ages as of the late 1980s confirm the persistence of religious differentials (Lehrer 1996b); these analyses also provide additional evidence that both the bargaining and marital stability effects play important roles in explaining the observed relationship between the religious composition of unions and fertility.

It is hoped that the findings in this study will stimulate further research on the role of religion in fertility behavior, both historically and for the more recent cohorts. For example, it would be useful to extend the analysis to investigate the nature of the bargaining process in interfaith marriages. Fertility might be modeled as a function of dummies for the religious composition of the union, the characteristics of husband and wife (including the nonearned income of each), and interaction terms between the two sets of variables. Such analyses would shed light on the determinants of the relative bargaining strength of each spouse in the area of fertility decisions. Current data on Mormons or information on Catholics before the 1970s would be particularly useful for this exercise.

Several studies find that women who anticipate a high likelihood of marital breakup respond by restricting their investments in spouse-specific human capital, children in particular, and by increasing their investments in labor market skills (Lillard and Waite 1993; Lehrer et al. 1996). The present results provide one more piece of evidence suggesting a negative relationship between the expected probability of marital dissolution and fertility, other factors held constant. Similarly, a companion study that focuses on the effects of the religious composition of unions on female labor supply (Lehrer 1995) suggests that, ceteris paribus, women who anticipate a high likelihood of divorce respond by increasing their attachment to the labor force. Clearly, a growing amount of evidence indicates that expected marital stability influences patterns of human capital investment and is an important determinant of both fertility and female time allocation decisions.

Acknowledgments

I am indebted to Carmel Chiswick, John Ermisch, Shoshana Grossbard-Shechtman, participants of the Demography Workshop at NORC, and two anonymous referees for many helpful comments and suggestions on earlier drafts of this paper. Responsible editor: John F. Ermisch.

Notes

1 The terminology for the two groups of Protestants follows Kelley (1972), who classifies religious groups along an ecumenical–exclusivist gradient depending on the clarity with which membership boundaries are drawn.

2 As Becker (1993) notes, with their very large families and high levels of achievement, Mormons represent a notable exception to the quantity–quality tradeoff.

3 The concept of religion-specific human capital refers to all those skills and experiences which are specific to a particular religion. These include not only knowledge about religious beliefs and practices, but also familiarity with the history and traditions of the group, as well as the development of social relationships and networks with coreligionists (Iannaccone 1990). As Schneider (1989) observes, whereas the theology of a new religion can be learned fairly rapidly, acquisition of some of the other components may take more time.

4 The importance of this selectivity effect may have been overrated, because affinity with the fertility norms of a particular religion is only one among many factors that have been identified as determinants of religious switching. Recent research has emphasized that placing a high priority on religious compatibility with the spouse is an important motive (Lehrer and Chiswick 1993). Other reasons include a desire to shift to a religion with more personally meaningful beliefs and ritual, a more compatible socioeconomic membership, or a more appropriate level of time intensity (Azzi and Ehrenberg 1975; Newport 1979).

5 Empirically, Lehrer and Chiswick (1993) find no significant difference in the stability of naturally homogamous and conversionary unions for exclusivist Protestants and Catholics. In the case of ecumenical Protestants, unions involving partners who shared the same faith before marriage are less stable, by a wide margin, than those that include a convert.

6 This survey was designed at the Center for Demography and Ecology at the University of Wisconsin-Madison under the direction of Larry Bumpass and James Sweet. The fieldwork was done by the Institute for Survey Research at Temple University.

7 Respondents were asked "What is your religious preference?" Where changes took place, there were further questions, including "Did you change your religion in connection with your (first) marriage?", "What was your religious preference before you changed at that time?" and "What religion did you change to at that time?" Similar information was obtained about the respondent's first spouse in the case of unions that had been dissolved by the time of the survey. For respondents whose first marriages were still intact, the survey documents the spouse's religious affiliation at the time of the interview, and just before the change if conversion took place in connection with the marriage.

8 Even in this more recent period from 1960 on, significant changes have taken place, notably a declining adherence of Catholics to the teachings of the Church. These changes are examined later in the text, in the model of Tables 4.11 and 4.12.

9 For marriages involving exclusivist Protestants of different denominations, the dummy variable for different religion takes the value 1, i.e., such unions are

considered to be heterogamous. On the other hand, interdenominational marriages involving ecumenical Protestants are treated as homogamous, as the distinguishing feature of these denominations is a loose definition of the boundaries that separate groups. This approach follows earlier research in which interdenominational marriages involving ecumenical Protestants have been found to be virtually as stable as unions in which both spouses have the identical denomination (Lehrer and Chiswick 1993).

10 For intact marriages (61 percent of the cases), duration is defined as the period between the date of marriage and the interview date. For other unions, duration is defined as the interval between the date of marriage and the date identified by the respondent as signaling the end of the union – through divorce (34 percent), separation (3 percent) or widowhood (2 percent).

11 Unfortunately the survey does not contain information on place of residence at the time of marriage. Based on region at age 16, the Pacific area turned out to have median fertility and is employed as benchmark in the regressions.

References

Azzi, C. and Ehrenberg, R. (1975) "Household Allocation of Time and Church Attendance." *Journal of Political Economy* 83(1):27–56.

Becker, G. S. (1991) *A Treatise on the Family*. Cambridge, MA: Harvard University Press.

Becker, G. S. (1993) *Human Capital: A Theoretical and Empirical Analysis with Special Reference to Education*. Chicago: University of Chicago Press.

Becker, G. S., Landes, E. M., and Michael, R. T. (1977) "An Economic Analysis of Marital Instability." *Journal of Political Economy* 85(6):1141–87.

Billette, A. (1967) "Conversion and Consonance: A Sociology of White American Catholic Converts." *Review of Religious Research* 8(2):100–4.

Castleton, A. and Goldscheider, F. K. (1989) "Are Mormon Families Different? Household Structure and Family Patterns." Pp. 93–109 in F. K. Goldscheider and C. Goldscheider (eds) *Ethnicity and the New Family Economy*. Boulder, CO: Westview Press.

Chiswick, C. (1997) "Determinants of Religious Intermarriage: Are Jews Really Different?" Pp. 247–57 in S. Della Pergola and J. Even (eds) *Papers in Jewish Demography 1993, in Memory of U. O. Schmelz*. Proceedings of the Demographic Sessions held at the 11th World Congress of Jewish Studies, Jerusalem, June 1993.

Della Pergola, S. (1980) "Patterns of American Jewish Fertility." *Demography* 17(3):261–73.

Goldscheider, C. and Mosher, W. D. (1991) "Patterns of Contraceptive Use in the United States: The Importance of Religious Factors." *Studies in Family Planning* 22(2):102–15.

Greeley, A. (1994) *Sex: The Catholic Experience*. Allen, TX: Tabor Publishing.

Heaton, T. B. (1986) "How Does Religion Influence Fertility? The Case of Mormons." *Journal for the Scientific Study of Religion* 25(2):248–58.

Heaton, T. B. and Goodman, K. L. (1985) "Religion and Family Formation." *Review of Religious Research* 26(4):343–59.

Heckert, A. and Teachman, J. D. (1985) "Religious Factors in the Timing of Second Births." *Journal of Marriage and the Family* 47(2):361–7.

Iannaccone, L. R. (1990) "Religious Practice: A Human Capital Approach." *Journal for the Scientific Study of Religion* 29(3):297–314.

Jones, E. F. and Westoff, C. F. (1979) "The End of 'Catholic' Fertility." *Demography* 16(2):209–18.

Kelley, D. M. (1972) *Why Conservative Churches are Growing*. New York: Harper and Row.

Lehrer, E. L. (1995) "The Effects of Religion on the Labor Supply of Married Women." *Social Science Research* 24:281–301. (Chapter 3 this volume.)

Lehrer, E. L. (1996a) "The Determinants of Marital Stability: A Comparative Analysis of First and Higher Order Marriages." Pp. 91–121 in T. P. Schultz (ed.) *Research in Population Economics*. Greenwich: JAI Press.

Lehrer, E. L. (1996b) "The Role of the Husband's Religion in the Economic and Demographic Behavior of Families." *Journal for the Scientific Study of Religion* 35(2):145–55.

Lehrer, E. L. and Chiswick, C. (1993) "Religion as a Determinant of Marital Stability." *Demography* 30(3):385–404. (Chapter 1 this volume.)

Lehrer, E. L., Grossbard-Shechtman, S., and Leasure, J. W. (1996) "Comment on 'A Theory of the Value of Children.' " *Demography* 33(1):133–6.

Lehrer, E. L. and Nerlove, M. (1984) "The Impact of Child Survival on Husbands' and Wives' Desired Fertility in Malaysia: A Log-Linear Probability Model." *Social Science Research* 13(3):236–49.

Lillard, L. and Waite, L. (1993) "A Joint Model of Marital Childbearing and Marital Disruption." *Demography* 30(4):653–82.

Lundberg, S. and Pollak, R. A. (1993) "Separate Spheres Bargaining and the Marriage Market." *Journal of Political Economy* 10(6):988–1010.

Manser, M. and Brown, M. (1980) "Marriage and Household Decision-Making: A Bargaining Analysis." *International Economic Review* 22:31–44.

Marcum, J. P. (1981) "Explaining Fertility Differences Among U.S. Protestants." *Social Forces* 60(2):532–43.

Marcum, J. P. (1988) "Religious Affiliation, Participation, and Fertility: A Cautionary Note." *Journal for the Scientific Study of Religion* 27(4):621–9.

Mayer, E. and Avgar, A. (1987) *Conversion among the Intermarried: Choosing to Become Jewish*. New York: American Jewish Committee.

McElroy, M. B. and Horney, M. J. (1981) "Nash-Bargained Household Decisions: Toward a Generalization of the Theory of Demand." *International Economic Review* 22:333–49.

Michael, R. (1979) "Determinants of Divorce." Pp. 223–54 in L. Levy-Garboua (ed.) *Sociological Economics*. Beverly Hills, CA: Sage.

Mosher, W. and Hendershot, G. (1984a) "Religion and Fertility: A Replication." *Demography* 21(2):185–91.

Mosher, W. and Hendershot, G. (1984b) "Religion and Fertility in the United States: The Importance of Marriage Patterns and Hispanic Origin." *Demography* 23(3):367–79.

Mosher, W., Johnson, D., and Horn, M. (1986) "Religion and Fertility in the United States: The Importance of Marriage Patterns and Hispanic Origin." *Demography* 23(3):367–79.

Mosher, W. D., Williams, L. B., and Johnson, D. P. (1992) "Religion and Fertility in the United States: New Patterns." *Demography* 29(2):199–214.

Mott, F. L. and Abma, J. C. (1992) "Differentials in Marriage and Fertility within the Jewish Population." Presented at the Annual Meetings of the Population Association of America, Denver.

Nerlove, M. and Razin, A. (1981) "Child Spacing and Numbers: An Empirical Analysis." Pp. 297–324 in A. Deaton (ed.) *Essays in the Theory and Measurement of Consumer Behavior in Honor of Sir Richard Stone*. Cambridge: Cambridge University Press.

Newport, F. (1979) "The Religious Switcher in the United States." *American Sociological Review* 44(4):528–52.

Sander, W. (1992) "Catholicism and the Economics of Fertility." *Population Studies* 46(3):477–89.

Sander, W. (1993) "Catholicism and Marriage in the United States." *Demography* 30(3):373–84.

Schneider, S. W. (1989) *Intermarriage – The Challenge of Living with Differences between Christians and Jews*. New York: Free Press.

Schultz, T. P. (1990) "Testing the Neoclassical Model of Family Labor Supply and Fertility." *Journal of Human Resources* 25(4):599–634.

Thornton, A. (1979) "Religion and Fertility: The Case of Mormonism." *Journal of Marriage and the Family* 41(1):131–42.

Thornton, A. (1985) "Reciprocal Influences of Family and Religion in a Changing World." *Journal of Marriage and the Family* 47(2):381–94.

Tomes, N. (1983) "Religion and the Rate of Return on Human Capital: Evidence from Canada." *Canadian Journal of Economics* 16(1):122–38.

Williams, L. and Zimmer, B. (1990) "The Changing Influence of Religion on U.S. Fertility: Evidence from Rhode Island." *Demography* 27(3):475–81.

Part III

The role of religion in education and well-being

5   The benefits from marriage and religion in the United States

A comparative analysis*

America is a religious nation. The vast majority of Americans, when asked, profess a belief in God and affirm that religion is at least "fairly important" in their lives (Myers 2000); about 60 percent of the population report membership in a religious organization and 45 percent state that they attend religious services at least monthly (Sherkat and Ellison 1999). Most American adults are currently married and almost all will marry at some time in their lives. About two-thirds of children live with their married (biological or adoptive) parents (US Census Bureau 2001). And marriage and a happy family life are almost universal goals for young adults.

This commentary presents a socioeconomic and demographic view of the research literature on the benefits of marriage and religious participation in the United States. We compare religion and marriage as social institutions, both clearly on everyone's shortlist of "most important institutions." Marriage is an either/or status. But marital unions differ in a multitude of ways, including the characteristics, such as education, earnings, religion, and cultural background, of each of the partners, and the homogamy of their match on these characteristics. Similarly, religion has multiple aspects. These include religious affiliation, a particular set of theological beliefs and practices, and religiosity. Religiosity may be manifested in various levels and forms of religious participation (attendance at religious services within a congregation, family observance, individual devotion) and in terms of the salience of religion, that is, the importance of religious beliefs as a guide for one's life. Our focus here is on broad comparisons between marriage (being married versus not) and religiosity (having some involvement in religious activities versus little or none). We argue that both marriage and religiosity generally have far-reaching, positive effects; that they influence similar domains of life; and that there are important parallels in the pathways through which each achieves these outcomes. Where applicable, we refer to other dimensions of marriage and religion, including the quality of the marital relationship and the type of religious affiliation.

*   This chapter is by L. Waite and E. Lehrer and is reprinted from *Population and Development Review* 29(2):255–275, 2003.

We begin with a comparison of the effects associated with marriage and involvement in religious activities, based on a literature review, followed by a comparison of the major channels through which each operates. We then discuss qualifications and important exceptions to the general conclusion that marriage and religious involvement have beneficial effects. We conclude with a consideration of the intersection between marriage and religion and suggestions for future research.

The effects of marriage and religious involvement

Marriage and religion influence various dimensions of life, including physical health and longevity, mental health and happiness, economic well-being, and the raising of children. Recent research has also examined connections to sex and domestic violence.

Physical health and longevity

One of the strongest, most consistent benefits of marriage is better physical health and its consequence, longer life. Married people are less likely than unmarried people to suffer from long-term illness or disability (Murphy et al. 1997), and they have better survival rates for some illnesses (Goodwin et al. 1987). They have fewer physical problems and a lower risk of death from various causes, especially those with a behavioral component; the health benefits are generally larger for men (Ross et al. 1990). A longitudinal analysis based on data from the Panel Study of Income Dynamics, a large national sample, documents a significantly lower mortality rate for married individuals (Lillard and Waite 1995). For example, simulations based on this research show that, other factors held constant, nine out of ten married women alive at age 48 would still be alive at age 65; by contrast, eight out of ten never-married women would survive to age 65. The corresponding comparison for men reveals a more pronounced difference: nine out of ten for the married group versus only six out of ten for those who were never married (Waite and Gallagher 2000).

Similarly, although there are exceptions and the matter remains controversial (Sloan et al. 1999), a growing body of research documents an association between religious involvement and better outcomes on a variety of physical health measures, including problems related to heart disease, stroke, hypertension, cancer, gastrointestinal disease, as well as overall health status and life expectancy. This research also points to differences by religious affiliation, with members of stricter denominations displaying an advantage (Levin 1994). Many of the early studies in this literature suffer from methodological shortcomings, including small, unrepresentative samples, lack of adequate statistical controls, and a cross-sectional design that confounds the direction of causality. Yet the conclusion of a generally positive effect of religious involvement on physical health and longevity also emerges from a new generation of studies that have addressed many of these methodological problems (Ellison and Levin 1998). In one of the most rigorous analyses to date, Hummer et al. (1999) use longitudinal data from a nationwide survey, the 1987 Cancer Risk Factor Supplement – Epidemiology Study, linked to the Multiple Cause of Death file. Their results show that the gap in life expectancy at age 20 between those who attend religious services more than once a week and those who never attend is more than seven years – comparable to the male–female and white–black differentials in the United States. Additional multivariate analyses of these data reveal a strong association between religious participation and the risk of death, holding constant socioeconomic and demographic variables, as well as initial health status. Other recent longitudinal studies also report a protective effect of religious involvement against disability among the elderly (Idler and Kasl 1992), as well as a positive influence on self-rated health (Musick 1996) and longevity (Strawbridge et al. 1997).

To the extent that marriage and religious involvement are selective of people with unobserved characteristics that are conducive to better health, their causal effects on health and longevity would be smaller than suggested by some of the estimates in this literature.

Mental health and happiness

Recent studies based on longitudinal data have found that getting married (and staying married to the same person) is associated with better mental health outcomes. Horwitz et al. (1996), Marks and Lambert (1998), and Simon (2002) present evidence of improvements in emotional well-being following marriage, and declines following the end of a union. Marks and Lambert (1998) report that marital gain affects men and women in the same way, but marital loss is generally more depressing for women. Analyses that control for the selection of the psychologically healthy into marriage, and also include a wider range of measures of mental well-being, find that although there are differences by sex in the types of emotional responses to marital transitions, the psychological benefits associated with marriage apply equally to men and women (Horwitz et al. 1996; Simon 2002).

Marriage is also associated with greater overall happiness. Analysis of data from the General Social Surveys of 1972–96 shows that, other factors held constant, the likelihood that a respondent would report being happy with life in general is substantially higher among those who are currently married than among those who have never been married or have been previously married; the magnitude of the gap has remained fairly stable over the past 35 years and is similar for men and women (Waite 2000).

The connection between religion and mental health has been the subject of much controversy over the years, and many psychologists and psychiatrists remain skeptical, in part because most of the research has been based on cross-sectional analyses of small samples. The studies to date are suggestive of an association between religious involvement and better mental health outcomes, including greater self-esteem, better adaptation to bereavement, a lower incidence of depression and anxiety, a lower likelihood of alcohol and drug abuse, and greater life satisfaction and happiness in general (Koenig et al. 2001). Recent longitudinal analyses of subgroups of the population provide additional evidence in support of this relationship (Zuckerman et al. 1984; Levin et al. 1996).

Economic well-being

A large body of literature documents that married men earn higher wages than their single counterparts. This differential, known as the "marriage premium," is sizable. A rigorous and thorough statistical analysis by Korenman and Neumark (1991) reports that married white men in America earn 11 percent more than their never-married counterparts, controlling for all the standard human capital variables. Between 50 and 80 percent of the effect remains, depending on the specification, after correcting for selectivity into marriage based on fixed unobservable characteristics. Other research shows that married people have higher family income than the nonmarried, with the gap between the family income of married and single women being wider than that between married and single men (Hahn 1993). In addition, married people on average have higher levels of wealth and assets (Lupton and Smith 2003). The magnitude of the difference depends on the precise measure used, but in all cases is far more than twice that of other household types, suggesting that this result is not merely due to the aggregation of two persons' wealth.

To the best of our knowledge, the effects of religious involvement on earnings and wealth have not been systematically analyzed. However, as we discuss below, an emerging literature shows a positive effect of religiosity on educational attainment, a key determinant of success in the labor market. These studies suggest a potentially important link between religious involvement during childhood and adolescence and subsequent economic well-being as an adult. Preliminary results from a new line of inquiry at the macro level are consistent with this hypothesis. Using a cross-country panel that includes information on religious and economic variables, Barro and McLeary (2006) find that enhanced religious beliefs affect economic growth positively, although growth responds negatively to increased church attendance. The authors interpret their findings as reflecting a positive association between "productivity" in the religion sector and macroeconomic performance.[1]

Children

Children raised by their own married parents do better, on average, across a range of outcomes than children who grow up in other living arrangements. There is evidence that the former are less likely to die as infants (Bennett et al. 1994), and have better health during childhood (Angel and Worobey 1988) and even in old age (Tucker et al. 1997). They are less likely to drop out of high school, they complete more years of schooling, they are less likely to be idle as young adults, and they are less likely to have a child as an unmarried teenager (McLanahan and Sandefur 1994).

Children who grow up in intact two-parent families also tend to have better mental health than their counterparts who have experienced a parental divorce. Using 17-year longitudinal data from two generations, Amato and Sobolewski (2001) find that the weaker parent–child bonds that result from marital discord mediate most of the association between divorce and the subsequent mental health outcomes of children. Cherlin et al. (1998) find that children whose parents would later divorce already showed evidence of more emotional problems prior to the divorce, suggesting that marriage dissolution tends to occur in families that are troubled to begin with. However, the authors also find that the gap continues to widen following the divorce, suggestive of a causal effect of family breakup on mental health. Summing up his assessment of the studies in this field, Cherlin (1999) concludes that growing up in a nonintact family can be associated with short- and long-term problems, partly attributable to the effects of family structure on the child's mental health, and partly attributable to inherited characteristics and their interaction with the environment.

Several studies have documented an association between religion and children's well-being. Recent research on differences in parenting styles by religious affiliation reveals that conservative Protestants display distinctive patterns: they place a greater emphasis on obedience and tend to view corporal punishment as an acceptable form of child discipline; at the same time, they are more likely to avoid yelling at children and are more prone to frequent praising and warm displays of affection (Bartowski et al. 2000). As to other dimensions of religion, Pearce and Axinn (1998) find that family religious involvement promotes stronger ties among family members and has a positive impact on mothers' and children's reports of the quality of their relationship.

A number of studies document the effects of children's own religious participation, showing that young people who grow up having some religious involvement tend to display better outcomes in a range of areas. Such involvement has been linked to a lower probability of substance abuse and juvenile delinquency (Donahue and Benson 1995), a lower incidence of depression among some groups (Harker 2001), delayed sexual debut (Bearman and Bruckner 2001), more positive attitudes toward marriage and having children, and more negative attitudes toward unmarried sex and premarital childbearing (Marchena and Waite 2002).

Religious participation has also been associated with better educational outcomes. Freeman (1986) finds a positive effect of churchgoing on school attendance in a sample of inner-city black youth. Regnerus (2000) reports that participation in religious activities is related to better test scores and heightened educational expectations among tenth-grade public school students. In the most comprehensive study to date, using data on adolescents from the National Education Longitudinal Study of 1988, Muller and Ellison (2001) find positive effects of various measures of religious involvement on the students' locus of control (a measure of self-concept), educational expectations, time spent on homework, advanced mathematics credits earned, and the probability of obtaining a high school diploma. Other research documents differences in educational attainment by religious affiliation (Chiswick 1988; Darnell and Sherkat 1997; Lehrer 1999; Sherkat and Darnell 1999) and suggests that the effects of religious participation on secular achievements may vary across denominations (Chiswick 1999; Lehrer 2004).

Studies of the influence of religiosity on schooling have raised the possibility that the estimated coefficients may overstate the positive causal effect of religious involvement on educational outcomes. This would be the case if religiosity is correlated with unobserved factors that encourage good behaviors in general: for example, the religiously more observant parents, who encourage their children to attend services as well, are also supportive of activities that are conducive to success in the secular arena. Freeman (1986) has emphasized this type of bias.

Biases operating in the opposite direction have also been identified (Lehrer 2004). Although this issue has not been studied systematically, there is some evidence that religious participation is especially beneficial for those who are more vulnerable, for reasons that might include poor health, unfavorable family circumstances, and adverse economic conditions (Hummer et al. 2002). To the extent that those who are vulnerable respond by embracing religion as a coping mechanism, the more religious homes would disproportionately have unobserved characteristics that affect educational outcomes adversely. If so, the estimated coefficients would understate the true effect of religiosity on educational attainment.[2]

Sex

Little attention has been given to the question of how marriage is related to the chances that people will have active, satisfying sex lives. Cross-tabulations based on data from the 1992 National Health and Social Life Survey show that levels of emotional and physical satisfaction with sex are highest for married people and lowest for noncohabiting singles, with cohabitors falling in between (Laumann et al. 1994). Additional evidence for the importance of commitment as a determinant of sexual satisfaction is provided by more recent multivariate analyses of these data (Waite and Joyner 2001). To date, these relationships have not been quantified using longitudinal data.

Our knowledge about the relationship between religion and sex is also limited. Cross-tabulations by religious denomination show that those with no affiliation (i.e., no involvement in religious activities) are least likely to report being extremely satisfied with sex either physically or emotionally (Laumann et al. 1994). Waite and Joyner (2001) find that emotional satisfaction and physical pleasure related to sex are higher for frequent attenders of religious services, holding other characteristics of the individual constant. Along similar lines, Greeley (1991) reports that couples who pray together say they have more "ecstasy" in their sex lives; he also finds that religious imagery and devotion is positively associated with sexual satisfaction. The small amount of evidence available is only suggestive of a connection between religious participation and the quality of people's sex lives.

Domestic violence

Using data from the 1987–88 National Survey of Families and Households, Stets (1991) finds a large difference between married people and cohabitors in the prevalence of domestic violence: 14 percent of people who have cohabiting arrangements say that they or their spouse hit, shoved, or threw things at their partner during the past year, compared to 5 percent of those who are formally married. The difference declines when age, education, and race are held constant. Additional analyses of these data show that engaged cohabiting couples display lower levels of physical violence than uncommitted cohabitors (Waite 2000).

Ellison et al. (1999) explore the relationship between religion and domestic violence in America, comparing reports of abuse for men and women by religious denomination, religious participation, and religious homogamy. They find that the likelihood of violence by males increases when the male is substantially more conservative (in beliefs about the inerrancy and authority of the Bible) than his female partner. Their results also show that the likelihood of reporting violence is lower for those who attend religious services more frequently. Additional confirmation for the hypothesis that religious participation is inversely associated with the perpetration of domestic violence is provided by a more recent analysis that uses information not only on self-reported domestic violence but also on abuse reported by the partner (Ellison and Anderson 2001).

As Ellison et al. (1999) note, it seems likely that part of the measured relationship between religiosity and domestic violence is due to selectivity: the more religious may well be disproportionately less prone to act violently; the same argument applies to the relationship between marriage and domestic violence.

Pathways of causality

Developing themes proposed by Durkheim (1951 [1897]), we argue that both marriage and religion lead to positive outcomes by providing social support and integration and by encouraging healthy behaviors and lifestyles. In addition, there is a mechanism that is unique to marriage, namely, the economic gains that result when two people make a commitment to become lifetime partners. There is also a pathway that is unique to religion: the positive emotions and spiritual richness that can come from personal faith and religious observance. In each case, although the various channels we discuss are conceptually distinct, they are not mutually exclusive.

Social integration and support

The argument for benefits from marriage stemming from its integrative influence runs as follows. Marriage implies love, intimacy, and friendship. The social integration and support it thus provides is a key channel through which it leads to improved mental and physical health. Being married means having someone who can provide emotional support on a regular basis, thereby decreasing depression, anxiety, and other psychological problems, and improving overall mental health. In turn, better emotional well-being contributes to enhanced physical wellness. Support from the spouse can also improve physical health directly, by aiding early detection and treatment and by promoting speedier recovery from illness (Ross et al. 1990). From the perspective of children, the mutual help that parents give to each other is part of the setting that provides advantages to youths who grow up in married-couple households. In addition to close support from the spouse, marriage connects people to other individuals, other social groups (e.g., in-laws), and other social institutions (Stolzenberg et al. 1995; Waite 1995), and this integration into a wider social network has additional positive effects on both spouses and on their children (McLanahan and Sandefur 1994).

The long-term commitment implied by marriage (as opposed to cohabitation) encourages the partners to invest in the relationship. Married couples indeed report higher levels of relationship quality than uncommitted cohabitors (Brown and Booth 1996) and better emotional well-being (Brown 2000). This pathway most likely explains the higher emotional satisfaction with sex generally reported by married individuals (Waite and Joyner 2001). Evidence of the impact of marriage on relationship quality comes also from studies on domestic violence: the stronger commitment implied by marriage (or even the promise of marriage in the form of engagement) inhibits aggression (Stets 1991; Waite 2000).

Like marriage, the institution of religion is an integrative force. Religious congregations offer regular opportunities to socialize and interact with friends who share similar values; they offer assistance to members in need; they foster a sense of community through which participants help one another. Ellison and George (1994) find that people who frequently attend religious services not only have larger social networks, but also hold more positive perceptions of the quality of their social relationships. The positive association between religious involvement and longevity is accounted for in part by this channel (Strawbridge et al. 1997; Hummer et al. 1999).

Recent research has emphasized that religion can play a pivotal role in the socialization of youth by contributing to the development of social capital. Religious congregations often sponsor family activities, stimulating the cultivation of closer parent–child relations; they also bring children together with grandparents and other supportive adults (parents of peers, Sunday-school teachers) in an environment of trust. This broad base of social ties can be a rich source of positive role models, confidants, useful information, and reinforcement of values that promote educational achievement. The positive impact of religious involvement on various measures of educational outcomes has been attributed largely to this pathway (Regnerus 2000; Muller and Ellison 2001; Lehrer 2004).

At the other end of the age spectrum, the social ties provided by religious institutions are of special value to the elderly, helping them deal with the many difficult challenges that tend to accompany old age: illness, dependency, loss, and loneliness (Levin 1994).

Healthy behaviors and lifestyles

Beyond its integrative function, emphasized above, marriage also has a regulative function. Married individuals, especially men, are more likely than their single counterparts to have someone who closely monitors their health-related conduct; marriage also contributes to self-regulation and the internalization of norms for healthful behavior (Umberson 1987). Positive and negative externalities within marriage also play a role: when an individual behaves in a way that is conducive to good health, the benefits spill over to the spouse; similarly, unhealthy behaviors inflict damage not only on the individual but also on the partner. In this way, marriage promotes healthy conduct. In addition, the enhanced sense of meaning and purpose provided by marriage inhibits self-destructive activities (Gove 1973). Consistent with this channel of causality, married individuals have lower rates of mortality for virtually all causes of death in which the person's psychological condition and behavior play a major role, including suicide and cirrhosis of the liver (Gove 1973). Lillard and Waite (1995) find that for men (but not for women) there is a substantial decline in the risk of death immediately after marriage, which suggests that the regulation of health behaviors is a key mechanism linking marriage to physical health benefits in the case of men.

Religion also serves a regulative function. Most faiths have teachings that encourage healthy behaviors and discourage conduct that is self-destructive; they also provide moral guidance about sexuality. Some religions have specific regulations limiting or prohibiting the consumption of alcohol, tobacco, caffeine, and potentially harmful foods. Several studies show that religious involvement is generally associated with health-promoting behaviors (Koenig et al. 2001) and that such behaviors explain in part the connection between religion and longevity (Strawbridge et al. 1997; Hummer et al. 1999).

Economic benefits from marriage

Marriage leads to increases in economic well-being for several reasons, including the pooling of risks (e.g., one spouse may increase the level of work in the labor force if the other becomes unemployed), economies of scale (e.g., renting a large apartment costs less than renting two small apartments), and public goods (e.g., a husband and wife can both enjoy all of the beauty of the pictures hanging on the wall). Division of labor and specialization are particularly important sources of gains from marriage, permitting the partners to produce and consume substantially more than twice the amount each could produce individually (Becker 1991). The long-term horizon implied by marriage gives each of the spouses the ability to neglect some skills and focus on the development of others. Gains from such specialization are responsible, in part, for the "marriage premium." Married men can specialize in labor market activities more than single men, thereby gaining a productivity advantage. Specialization also encourages women to make human capital investments that advance their husbands' careers (Grossbard-Shechtman 1993).

For all of these reasons, marriage promotes higher levels of economic well-being. This factor accounts to a large extent for the advantages that accrue to children raised by two parents (McLanahan and Sandefur 1994). From an economic perspective, a two-parent household is also the optimal institutional arrangement for raising children for another reason: there is a tendency for the level of expenditures on children to be inefficiently low when the father is not present. Inadequate provision of the couple's collective good – child expenditures – occurs because of the father's lack of control over the allocation of resources by the mother (Weiss and Willis 1985).

The very substantial increase in economic resources that marriage implies for women may lead to better health directly, by improving general standards of living and access to medical resources, as well as indirectly by reducing levels of stress (Hahn 1993). Consistent with this research, Lillard and Waite (1995) find that the greater financial resources available in married-couple households account for most of the positive effect of marriage on longevity for women, but not for men.

Spiritual benefits from religion

Some facets of religion lead to spiritual benefits that are unique to religious experiences. Idler and Kasl (1992) underscore the importance of religious rituals, such as the annual observance of religious holidays, noting that the periodicity of these celebrations reminds members of their shared past and their connection to preceding generations. Religious belief can also serve as a coping mechanism that helps individuals deal with conflict and difficult life-cycle stages, such as the assertion of independence by adolescent children (Pearce and Axinn 1998), as well as bereavement and major health problems (Pargament et al. 1990). In addition, personal faith can provide a sense of meaning that tends to reduce helplessness and heighten optimism. As Koenig (1994) notes, the religious prescription to love and forgive others can also have positive consequences for emotional well-being. The intangible nature of these effects defies easy quantification.

Caveats

Overall, there is evidence of a strong association between stable marriages and a wide range of positive outcomes for children and adults, and the same is true in the case of religious involvement. However, the benefits are by no means uniform for all individuals, and significant exceptions may be cited. In addition, issues of selection bias deserve special attention.

Variations across individuals and exceptions

The benefits of religious involvement vary across individuals, as do the costs. The costs are higher for those with a more secular orientation, and to the extent that religious involvement is a time-intensive activity, costs are also higher for those with a higher wage rate and opportunity cost of time. As to the benefits, the spiritual gains associated with religious activity increase with the stock of religious capital: those who have made greater investments in religion stand to benefit more from religious participation (Iannaccone 1990). Regnerus and Elder (2001) find support for the hypothesis that by providing functional communities amidst dysfunction, religious institutions are especially valuable in enhancing social capital for disadvantaged youths. The elderly and those with serious physical health problems also appear to derive substantial benefits from religious involvement (Koenig 1994; Musick 1996).

Membership in some religious groups may reduce rather than enhance economic well-being. For example, the religious beliefs of conservative Protestants can discourage intellectual inquiry and have been linked with lower educational attainment (Darnell and Sherkat 1997; Sherkat and Darnell 1999; Lehrer 1999, 2004), implying negative consequences for earnings. There is also evidence that certain forms of religious beliefs and practices may not be beneficial for mental and physical health. Pargament et al. (1998) examine the role of religion as a coping tool, making a distinction between positive and negative religious coping. The former includes methods that reflect a secure relationship with God and a sense of spiritual connectedness with others. The latter is based on a pessimistic world view, a tenuous relationship with God, and a perception that God can inflict punishment. While the positive religious coping methods are associated with higher levels of mental well-being, the opposite is true of the negative methods – an indication that religion has the capacity to cause distress and make things worse. Some religious teachings also promote the avoidance of medical services and can lead to serious adverse consequences for health (e.g., see Asser and Swan 1998).

The benefits of marriage are also far from uniform. While the economic gains stemming from the joint consumption of public goods and from economies of scale are likely to vary only weakly with the quality of the union, most of the benefits from marriage vary closely with marital quality. For example, Gray and Vanderhart (2000) find that the marriage premium increases with marital stability: when the marriage is perceived to be solid, a woman is much more likely to make investments that enhance her husband's career. The mental and physical health benefits of marriage have also been found to vary with the quality of the relationship (Horwitz et al. 1996; Wickrama et al. 1997). In the extreme case of very poor marital quality, the consequences for health and well-being are clearly negative. For instance, Kiecolt-Glaser et al. (1993) show that serious conflict within a marriage can lead to adverse immunological changes, increasing the risk of illness. When marital quality becomes very low, so that one or both partners conclude that the benefits from remaining married have come to be smaller than the costs, the result may well be divorce. Lehrer (2003) reviews the characteristics and behaviors of individuals and couples that make this scenario most likely.

An understanding of the circumstances under which marriage is or is not beneficial can shed some light on the current policy debate in the United States regarding the promotion of marriage. One of the goals of the Personal Responsibility and Work Opportunity Reconciliation Act of 1996 was to reduce out-of-wedlock childbearing and to encourage the formation and maintenance of two-parent families.[3] More recently, the Bush administration has proposed spending more than $1 billion over five years on programs to promote "healthy marriages" (Carlson et al. 2004; McLanahan et al. 2001). Under the proposed plan, states may be eligible for federal funds if they develop programs to promote marriage. Such programs might include pre-marital counseling, marriage workshops, programs to enhance mental well-being, and additional welfare benefits for couples who enter formal marriage. Our review of the literature suggests that initiatives that enhance relationship skills may be helpful, as such skills are important to a stable marriage and young adults who grew up in non-intact homes may well be weak in this area (Amato 1996). Complementary programs to address problems of depression and drug use may also help, on this as well as other fronts (Lehrer et al. 2002a, 2002b). On the other hand, financial incentives or negative economic pressures to enter formal marriage are likely to do more harm than good, by encouraging unions of poor marital quality.[4]

Issues of selection bias

As we indicated earlier in this commentary, problems of selection bias affect many of the studies in both bodies of literature. The better outcomes observed for individuals in stable marriages may result in part from the greater likelihood that healthy, happy, and wealthy people marry and stay married. Results from analyses of marriage that have addressed the issue of selection biases suggest that they are indeed sizable in magnitude (e.g., Korenman and Neumark 1991; Horwitz et al. 1996; Lillard and Panis 1996; Simon 2002). The biases, however, do not always operate in the direction suggested by conventional wisdom.[5] An important item in the agenda for future research is to do more along the lines of the studies cited above, in an effort to better sort out the associational and causal relationships between marriage and well-being. Of particular value would be studies that specifically model the processes through which some individuals select or are selected into stable marriages and others are not. The corresponding gaps in our knowledge are even more pronounced in the case of the literature on religion.

The intersection of religion and marriage

In thinking about the role of religion in the lives of married people, a good point of departure is the concept that religion is a complementary trait within marriage. Religion affects many activities that husband and wife engage in as a couple beyond the purely religious sphere (Becker 1991). Religion influences the education and upbringing of children, the allocation of time and money, the cultivation of social relationships, and often even the place of residence. Thus there is a greater efficiency and less conflict in a household if the spouses share the same religious beliefs. Furthermore, as Pearce and Axinn (1998) emphasize, just as religion is an integrative force in society, so it can have this effect also within the family: shared religious experiences can increase cohesion among family members.

The other side of this argument is that a difference in religion between partners may be a destabilizing force within a marriage. Empirical analyses have found that religious heterogamy increases the risk of marital conflict and instability (Michael 1979; Lehrer 1996). A more detailed analysis that examines different types of interfaith unions shows that intermarriage comes in various forms and shades. Some interfaith marriages, such as those involving members of different ecumenical Protestant denominations, are quite stable. In contrast, the probability of divorce is high for unions in which the partners have very different religious beliefs or are members of religious groups that have sharply defined boundaries. Additional analyses for Catholics and Protestants reveal that unions that achieve homogamy through conversion are at least as stable as those involving partners who were raised in the same faith (Lehrer and Chiswick 1993).

The hypothesis that religious involvement may enhance marital happiness and stability has also received considerable attention in the literature. A large number of studies report a positive relationship between measures of religiosity and indicators of marital satisfaction and stability (e.g., Glenn and Supancic 1984; Heaton and Pratt 1990). However, the cross-sectional design of these analyses, with both key variables measured at the same point in time, implies that the estimates confound the direction of causality. Two recent studies have addressed this shortcoming. Using data from waves 1 and 2 of the National Surveys of Families and Households, Call and Heaton (1997) find that higher levels of husband's and wife's church attendance as found at the initial interview reduce the likelihood that the union will have been dissolved by the second wave, about five years later; differences between the spouses in attendance levels are found to be destabilizing. In contrast, in their analysis of a 12-year longitudinal sample, Booth et al. (1995) find that although an increase in religious activity over time reduces the chance of considering divorce, it does not increase marital happiness or decrease marital conflict.

The studies in this literature, however, are subject to a critical limitation: none of them has modeled the effects of religious participation on marital satisfaction or stability in a way that allows the relationship to vary depending on the religious composition of the union. Theoretically, if a marriage is homogamous, more religious involvement by one of the spouses, and especially by both spouses, should be a positive force within the union. The opposite would be expected if the marriage is heterogamous, involving two faiths that are quite different. Thus a clear understanding of how religious participation influences marital harmony must await analyses that are conducted separately for these two very different groups. Improving our knowledge about these relationships, especially as they pertain to children growing up in interfaith homes, should have high priority in the agenda for future research.

Conclusions

Our comparative analysis of religion and marriage in the United States reveals remarkable similarities in the benefits that are associated with these two social institutions, and also in the pathways through which they operate. Being married and being involved in religious activities are generally associated with positive effects in several areas, including physical and mental health, economic outcomes, and the process of raising children. For some of these influences, such as the effect of religion and marriage on longevity, substantial evidence has been accumulated. For other relationships, such as the effect of religious involvement on mental health, the evidence is not as strong. A large body of research points to social integration and the regulation of health behaviors as key pathways through which both institutions exert an influence. In addition, there is evidence of substantial economic gains from marriage, while religious experiences can significantly improve and enrich people's spiritual lives.

Marriage and religion work independently as integrative forces. They also seem to work together as integrative forces. At present, married adults and the children living with them may be greater beneficiaries of the integration and social support from religious organizations; having children of school age seems to move married couples toward stronger ties with their church, synagogue, or mosque. But adults and children in other types of families seem to move away from religious participation (Stolzenberg et al. 1995). In a recent article, Wilcox (2000) points out that although mainline Protestant denominations talk a great deal about acceptance of single-parent or other alternative family forms, and about the needs of single adults, almost all of their formal activities are aimed at married-couple families. Lacking the social ties provided by marriage, single individuals, especially those who are raising children, could potentially derive important benefits from the support that religious institutions can provide.

There is much that we do not know about the intersection between religion and marriage, and about interfaith couples in particular. Such couples often face a choice between raising their children in a home without religion and raising them in the faith of one of the parents. The research to date suggests that some religious involvement is generally beneficial for young people. At the same time, religious heterogamy is known to be a destabilizing force in a marriage, and it seems likely that active participation in religious activities by only one parent and the children would accentuate the differences. Estimates of the magnitudes of these effects would be of value in guiding the choices of interfaith couples.

Religiosity has many dimensions, including attendance at religious services, private devotion, and the salience of religion in the individual's life. The literature contains conflicting findings regarding which of these aspects is most important, and the effects associated with the various dimensions are not always consistent. Research seeking to clarify these differences and to identify patterns among the discrepant results would be desirable.

With regard to marriage, most of the studies to date have focused on comparing outcomes for those who are currently married with those who have never married or are widowed or divorced. We know much less about the implications of formal marriage versus informal cohabiting arrangements, especially from the perspective of the children growing up in these two types of households. A substantial amount of recent work seeks to fill this gap (e.g., Lerman 2002; Duncan et al. 2003; Kiernan 2003; Manning and Brown 2003).

As we continue to advance our knowledge in each of these fields, it will be helpful to integrate them to a much larger extent than has been done to date. At a minimum, it would be useful if researchers who are focusing on issues pertaining to marriage would include a richer set of controls for religion, and vice versa. Additional research seeking to improve our understanding of the complex relationships between religion and marriage would be especially valuable.

Acknowledgments

This research was supported by the National Institute on Aging through Grant No. P-01 AG18911 and through the Alfred P. Sloan Center for Parents, Children and Work at the University of Chicago. A previous version was presented at a workshop on Ties That Bind: Religion and Family in Contemporary America, May 2001, Princeton University. We are indebted to Barry Chiswick and participants in the Microeconomics and Human Resources Workshop at the University of Illinois at Chicago for many helpful comments on earlier drafts. Sarinda Taengnoi provided skillful research assistance.

Notes

1 The "religion sector" encompasses all aspects of religion in a given country, including denominational composition and the nature and extent of religiousness.
2 Another way of stating this argument is to note that inputs that may improve health and well-being, such as religion, are most likely to be "purchased" by those individuals who need their protection the most; see Lillard and Panis (1996) for a parallel argument in the marriage literature.
3 See Gennetian and Knox (2003) for a preliminary examination of the effects of the Act in the area of union formation and dissolution.
4 A firestorm of public debate surrounds these various efforts by the George W. Bush US administration to strengthen marriage. Proponents argue that marriage is good (for all the reasons outlined here) and therefore should be encouraged by the government. Opponents argue that government intervention in this area is inappropriate. Many view these initiatives as inconsistent with equality for women (Stacey 1993) and as a waste of money that could be used for job training or programs to prevent domestic violence. Support for marriage (as opposed to families) seems to some to discriminate against single mothers, those who choose to remain single or want to marry but have been unable to do so, gay and lesbian individuals and couples, cohabitors, the poor, and minorities. (See "Young feminists take on the family," part of a special issue of *The Scholar & Feminist Online*, www.barnard.edu/sfonline). For additional discussion of this issue, see Carlson et al. (2001), Seiler (2002), and Amato (2003). Similarly, the faith-based initiatives advanced by President Bush early in his presidency were highly controversial.
5 For example, in their simultaneous-equations model of marital transitions, health, and mortality, Lillard and Panis (1996) find empirical support for the argument that unhealthy men have a particularly strong incentive to seek out the health protection offered by marriage. Their results show adverse selection into marriage based on self-perceived general health. At the same time, they also find evidence of positive selection into marriage based on unobserved characteristics, such as preferences for risk and adventure and for social contact.

References

Amato, P. R. (1996) "Explaining the Intergenerational Transmission of Divorce." *Journal of Marriage and the Family* 58:628–40.
Amato, P. R. (2003) "Relationship Skills Training and Marriage Among Low-Income Couples." Presented at the annual meetings of the Population Association of America, Minneapolis.
Amato, P. R. and Sobolewski, J. (2001) "The Effects of Divorce and Marital Discord on Adult Children's Psychological Well-Being." *American Sociological Review* 66:900–21.
Angel, R. and Worobey, J. L. (1988) "Single Motherhood and Children's Health." *Journal of Health and Social Behavior* 29:38–52.
Asser, S. M. and Swan, R. (1998) "Child Fatalities from Religion-Motivated Medical Neglect." *Pediatrics* 101(4):625–9.
Barro, R. J. and McCleary, R. M. (2006) "Religion and Political Economy in an International Panel." *Journal for the Scientific Study of Religion* 45(2):149–75.
Bartowski, J. P., Wilcox, B., and Ellison, C. G. (2000) "Charting the Paradoxes of Evangelical Family Life: Gender and Parenting in Conservative Protestant Households." *Family Ministry* 14(4):9–21.

Bearman, P. S. and Bruckner, H. (2001) "Promising the Future: Virginity Pledges and First Intercourse." *American Journal of Sociology* 106(4):859–912.

Becker, G. (1991) *A Treatise on the Family.* Cambridge, MA: Harvard University Press.

Bennett, T., Braveman, P., Egerter, S., and Kiely, J. L. (1994) "Maternal Marital Status as a Risk Factor for Infant Mortality." *Family Planning Perspectives* 26:252–6.

Booth, A., Johnson, D. R., Branaman, A., and Sica, A. (1995) "Belief and Behavior: Does Religion Matter in Today's Marriage?" *Journal of Marriage and the Family* 57(3):661–71.

Brown, S. (2000) "The Effects of Union Type on Psychological Well-Being: Depression Among Cohabitors versus Marrieds." *Journal of Health and Social Behavior* 41:241–55.

Brown, S. and Booth, A. (1996) "Cohabitation versus Marriage: A Comparison of Relationship Quality." *Journal of Marriage and the Family* 58(3):668–78.

Call, V. R. and Heaton, T. B. (1997) "Religious Influence on Marital Stability." *Journal for the Scientific Study of Religion* 36(3):382–92.

Carlson, M., McLanahan, S., and England, P. (2004) "Union Formation in Fragile Families." *Demography* 41(2):237–61.

Cherlin, A. J. (1999) "Going to Extremes: Family Structure, Children's Well-Being, and Social Science." *Demography* 36(4):421–8.

Cherlin, A. J., Chase-Lansdale, L., and McRae, C. (1998) "Effects of Parental Divorce on Mental Health Throughout the Life Course." *American Sociological Review* 63:239–49.

Chiswick, B. R. (1988) "Differences in Education and Earnings Across Racial and Ethnic Groups: Tastes, Discrimination, and Investments in Child Quality." *Quarterly Journal of Economics* 103(3):571–97.

Chiswick, C. U. (1999) "An Economic Model of Jewish Continuity." *Contemporary Jewry* 20:30–56.

Darnell, A. and Sherkat, D. E. (1997) "The Impact of Protestant Fundamentalism on Educational Attainment." *American Sociological Review* 62:306–15.

Donahue, M. J. and Benson, P. L. (1995) "Religion and the Well-Being of Adolescents." *Journal of Social Issues* 51(2):145–60.

Duncan, G., England, P., and Wilkerson, B. (2003) "Cleaning up their Act: The Impacts of Marriage, Cohabitation, and Fertility on Licit and Illicit Drug Use." Presented at the annual meetings of the Population Association of America, Minneapolis.

Durkheim, E. (1951 [1897]) *Suicide.* Glencoe, IL: The Free Press.

Ellison, C. G. and Anderson, K. L. (2001) "Religious Involvement and Domestic Violence Among U.S. Couples." *Journal for the Scientific Study of Religion* 40(2):269–86.

Ellison, C. G., Bartkowski, J. P., and Anderson, K. L. (1999) "Are There Religious Variations in Domestic Violence?" *Journal of Family Issues* 20(1):87–113.

Ellison, C. G. and George, L. K. (1994) "Religious Involvement, Social Ties, and Social Support in a Southeastern Community." *Journal for the Scientific Study of Religion* 33(1):46–61.

Ellison, C. G. and Levin, J. S. (1998) "The Religion–Health Connection: Evidence, Theory, and Future Directions." *Health Education and Behavior* 25(6):700–20.

Freeman, R. B. (1986) "Who Escapes? The Relationship of Churchgoing and Other Background Factors to the Socioeconomic Performance of Black Male Youths from Inner-City Tracts." Pp. 353–76 in R. B. Freeman and H. J. Holzer (eds.) *The Black Youth Employment Crisis*. Chicago: University of Chicago Press.

Gennetian, L. A. and Knox, V. (2003) "Can Social Welfare Policy Increase Marriage or Decrease Divorce?" Presented at the annual meeting of the Population Association of America, Minneapolis.

Glenn, N. D. and Supancic, M. (1984) "The Social and Demographic Correlates of Divorce and Separation in the United States: An Update and Reconsideration." *Journal of Marriage and the Family* August:563–75.

Goodwin, J. S., Hunt, W. C., Key, C. R., and Samet, J. M. (1987) "The Effect of Marital Status on Stage, Treatment, and Survival of Cancer Patients." *Journal of the American Medical Association* 258(21):3125–30.

Gove, W. R. (1973) "Sex, Marital Status, and Mortality." *American Journal of Sociology* 79:45–67.

Gray, J. S. and Vanderhart, M. J. (2000) "On the Determination of Wages: Does Marriage Matter?" Pp. 356–67 in L. J. Waite, C. Bachrach, M. Hindin, E. Thomson, and A. Thornton (eds) *The Ties that Bind: Perspectives on Marriage and Cohabitation*. New York: Aldine de Gruyter.

Greeley, A. M. (1991) *Faithful Attraction: Discovering Intimacy, Love, and Fidelity in American Marriage*. New York: Tom Doherty Associates.

Grossbard-Shechtman, S. (1993) *On the Economics of Marriage: A Theory of Marriage, Labor, and Divorce*. Boulder, CO: Westview Press.

Hahn, B. A. (1993) "Marital Status and Women's Health: The Effect of Economic Marital Acquisitions." *Journal of Marriage and the Family* 55:495–504.

Harker, K. (2001) "Immigrant Generation, Assimilation, and Adolescent Psychological Well-Being." *Social Forces* 79(3):969–1004.

Heaton, T. B. and Pratt, E. L. (1990) "The Effects of Religious Homogamy on Marital Satisfaction and Stability." *Journal of Family Issues* 11(2):191–207.

Horwitz, A. V., White, H. R., and Howell-White, S. (1996) "Becoming Married and Mental Health: A Longitudinal Analysis of a Cohort of Young Adults." *Journal of Marriage and the Family* 58:895–907.

Hummer, R. A., Padilla, Y. C., Echevarria, S., and Kim, E. (2002) "Does Parental Religious Involvement Affect the Birth Outcomes and Health Status of Young Children?" Presented at the annual meetings of the Population Association of America, Atlanta.

Hummer, R.A., Rogers, R. G., Nam, C. B., and Ellison, C. G. (1999) "Religious Involvement and U.S. Adult Mortality." *Demography* 36(2):273–85.

Iannaccone, L. R. (1990) "Religious Practice: A Human Capital Approach." *Journal for the Scientific Study of Religion* 29:297–314.

Idler, E. and Kasl, S. V. (1992) "Religion, Disability, Depression, and the Timing of Death." *American Journal of Sociology* 97(4):1052–79.

Kiecolt-Glaser, J., Malarkey, W. B., Chee, M., Newton, T., Cacioppo, J. T., Mao, H. Y., and Glaser, R. (1993) "Negative Behavior During Marital Conflict is Associated With Immunological Down-Regulation." *Psychosomatic Medicine* 55:395–409.

Kiernan, K. (2003) "Unmarried Parenthood: Does it Matter?" Presented at the annual meeting of the Population Association of America, Minneapolis.

Koenig, H. G. (1994) "Religion and Hope for the Disabled Elder." Pp. 18–51 in J. S. Levin (ed.) *Religion in Aging and Health: Theoretical Foundations and Methodological Frontiers*. Thousand Oaks, CA: Sage.

Koenig, H. G., McCullough, M. E., and Larson, D. B. (2001) *Handbook of Religion and Health*. New York: Oxford University Press.

Korenman, S. and Neumark, D. (1991) "Does Marriage Really Make Men More Productive?" *Journal of Human Resources* 26(2):282–307.

Laumann, E. O., Gagnon, J. H., Michael, R. T., and Michaels, S. (1994) *The Social Organization of Sexuality: Sexual Practices in the United States*. Chicago: University of Chicago Press.

Lehrer, E. L. (1996) "The Determinants of Marital Stability: A Comparative Analysis of First and Higher Order Marriages," Pp. 91–121 in T. P. Schultz (ed.) *Research in Population Economics*, vol. 8. Greenwich: JAI Press.

Lehrer, E. L. (1999) "Religion as a Determinant of Educational Attainment: An Economic Perspective." *Social Science Research* 28:358–79.

Lehrer, E. L. (2003) "The Economics of Divorce." Pp. 55–74 in S.Grossbard-Shechtman (ed.) *Marriage and the Economy: Theory and Evidence from Industrialized Societies*. Cambridge: Cambridge University Press.

Lehrer, E. L. (2004) "Religiosity as a Determinant of Educational Attainment: The Case of Conservative Protestant Women in the United States." *Review of Economics of Houeshold* 2(2):203–19.

Lehrer, E. and Chiswick, C. U. (1993) "Religion as a Determinant of Marital Stability." *Demography* 30(3):385–404. (Chapter 1 this volume.)

Lehrer, E., Crittenden, K., and Norr, K. (2002a) "Depression and Welfare Dependency Among Inner-City Minority Mothers." *Social Science Research* 31:285–309.

Lehrer, E., Crittenden, K., and Norr, K. (2002b) "Illicit Drug Use and Reliance on Welfare." *Journal of Drug Issues* 32(1):179–207.

Lerman, R. (2002) *How do Marriage, Cohabitation, and Single Parenthood Affect the Material Hardships of Families with Children?* On-line book found at: http://www.urban.org/UploadedPDF/410539_SippPaper.pdf (accessed February 23, 2008).

Levin, J. S. (1994) "Religion and Health: Is There an Association, Is It Valid, and Is It Causal?" *Social Science and Medicine* 38(11):1475–82.

Levin, J. S., Markides, K. S., and Ray, L. A. (1996) "Religious Attendance and Psychological Well-Being in Mexican-Americans: A Panel Analysis of Three-Generations Data." *The Gerontologist* 36(4):454–63.

Lillard, L. A. and Panis, C. (1996) "Marital Status and Mortality: The Role of Health." *Demography* 33(3):313–27.

Lillard, L. A. and Waite, L. J. (1995) "' Til Death Do Us Part': Marital Disruption and Mortality." *American Journal of Sociology* 100(5):1131–56.

Lupton, J. and Smith, J. P. (2003) "Marriage, Assets, and Savings." Pp. 129–52 in S. Grossbard-Shechtman (ed.) *Marriage and the Economy: Theory and Evidence from Industrialized Societies*. Cambridge: Cambridge University Press.

Manning, W. D. and Brown, S. L. (2003) "Children's Economic Well-Being in Cohabiting Parent Families: An Update and Extension." Presented at the annual meeting of the Population Association of America, Minneapolis.

Marchena, E. and Waite, L. J. (2002) "Re-Assessing Family Goals and Attitudes in Late Adolescence: The Effects of Natal Family Experiences and Early Family Formation." Pp. 97–127 in R. Lesthaeghe (ed.) *Meaning and Choice: Value Orientations and Life Course Decisions*. Brussels: The Netherlands Interdisciplinary Demographic Institute.

Marks, N. F. and Lambert, J. D. (1998) "Marital Status Continuity and Change

Among Young and Midlife Adults: Longitudinal Effects on Psychological Well-Being." *Journal of Family Issues* 19:652–86.

McLanahan, S. and Sandefur, G. (1994) *Growing Up with a Single Parent: What Hurts, What Helps*. Cambridge, MA: Harvard University Press.

McLanahan, S., Garfinkel, I., and Mincy, R. (2001) "Fragile Families, Welfare Reform, and Marriage." Policy Brief No. 10. Washington: The Brookings Institution.

Michael, R. T. (1979) "Determinants of Divorce." Pp. 223–69 in L. Levy-Garboua (ed.) *Sociological Economics*. London: Sage.

Muller, C. and Ellison, C. G. (2001) "Religious Involvement, Social Capital, and Adolescents' Academic Progress: Evidence From the National Education Longitudinal Study of 1988." *Sociological Focus* 34(2):155–83.

Murphy, M., Glaser, K., and Grundy, E. (1997) "Marital Status and Long-Term Illness in Great Britain." *Journal of Marriage and the Family* 59(1):156–64.

Musick, M. A. (1996) "Religion and Subjective Health Among Black and White Elders." *Journal of Health and Social Behavior* 37:221–37.

Myers, D. G. (2000) *The American Paradox: Spiritual Hunger in an Age of Plenty*. New Haven, CT: Yale University Press.

Pargament, K. I., Ensig, D. S., Falgout, K., Olsen, H., Reilly, B., Van Haitsma, K. and Warren, R. (1990) "God Help Me: Religious Coping Efforts as Predictors of the Outcomes to Significant Negative Life Events." *American Journal of Community Psychology* 18(6):793–824.

Pargament, K. I., Smith, B. R., Koenig, H. G., and Perez, P. (1998) "Patterns of Positive and Negative Religious Coping With Major Life Stressors." *Journal for the Scientific Study of Religion* 37(4):710–24.

Pearce, L. D. and Axinn, W. G. (1998) "The Impact of Family Religious Life on the Quality of Mother–Child Relations." *American Sociological Review* 63:810–28.

Regnerus, M. D. (2000) "Shaping Schooling Success: Religious Socialization and Educational Outcomes in Metropolitan Public Schools." *Journal for the Scientific Study of Religion* 39:363–70.

Regnerus, M. D. and Elder, G. (2001) "Staying on Track: Religious Influences in High- and Low-Risk Settings." *Journal for the Scientific Study of Religion* 42(4):633–49.

Ross, C. E., Mirowsky, J., and Goldsteen, K. (1990) "The Impact of the Family on Health: A Decade in Review." *Journal of Marriage and the Family* 52:1059–78.

Seiler, N. (2002) "Is Teen Marriage a Solution?" Unpublished manuscript, Center for Law and Social Policy.

Sherkat, D. E. and Darnell, A. (1999) "The Effects of Parents' Fundamentalism on Children's Educational Attainment: Examining Differences by Gender and Children's Fundamentalism." *Journal for the Scientific Study of Religion* 38:23–35.

Sherkat, D. E. and Ellison, C. G. (1999) "Recent Developments and Current Controversies in the Sociology of Religion." *Annual Review of Sociology* 25:363–94.

Simon, R. W. (2002) "Revisiting the Relationship Among Gender, Marital Status, and Mental Health." *American Journal of Sociology* 107:1065–96.

Sloan, R., Bagiella, E., and Powell, T. (1999) "Religion, Spirituality, and Medicine." *Lancet* 353:664–7.

Stacey, J. (1993) "Good Riddance to 'The Family': A Response to David Popenoe." *Journal of Marriage and the Family* 55:545–7.

Stets, J. E. (1991) "Cohabiting and Marital Aggression: The Role of Social Isolation." *Journal of Marriage and the Family* 53:669–80.

Stolzenberg, R. M., Blair-Loy, M., and Waite, L. J. (1995) "Religious Participation Over the Life Course: Age and Family Life Cycle Effects on Church Membership." *American Sociological Review* 60:84–103.

Strawbridge, W. J., Cohen, R. D., Shema, S. J., and Kaplan, G. A. (1997) "Frequent Attendance at Religious Services and Mortality Over 28 Years." *American Journal of Public Health* 87(6):957–61.

Tucker, J. S., Friedman, H. S., Schwartz, J. E., Criqui, M. H., Tomlinson-Keasey, C., Wingard, D. L., and Martin, L. R. (1997) "Parental Divorce: Effects on Individual Behavior and Longevity." *Journal of Personality and Social Psychology* 73(2):381–91.

Umberson, D. (1987) "Family Status and Health Behaviors: Social Control as a Dimension of Social Integration." *Journal of Health and Social Behavior* 28:306–19.

US Census Bureau. (2001) *Living Arrangements of Children Under 18 Years Old: 1960 to Present.* US Census Bureau, online. Available at: http://www.census.gov/population/socdemo/hh-fam/tabCH-1.xls (accessed February 23, 2008).

Waite, L. J. (1995) "Does Marriage Matter?" *Demography* 32(4):483–507.

Waite, L. J. (2000) "Trends in Men's and Women's Well-Being in Marriage." Pp. 368–92 in L. J. Waite, C. Bachrach, M. Hindin, E. Thomson, and A. Thornton (eds) *The Ties that Bind: Perspectives on Marriage and Cohabitation.* New York: Aldine de Gruyter.

Waite, L. J. and Gallagher, M. (2000) *The Case for Marriage: Why Married People Are Happier, Healthier, and Better Off Financially.* New York: Doubleday.

Waite, L. J. and Joyner, K. (2001) "Emotional Satisfaction and Physical Pleasure in Sexual Unions: Time Horizon, Sexual Behavior and Sexual Exclusivity." *Journal of Marriage and the Family* 63:247–64.

Weiss, Y. and Willis, R. J. (1985) "Children as Collective Goods." *Journal of Labor Economics* 3:268–92.

Wickrama, K. A. S., Lorenz, F. O., Conger, R. D., and Elder, G. H. (1997) "Marital Quality and Physical Illness: A Latent Growth Curve Analysis." *Journal of Marriage and the Family* 59:143–55.

Wilcox, W. B. (2000) "For the Sake of the Children? Family-Related Discourse and Practice in the Mainline." Draft prepared for the "Public Role of Mainline Protestantism Project," Princeton University.

Zuckerman, D. M., Kasl, S. V., and Ostfeld, A. M. (1984) "Psychosocial Predictors of Mortality Among the Elderly Poor: The Role of Religion, Well-Being, and Social Contacts." *American Journal of Epidemiology* 119(3):410–23.

6 Religion as a determinant of educational attainment

An economic perspective*

Several studies have documented that religion plays an important role in the economic and demographic behavior of American families, ranging from marriage and divorce to fertility and female employment (see reviews of this literature in Lehrer 1996a; Iannaccone 1998). A large body of research has also explored the effects of religion on education, earnings, and other measures of socioeconomic attainment. Early studies consistently found that Jews have substantially higher levels of schooling and earnings than other groups (Chiswick 1983, 1988, 1993; Tomes 1983, 1985). Comparisons between Protestants and Catholics, however, yielded conflicting rankings (Featherman 1971; Greeley 1976, 1981; Roof 1979, 1981; Tomes 1985; Steen and Dubbink 1994). Partly because of this lack of clear patterns, the effects of religion on educational attainment have received little attention in recent years. Thus it is not surprising that, in an extensive survey of the determinants of children's attainments, religion is conspicuously absent from the family background factors reviewed (Haveman and Wolfe 1995).

At the same time that researchers were finding no systematic Catholic–Protestant differentials in socioeconomic status, scholars also began to note that the demographic behavior of Catholics in the United States was losing its former distinctiveness. Convergence was documented in several areas, including fertility (Jones and Westoff 1979; Mosher et al. 1992; Lehrer 1996b), union formation (Sander 1995; Lehrer 2000), separation and divorce (Thornton 1985a; Lehrer and Chiswick 1993), and female time allocation and labor supply behavior (Brinkerhoff and MacKie 1984, 1988; Lehrer 1995).[1]

However, while many of the special characteristics that singled out Catholics were disappearing, a large and influential group within Protestantism was becoming more distinct. As Thornton observes:

> During the last two decades – when there were important trends toward more egalitarian sex role attitudes, more acceptance of divorce, more

* Reprinted from *Social Science Research* 28:358–379, 1999.

acceptance of childlessness, and a desire for smaller families – fundamentalist Protestants changed along with the rest of the American population, but the extent of their change was smaller. The result is that they are now generally more traditional than other Americans on many aspects of family life [. . .] This group of Protestants also continues to have somewhat higher fertility than others [. . .]

(1985b, p. 386)

In addition, their patterns of union formation and maternal employment remain distinct. Compared to mainline Protestants, fundamentalist Protestant women enter marriage at younger ages (Lehrer 2000) and display a lower level of attachment to the labor market when young children are present in the home (Lehrer 1995). Moreover, the boundaries that separate fundamentalist Protestants from other groups remain sharp. Thus, while the prevalence of intermarriage has increased over the past decades among mainline Protestants, Catholics, and Jews, the rate has remained remarkably stable for fundamentalist Protestants (Glenn 1982; Kalmijn 1991; Sander 1993; Chiswick 1997; Lehrer 1998).

Recent research has reopened the question of how religion affects schooling and income, by shifting the focus of attention away from Catholic–Protestant comparisons, toward the distinction between fundamentalist and nonfundamentalist Protestants. Using data from the Youth Parent Socialization Panel, collected in 1965, 1973, and 1982, Darnell and Sherkat (1997) and Sherkat and Darnell (1999) document a strong negative effect of fundamentalism on educational achievement, net of other social background variables. Similarly, based on a pooled cross-section of data at the state level for 1952, 1971, and 1980, Waters et al. (1995) report an adverse impact of fundamentalism on income, other factors held constant.

The present research uses data from the 1987–88 National Survey of Families and Households (NSFH) to explore further the role of religion in human capital investment decisions, with particular emphasis on the effects associated with membership in fundamentalist Protestant denominations. The study compares the educational achievement of individuals raised in four major religious groups: Catholics, Jews, mainline Protestants, and fundamentalist Protestants.[2] Table 6.1 provides an overview by reporting mean years of schooling and the distribution of this variable by religion and gender. For both men and women, educational attainment is clearly highest among Jews and lowest among fundamentalist Protestants, with Catholics and mainline Protestants at the center of the distribution. This study examines these differences in some detail, showing that they are significant and do not disappear when other background factors are held constant. The study also identifies the stages of the schooling process at which the divergences occur and assesses the relative weights of various causal mechanisms through which religion may affect educational attainment.

Table 6.1 Educational attainment by religion

	Mean years of schooling	*Less than 12 years*	*12 years*	*13–15 years*	*16 years or more*
	Men (N = 1,313)				
Mainline Protestant	14.46	0.04	0.29	0.29	0.38
Fundamentalist Protestant	13.33	0.11	0.42	0.23	0.25
Catholic	14.34	0.03	0.32	0.28	0.36
Jewish	16.85	0.00	0.07	0.18	0.75
	Women (N = 1,831)				
Mainline Protestant	13.97	0.04	0.40	0.26	0.30
Fundamentalist Protestant	12.89	0.14	0.46	0.24	0.16
Catholic	13.72	0.04	0.43	0.27	0.26
Jewish	15.78	0.00	0.17	0.21	0.62

Analytical framework

The human capital model developed by Becker and Chiswick (1966) and Becker (1967) provides a useful framework for understanding the various channels through which religion may influence educational decisions and for testing which set of factors is most important in each case. In this model, the optimal level of schooling for a given individual is that where the demand for funds for investment in education intersects the supply.[3] The shape of these curves, illustrated in Figure 6.1, is as typical in economic applications. The demand schedule shows the marginal rate of return derived from each additional dollar spent on schooling. It is drawn with a negative slope because, as more years of schooling are obtained and productivity in the labor market rises, the cost in terms of forgone earnings increases. In addition, since a person's mental capacity is fixed and life is finite, diminishing marginal returns eventually set in as additional education is acquired. The supply curve shows the marginal rate of interest on funds borrowed (or not lent) to finance investments in education. It is drawn with an upward slope under the assumption that obtaining additional funds is increasingly expensive as more human capital investments are undertaken.

Differences among individuals in schooling levels can be understood in terms of variations in the circumstances that influence the position of these curves. Figure 6.2a illustrates that, other factors held constant, persons who have a demand curve that is farther to the right acquire more schooling and earn a higher rate of return on their investment. This situation may result from a high level of ability (due to inherited talents or parental investments in child quality) which would lower the psychological costs of acquiring education, and cause any given input of schooling to be translated into a larger increase in earning capacity. It could also arise from easier access to schooling

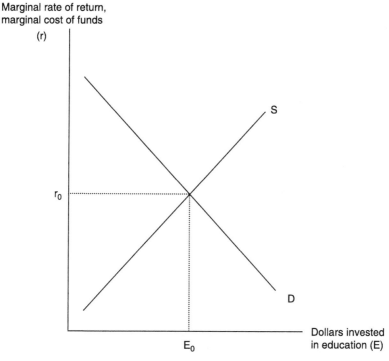

Figure 6.1 The supply and demand of funds for investments in schooling. The optimal level of schooling for this individual is E_0. At this point, the marginal
interest cost of funds is equal to the marginal rate of return (r_0).

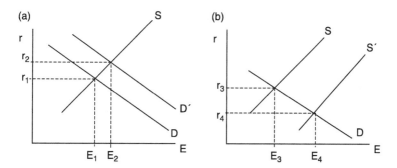

Figure 6.2 The effects of differences among groups in demand and supply conditions.
(a) Ceteris paribus, individuals with a D curve further to the right invest
more in schooling and earn a higher rate of return. This could result from
greater ability or from access to schooling of higher quality, among other
factors. (b) Ceteris paribus, individuals with an S curve further to the right
invest more in schooling and earn a lower rate of return. This could result
from a high level of family wealth or from a high priority placed on education, among other factors.

or to schooling of a higher quality. If two persons of equal ability make the same dollar expenditures on education but one receives better training, that individual would obtain a higher earning capacity and a greater rate of return.

Figure 6.2b shows that ceteris paribus, individuals for whom the supply curve is farther to the right make greater investments in schooling and earn a lower rate of return. This situation may be due to a higher level of family wealth, which makes it possible to self-finance investments in education or borrow funds at relatively low rates. It may also arise from a strong preference for schooling: an individual who places a high priority on education would be willing to invest more in human capital at any given interest rate.

Religion may influence schooling decisions by affecting the positions of the demand and supply curves. Using mainline Protestants as the comparison group, the sections below analyze in turn the cases of Jews, fundamentalist Protestants, and Catholics.

Jews

A detailed analysis of how the human capital framework explains the high educational attainment of Jews is presented by Chiswick (1988) and is reviewed here only briefly. On the one hand, the "diaspora" hypothesis suggests that the supply curve for Jews is farther to the right. For reasons related to their history, Jewish individuals have a strong preference for investments in human capital, as they are more portable and transferable than are investments in physical capital (Brenner and Kiefer 1981). On the other hand, the lower fertility of Jews (Goldscheider 1967; Della Pergola 1980), coupled with their lower rates of female employment when children are young (Chiswick 1986), implies high levels of home investments in child quality. Such investments increase the productivity of formal education and lead to a demand curve for human capital that is farther to the right than for other groups.

Both effects probably operate, and which one dominates is an empirical matter. Figure 6.3 illustrates the various possibilities. The three cases are consistent with the observation that the level of schooling is higher for Jews $(E_J > E_M)$, but they differ in what they imply about the rate of return from investments in education. If the diaspora effect is stronger, the observed rate of return should be lower for Jews, as shown in Figure 6.3a. On the other hand, if the dominant force is the alternative view that Jews are more productive in converting the schooling process into earnings, then the observed rate of return should be higher for Jews, as in Figure 6.3b. If both influences are of equal strength, the observed rate of return should be the same for Jews and other religious groups, as illustrated in Figure 6.3c. Empirically, Tomes (1983), Meng and Sentance (1984), and Chiswick (1988) all find that the rate of return for Jews exceeds that of other groups by a wide margin. These results suggest that Figure 6.3b is the relevant case and imply that demand

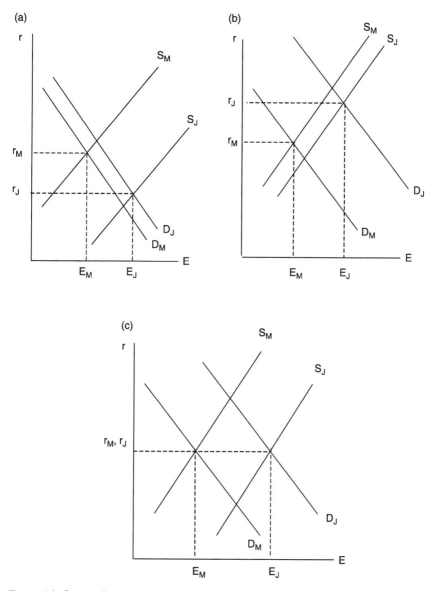

Figure 6.3 Comparisons between Jews (J) and mainline Protestants (M). (a) If supply forces dominate, the observed rate of return should be lower for Jews. (3b) If demand forces dominate, the observed rate of return should be higher for Jews. (3c) If supply and demand forces are of equal strength, the observed rate of return should be equal for the two groups.

factors are more important than supply considerations in explaining the unusually high educational achievement of Jews.

Fundamentalist Protestants

The human capital framework may also be used to shed light on the relative importance of various factors in explaining the low schooling levels of fundamentalist Protestants. Fundamentalist beliefs, rooted in strong faith on the inerrancy of the Bible, may affect the supply of investable funds for several reasons emphasized by Darnell and Sherkat (1997). As the authors note, a literal interpretation of the Bible leads to hostility toward the scientific method, because this approach to learning "seeks to *discover* truths rather than claiming to *know* 'The Truth.' Scientific discoveries are seen as promoting alternatives to divine truths already specified in scripture" (1997, p. 308). Fundamentalist Protestants are also concerned about the challenge to their beliefs posed by humanistic education. Their reservations about the learning that takes place in secular institutions are particularly pronounced at the college level; at the same time, the opportunities to attend religious institutions of higher education are limited and expensive. These various concerns about possible negative effects of secular schooling imply that, at any given interest cost, fundamentalist parents would be willing to invest less funds for the education of their children – i.e., they imply that their supply curve is farther to the left than for other religious groups.

Affiliation with a fundamentalist Protestant denomination may also affect the position of the demand curve for schooling. On the one hand, fundamentalist beliefs are associated with more traditional attitudes toward gender roles and the appropriate intrafamily division of labor (McMurry 1978; Brinkerhoff and MacKie 1988). Levels of employment during the child-rearing years are correspondingly somewhat lower among fundamentalist Protestant mothers than among women of other religious affiliations (Lehrer 1995). This effect suggests that the former make greater home investments in child quality during the formative years. This influence may be offset, however, by the fact that fertility levels among fundamentalist Protestants are higher by a small margin than for other Protestant groups (Marcum 1981; Heaton and Goodman 1985; Lehrer 1996b).

Productivity effects associated with the nature of early investments in human capital are likely to be more important demand-side forces than the influences described above. Because of its authoritarian approach to knowledge and its rejection of critical inquiry and unconventional modes of thinking, a fundamentalist upbringing may imply lower levels of certain types of home investments in child quality that increase the productivity of formal schooling. Further, fundamentalist orientations have been found to have a strong adverse effect on the probability that a student will take college preparatory work during high school (Darnell and Sherkat 1997). As the authors note, "these college preparatory courses are the ones fundamentalists find most harmful to their children, because of their advocacy of humanism, evolution, cultural tolerance, and variable based approaches to mathematics" (Sherkat and Darnell 1999, p. 7). Children raised in fundamentalist homes may thus find that their access to high-quality universities is restricted. Such access may be limited even further to the extent that secular institutions of higher education discriminate against fundamentalist Protestants.[4] Together, all of these considerations imply that the demand curve for fundamentalist Protestants is to the left of that for other groups.

Among fundamentalist Protestants, the demand curve is expected to be farthest to the left for members of sects. For such individuals, the expected benefits from investments in education may be depressed by various constraints that limit secular activities and rewards (Iannaccone 1992). A difference by gender within the fundamentalist Protestant group may also be expected. Fundamentalist beliefs are associated with traditional views regarding the intrafamily division of labor. Thus, the length of labor market activity and the rewards from formal investments in school are expected to be lower for fundamentalist women than for their male counterparts.

Both the supply- and demand-side considerations outlined above are consistent with the relatively low level of educational attainment of children raised in fundamentalist Protestant homes. Empirically, it is possible to assess the relative strength of the two sets of forces by estimating the rate of return from investments in schooling. If the factors that place the supply curve further to the left for fundamentalist Protestants dominate, then the observed rate of return should be higher for this group, as shown in Figure 6.4a. The opposite would hold if the influences that tend to push the demand curve downward were strongest, as in Figure 6.4b. It is also possible that the two sets of factors are of approximately equal weight. In this case, the rate of return for fundamentalist Protestants should not be very different from that of other religious groups, as shown in Figure 6.4c.

Catholics

Figure 6.5 shows the S and D curves for Catholics as coinciding with the respective curves for mainline Protestants. This hypothesis is based on the premise that there has been a convergence between Catholics and mainline Protestants in most areas of economic and demographic behavior and is consistent with evidence that the schooling levels of the two groups are very similar. If true, the empirical results should show that the rate of return from investments in education is also roughly the same ($r_C = r_M$).

Methods

The empirical analysis is based on data from the 1987–88 National Survey of Families and Households (NSFH), an extensive questionnaire addressed to a main sample of 9,643 male and female respondents, representative of the US

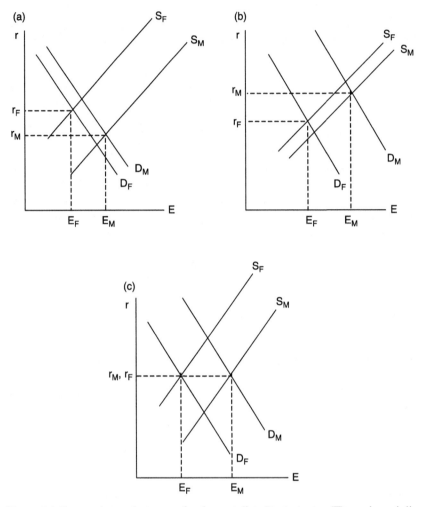

Figure 6.4 Comparisons between fundamentalist Protestants (F) and mainline Protestants (M). (a) If supply forces dominate, the observed rate of return should be higher for fundamentalist Protestants. (b) If demand forces dominate, the observed rate of return should be lower for fundamentalist Protestants. (4c) If supply and demand forces are of equal strength, the observed rate of return should be equal for the two groups.

population aged 19 and above. An additional 3,374 cases correspond to an oversampling of special groups including African Americans, Hispanics, and families with stepchildren.[5] The survey is rich in economic, demographic, and family background variables. For the purposes of the present research, an important feature of this data set is that it documents not only the current religious affiliation of respondents but also the faith in which they were brought up.[6]

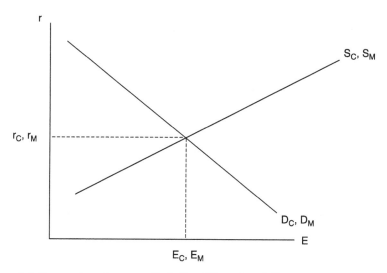

Figure 6.5 Comparison between Catholics (C) and mainline Protestants (M). The S and D curves for Catholics are shown as coinciding with the respective curves for mainline Protestants.

The study is restricted to non-Hispanic white respondents who resided in the United States at age 16. Even though African Americans and Hispanics were oversampled, the number of observations available for these groups is not sufficient to permit separate analyses; similarly, the number of respondents raised in foreign countries is small.[7] The sample is further restricted to individuals born in the period 1945–60. This post-World War II cohort attained significantly higher levels of schooling than did previous generations; this is also the group that marked the end of the distinctive demographic behavior of Catholics. Respondents born after 1960 are excluded, because at the survey date they were in age categories where the schooling process is often not yet complete. All analyses are weighted and conducted separately for males and females, to allow for possible differences by gender in the effects of religion on educational attainment.

The resulting sample sizes are N = 1,313 for males and N = 1,831 for females. These cases correspond to individuals raised in the four major religious groups considered in this study: Catholicism, Judaism, mainline Protestantism, and fundamentalist Protestantism.[8] The classification of Protestants is based on the categories employed by Lehrer and Chiswick (1993) for these data. Episcopalians, Methodists, Presbyterians, Lutherans, Unitarians, and various other ecumenical bodies are classified as mainline Protestants. The fundamentalist group includes Baptists, Jehovah's Witnesses, Seventh-Day Adventists, Christian Scientists, and a large number of other exclusivist groups. The NSFH includes all Baptists in one category, so it is not possible to make finer distinctions within this group.[9] This limitation of the data implies that the respondents classified in this study as fundamentalist Protestant include a small number of nonfundamentalists, suggesting a bias toward zero in the coefficient on the fundamentalist dummy variable. Thus, the negative effect of membership in fundamentalist denominations on education is more pronounced than indicated by the estimates in this study.[10]

Previous research suggests that current religious affiliation is determined simultaneously with the education process (Newport 1979; Waters et al. 1995; Lehrer 1998). The analyses presented here are thus based on the faith in which the individual was raised, a measure not affected by problems of endogeneity.

Table 6.2 presents definitions and means for the religion variables and for other factors used in the empirical analysis as controls. These include the mother's and father's years of schooling,[11] the father's socioeconomic status as measured by the Stevens–Cho (1985) index, dummy variables to indicate a nonintact family of origin, and reliance on welfare during the respondent's childhood, the number of siblings, dummies for whether the mother worked in the labor market when the respondent was a preschooler and during the school years, and variables to control for the region of residence at age 16.

Results

Table 6.3 presents ordinary least squares regressions with years of regular schooling as the dependent variable, estimated separately for men and women. In the first set of equations, only the religion variables are included as regressors (with mainline Protestants as the reference category). These results correspond exactly to the descriptive statistics reported in Table 6.1 and restate the findings therein: educational attainment is highest for Jews by a margin of about two years and lowest for fundamentalist Protestants by a margin of approximately one year. As the t-tests show, the differences are highly significant. In addition, the regression for women indicates that the educational attainment of Catholics is lower than that of mainline Protestants by about a fourth of a year.

When all the control factors are included, in the second set of regressions, the measured effects of religion decline considerably. But while the Catholic differential uncovered by the previous model in the female sample disappears completely, significant Jewish and fundamentalist Protestant effects persist. Compared to the benchmark, the educational attainment of Jews is higher by 1.330 years among men and by 1.219 years among women; for fundamentalist Protestants, it is lower by 0.328 and 0.383 years among men and women, respectively. While these influences are smaller than those found in the models with no controls, they are still sizable in the case of Jews and not trivial in the case of fundamentalist Protestants. One way of assessing the relative importance of the fundamentalist effect is by comparison with the influences of the control variables. For example, it is roughly in the same order of magnitude as the impact of having a mother or father with less than 12 years of schooling

Table 6.2 Variable definitions and means

		Men	*Women*
Control variables			
Mother's education	=1 if mother's years of regular schooling is in category indicated (benchmark: 12 years)		
<12		0.198	0.264
13–15		0.121	0.121
≥16		0.182	0.155
Missing		0.059	0.053
Father's education	=1 if years of regular schooling completed by the father is in category indicated (benchmark: 12 years). The "father" is the biological father in the case of intact families or the stepfather if he lived with the respondent at age 16.		
<12		0.278	0.295
13–15		0.109	0.098
≥16		0.269	0.282
Missing		0.059	0.064
Father not present	=1 if neither biological father nor stepfather was present at age 16	0.039	0.056
Nonintact family	=1 if respondent did not live with both biological parents at age 16	0.194	0.194
Father's SES	Steven and Cho's (1985) index of socioeconomic status corresponding to the occupation of the biological father, or the stepfather if he lived with the respondent at age 16. The lowest value is assigned if neither was present.	34.817	33.710
Ever on welfare	=1 if respondent's family ever relied on welfare	0.060	0.061
Number of siblings	Total number of biological siblings and step-siblings	3.014	3.109
Mother worked	=1 if mother ever worked when respondent was in the age category indicated		
0–5		0.312	0.227
6–17		0.586	0.566
Residence at age 16	=1 if respondent lived in the region indicated at age 16		
North Central		0.339	0.348
Northeast		0.236	0.242
West		0.147	0.131
Religion variables	=1 if faith in which respondent was raised belongs to the category indicated (benchmark: mainline Protestant)		
Fundamentalist Protestant		0.236	0.246
Catholic		0.309	0.328
Jewish		0.035	0.026
N		1,313	1,831

Table 6.3 The effects of religious upbringing on years of schooling: OLS regressions (t-values in parentheses)

	Men	Women
Control variables		
Mother's education		
<12	-0.203 (-1.1)	-0.414 (-3.3)**
13–15	0.566 (2.7)**	0.921 (5.8)**
≥16	1.310 (6.0)**	1.402 (7.8)**
Missing	-1.845 (-4.9)**	-2.429 (-8.1)**
Father's education		
<12	-0.390 (-2.3)**	-0.510 (-4.0)**
13–15	0.420 (1.9)*	0.364 (2.0)**
≥16	0.651 (2.8)**	0.867 (4.8)**
Missing	-2.295 (-6.0)**	-1.751 (-6.2)**
Father not present	-0.688 (-1.6)*	-0.642 (-2.1)**
Nonintact family	-0.282 (-1.6)*	-0.690 (-5.0)**
Father's SES	0.014 (3.1)**	0.012 (3.6)**
Ever on welfare	-0.524 (-1.9)*	-0.390 (-1.9)*
Number of siblings	-0.209 (-6.8)**	-0.146 (-6.4)**
Mother worked		
0–5	-0.254 (-1.7)*	0.216 (1.7)*
6–17	-0.238 (-1.7)*	-0.105 (-1.0)
Residence at age 16		
North Central	-0.014 (-0.08)	-0.034 (-0.3)
Northeast	0.240 (1.3)	-0.162 (-1.1)
West	0.059 (0.3)	-0.171 (-1.0)
Religion variables		
Fundamentalist Protestant	-0.328 (-1.9)*	-0.383 (-2.9)**
Catholic	0.222 (1.4)	0.084 (0.7)
Jewish	1.330 (3.7)**	1.219 (3.9)**
Constant	14.492 (57.1)**	13.914 (67.9)**
R^2	0.280	0.315
N	1,313	1,831

* $p < 0.10$; ** $p < 0.05$.

rather than a high school degree, or of having to compete with an additional sibling for resources.

In general, the coefficients of the control variables reveal few surprises. For both men and women, the parents' years of schooling and the father's socio-economic status (SES) have the expected positive influence on educational attainment; a broken family background, reliance on welfare, and the number of siblings all affect schooling negatively. Region of residence at age 16 has no significant impact. Whereas mother's employment during the preschool years influences schooling positively for women, among men the effect is negative and extends also to the case of maternal work during the years of elementary and secondary school. This result lends support to earlier research suggesting that women's labor market activities may adversely affect the cognitive development and schooling level of their male offspring (Hill and Duncan 1987; Desai et al. 1989).

The results in Table 6.3 provide an initial overview of the role of religious upbringing in educational attainment by focusing on the total number of years of schooling completed. The estimates are consistent with recent work by Sander (1995) that focuses on various aspects of the economic behavior of Catholics. His classification of Protestants consists of two groups: Baptist vs. all other; the latter is clearly dominated by mainline Protestants. His education regressions show that attainment is lowest among Baptists and highest among Jews; they also reveal no significant difference between Catholics and other Protestants.

The relationship between religion and schooling is explored further in Tables 6.4 and 6.5, which show the influences of the faith of upbringing at each of the main stages of the educational process. These analyses examine the effects of religion on the likelihood of obtaining a high school degree, of going on to college among those who completed their secondary education, and of obtaining a college degree among those who attended college. The logit regression results reported in Table 6.4 provide information on the direction and significance of the effects. The magnitude of each influence may be assessed more easily by examining the estimated probabilities shown in Table 6.5.

Tables 6.4 and 6.5 indicate that the positive effects on schooling associated with a Jewish upbringing are present at all stages of the educational process, for both men and women. A marginally significant coefficient is observed for Catholics in the college attendance regression for the female sample. However, the impact is not strong enough to have a perceptible influence on completed education, as Table 6.3 shows.

In the case of fundamentalist Protestants, these analyses reveal differences by gender that were not evident in the earlier regressions. Among men, the negative effect of fundamentalism on schooling occurs most strongly at the stage of deciding whether or not to attend college (t = −2.1): conditional on completing secondary school, the probability of going on to higher education is 0.61 for fundamentalist Protestant men, compared to 0.70 for mainline

Table 6.4 The effects of religious upbringing on schooling transitions: logit regressions[a] (t-values in parentheses)

	Men			Women		
	High school degree	College attendance	College degree	High school degree	College attendance	College degree
Fundamentalist Protestant	−0.589 (−1.7)*	−0.372 (−2.1)**	0.150 (0.7)	−0.841 (−3.3)**	0.016 (0.1)	−0.357 (1.7)*
Catholic	0.355 (0.9)	0.180 (1.1)	0.135 (0.7)	0.080 (0.3)	0.200 (1.4)#	0.033 (0.2)
Jewish	−[b]	1.233 (2.0)**	0.659 (1.5)#	−[b]	1.148 (2.6)**	0.961 (2.3)**
Log-likelihood function	−207.244	−676.257	−479.553	−340.343	−927.676	−577.165
N	1,313	1,240	806	1,831	1,686	927
Sample:	all respondents	respondents who completed at least 12 years of schooling	respondents who attended college at least one year	all respondents	respondents who completed at least 12 years of schooling	respondents who attended college at least one year

# p < 0.15; * p < 0.10; ** p < 0.05.

Notes

a All the control variables shown in Table 6.2 are included in these regressions.
b The Jewish variable was excluded as it has no variance: all Jews in the sample have at least a high school degree.

Table 6.5 Estimated probabilities of schooling transitions[a]

	Men			Women		
	High school degree	College attendance	College degree	High school degree	College attendance	College degree
Mainline Protestant	0.98	0.70	0.56	0.98	0.56	0.52
Fundamentalist Protestant	0.96	0.61	(0.59)	0.95	(0.57)	0.43
Catholic	(0.98)	(0.73)	(0.59)	(0.98)	0.61	(0.53)
Jewish	_b	0.89	0.71	_b	0.80	0.74

Notes

a These probabilities are calculated from the equations in Table 6.4 by setting all the explanatory variables at the mean and the religion variables at the categories indicated in the stub. Figures in parentheses correspond to coefficients that are not significantly different from the mainline Protestant category in Table 6.4.

b The Jewish variable is excluded; see Table 6.4, note b.

Protestants. In contrast, in the case of women, the most marked negative impact of fundamentalism takes place later, at the stage of completing a college degree or not (t = −1.7). Conditional on having enrolled in an institution of higher education, fundamentalist Protestant women have a 0.43 probability of obtaining a college degree, compared to 0.52 for their mainline Protestant counterparts.

Sherkat and Darnell's (1999) analysis suggests a possible explanation for this difference by gender. As the authors point out, fundamentalist parents are more willing to make investments in higher education when their children follow their faith. The present data suggest that this outcome is somewhat more likely in the case of female offspring. Among women raised in fundamentalist denominations, 83 percent reported affiliation with a fundamentalist group at the time of the survey. The corresponding figure for men is 77 percent, a difference that is statistically significant at the 0.05 level. Perhaps more importantly, the pronounced fundamentalist effect that is uncovered at a later stage for women is likely to reflect the stronger emphasis placed by this group on the traditional division of labor within the family. As the childrearing years approach, the incentives among fundamentalist Protestant women to remain in school may begin to weaken.

As indicated earlier, the relative strength of supply- and demand-side influences on human capital decisions may be assessed by estimating the rate of return from investments in schooling. As a first approximation, the coefficient on the education variable in a wage regression provides an estimate of such rate.[12] Table 6.6 reports regressions for men and women, estimated separately by religious affiliation, with the natural logarithm of the wage rate as the dependent variable.[13] The inverse of Mill's ratio is included in the analyses for women to correct for possible selectivity biases. The probit labor force participation equations used to perform the correction are reported in Appendix 6.1.

The estimates for Jews must be interpreted with caution, as the sample sizes are very small: only 33 cases for men and 28 cases for women. For both genders, the point estimates suggest that the rate of return from schooling is highest for Jews by a wide margin. In the male sample, the coefficient on education is 0.145, compared to between 0.068 and 0.098 for the other groups. Similarly, in the female sample, their coefficient is 0.132, compared to between 0.084 and 0.108 for the other groups. The sample size limitations are severe and most of the pairwise differences between the coefficients for Jews and other religious groups do not attain significance at conventional levels. The point estimates, however, are consistent with results of other researchers (Chiswick 1983, 1988; Tomes 1983; Meng and Sentance 1984) and lend further support to their conclusion that the high educational achievement of Jews is primarily due to demand side forces (as in Figure 6.3b).

The estimates in Table 6.6 suggest relatively small differences between the coefficients on schooling for fundamentalist and mainline Protestants and statistically these differences are not significant. Together with the fact noted

Table 6.6 Wage regressions by religion (dependent variable: ln wage; t-values in parentheses)

	Men				Women			
	Mainline Protestant	Fundamentalist Protestant	Catholic	Jewish	Mainline Protestant	Fundamentalist Protestant	Catholic	Jewish
Years of schooling	0.094**	0.098**	0.068**	0.145**	0.084**	0.108**	0.099**	0.132*
	(11.2)	(7.7)	(6.2)	(3.3)	(10.1)	(8.9)	(9.1)	(1.7)
Years of experience[a]	0.020**	0.011**	0.016**	0.057**	0.011**	0.016**	0.013**	0.011
	(6.0)	(2.2)	(3.6)	(2.4)	(2.7)	(2.5)	(2.7)	(0.3)
Outside SMSA	-0.237**	-0.209**	-0.285**	-0.158	-0.158**	-0.110**	-0.191**	—[b]
	(-5.1)	(-3.2)	(-3.9)	(-0.2)	(-3.1)	(-2.0)	(-2.8)	
Residence								
North Central	0.048	0.054	0.079	0.460	-0.002	0.054	0.066	-0.495
	(1.0)	(0.8)	(1.0)	(1.3)	(0.05)	(0.9)	(0.9)	(-0.7)
Northeast	0.110*	0.031	0.072	0.794**	0.060	0.020	0.106#	-0.179
	(1.8)	(0.2)	(1.0)	(2.6)	(0.9)	(0.2)	(1.5)	(-0.3)
West	0.028	0.100	0.032	0.442	0.111*	0.032	0.294**	-0.258
	(0.5)	(1.1)	(0.4)	(1.2)	(1.9)	(0.4)	(3.6)	(-0.4)
Constant	0.897**	0.988**	1.298**	-0.836	0.932**	0.398*	0.600**	0.709*
	(6.0)	(4.8)	(6.8)	(-0.9)	(6.2)	(1.7)	(3.1)	(1.7)
Lambda	—	—	—	—	-0.174**	0.101	0.045	-0.240
					(-2.1)	(0.9)	(0.4)	(-0.3)
R^2	0.289	0.254	0.166	0.496	0.250	0.289	0.265	0.202
N	460	260	339	33	473	283	407	28

# p < 0.15; * p < 0.10; ** p < 0.05.

Notes
a In preliminary runs, a variable for years of experience squared was also included. The coefficients in all equations were insignificant, probably due to the limited age range of the respondents in the sample (27–43).
b Variable had no variance and was omitted.

earlier, that fundamentalist Protestants have a significantly lower level of schooling (Table 6.3), this finding supports the hypothesis illustrated in Figure 6.4c. Thus supply and demand effects appear to have similar weight in explaining the relatively low educational attainment of fundamentalist Protestants.

Turning now to comparisons between Catholics and mainline Protestants, Table 6.3 showed that there is no significant difference in their educational attainment, and Table 6.6 indicates that there is no significant difference in their rate of return. Thus the empirical findings support the hypothesis maintained in Figure 6.5, namely, that the supply and demand curves for the two religious groups roughly coincide.

Overall, the bulk of the evidence presented here and in previous research suggests the scenario summarized in Figure 6.6. The configuration of supply and demand curves shown there is consistent with the two main stylized facts, namely: (a) educational attainment is highest for Jews (E_J), lowest for fundamentalist Protestants (E_F), with mainline Protestants and Catholics at the center of the distribution ($E_M = E_C$); and (b) the rate of return from investments in schooling is roughly the same for fundamentalist Protestants, mainline Protestants, and Catholics ($r_F = r_M = r_C$), and is higher for Jews (r_J).

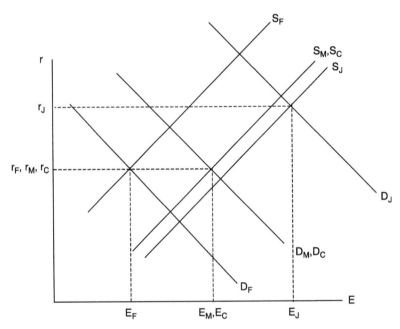

Figure 6.6 Comparisons among Jews, mainline Protestants, Catholics, and fundamentalist Protestants. The configuration of S and D curves shown in this diagram is consistent with the empirical evidence on the relative schooling levels and rates of return earned by the various groups.

Conclusions

Using data from the 1987–88 National Survey of Families and Households, this study presents a comparative analysis of educational attainment by religious upbringing. Previous studies have documented a convergence between Catholics and mainline Protestants in many areas of economic and demographic behavior. Consistent with this trend, the present study finds no significant difference in years of schooling between the two groups, other factors held constant. Two religious bodies, however, display distinct patterns of investments in human capital. Ceteris paribus, the educational attainment of Jews exceeds that of mainline Protestants by approximately 1.2–1.3 years; at the same time, the schooling level of fundamentalist Protestants is lower than that of mainline Protestants by about 0.3–0.4 years. The fundamentalist Protestant effect is comparable in magnitude to the influence of having a parent with less than 12 years of schooling as opposed to a high school diploma, or of having to compete with an additional sibling for resources.

A detailed analysis of schooling transitions suggests that the Jewish effect is present at all stages of the educational process. For fundamentalist Protestants, a difference by gender emerges. Among men, the negative effect on schooling occurs most strongly at the stage of deciding whether or not to attend college, whereas for women, the most pronounced impact takes place later, at the time of deciding whether or not to complete a college degree.

The study uses a human capital model to interpret the observed differences in educational attainment by religion. This framework views schooling decisions as being influenced by demand and supply factors, and offers a way to ascertain which are more important. The empirical evidence on the rate of return from investments in schooling for the various groups suggests that, while demand side influences are dominant in explaining the high educational attainment of Jews, the relatively low schooling level of fundamentalist Protestants reflects supply and demand forces of similar strength.

Overall, the empirical results underscore the importance of religion and suggest that future studies on the determinants of educational attainment should include it among the background factors considered, paying special attention to divide the Protestant group into at least the two categories employed here. Replication of the present analyses with data containing larger sample sizes for the four religions that were considered in this study would be desirable. It would also be useful to extend this work to focus on other groups that exhibit distinctive behaviors, such as Mormons, agnostics, and atheists. Given the mounting evidence on the importance of religion as a background factor, future surveys will hopefully collect more detailed information on this variable. Further research with such data would not only contribute to our knowledge of the relationship between religious affiliation and schooling, but would also provide additional insights into the various ways in which the environment in which children are raised influences their educational achievement.

The analyses presented in this study focus entirely on how the religion of upbringing influences education as measured at the survey date. Other research has examined causality running in the opposite direction: from schooling decisions to religious choices. Sherkat and Wilson (1995) study two dimensions of education: relative to one's parents and relative to other members of the denomination of origin. They find that intergenerational educational mobility does not affect the choice of religious affiliation. However, departures from the average schooling level in the religion of origin have a significant impact: attaining less education than the average raises the odds of switching to a conservative Protestant denomination; achieving a higher level of schooling than the average increases the likelihood of apostasy. Exploratory work using data from the 1987–88 NSFH reveals that religious switching into and out of fundamentalist Protestant denominations is more likely among those who attain schooling levels that are very different from those that would be expected, given their observed background characteristics. The direction of the conversion flows tends to achieve congruence between the individual's educational achievement and the schooling level that is typical of the new religious group (results not shown).

An important goal for future investigations is to begin integrating these lines of research. As data sets with more detailed information on the timing of both schooling and religious switching events become available, it will be possible to obtain a more complete picture of the complex reciprocal relationships between investments in secular human capital and religious affiliation.

Appendix 6.1

Appendix 6.1 Female labor force participation: probit regressions

	Mainline Protestant	Fundamentalist Protestant	Catholic	Jewish
Years of schooling	0.073**	0.076**	0.137**	0.284**
	(2.8)	(2.3)	(4.4)	(2.5)
Years of experience	0.054**	0.104**	0.039**	0.091*
	(4.5)	(7.1)	(2.7)	(1.6)
Outside SMSA	−0.183	−0.071	0.490**	_−[a]
	(−1.3)	(−0.5)	(2.2)	
Residence				
North-central	0.281*	0.460**	−0.157	8.703
	(1.9)	(2.6)	(−0.7)	(0.1)
Northeast	0.151	0.120	−0.263	−0.859
	(0.8)	(0.5)	(−1.1)	(−0.6)
West	−0.180	0.039	−0.120	−0.682
	(−1.1)	(0.2)	(−0.4)	(−0.5)
Unmarried	0.048	−0.143	0.024	0.015
	(0.3)	(−0.6)	(0.1)	(0.01)

Married, husband's earnings				
in lowest quartile	0.206	−0.427*	0.109	−[a]
	(1.0)	(−1.8)	(0.4)	
in second quartile	−0.219	0.219	0.341#	−5.02
	(−1.2)	(0.8)	(1.5)	(−0.1)
in highest quartile	−0.735**	−0.237	−0.569**	0.336
	(−4.5)	(−0.9)	(−2.9)	(0.5)
Missing	−1.587**	−1.034**	−1.116**	−[a]
	(−4.3)	(−3.0)	(−3.8)	
Number of children	−0.216**	−0.113*	−0.248**	−0.399
	(−3.9)	(−1.8)	(−4.4)	(−1.0)
Presence of child under age 6	−0.610**	−0.645**	−0.568**	−0.649
	(−4.9)	(−4.2)	(−4.0)	(−1.1)
Constant	−0.027	−0.787#	−0.490	−3.244#
	(−0.1)	(−1.5)	(−0.9)	(−1.5)
Log-likelihood function	−311.388	−223.363	−237.090	−14.235
N	649	443	547	41

\# $p < 0.15$; * $p < 0.10$; ** $p < 0.05$.

Note
a Variable had zero variance and was omitted.

Acknowledgments

I am indebted to Barry Chiswick, Carmel Chiswick, and two anonymous referees for many helpful comments and suggestions on earlier drafts of this chapter.

Notes

1 Alwin (1984) suggests that convergence has also taken place in childrearing orientations. However, recent research that separates liberal from conservative Protestant groups and uses Lenski's (1961) measures of valuation of obedience and autonomy finds that Catholics continue to have more authoritarian values and practices, compared with nonfundamentalists (Ellison and Sherkat 1993).
2 Details on the classification of Protestants are presented in the section on Methods.
3 A supply-demand framework has also been used in rational choice theories of religion. In this literature, religious behavior and choices are modeled as a function of individuals' preferences (the "demand side") and macrolevel conditions that affect the quality and diversity of the options available (the "supply side"). The demand side is most clearly developed by Sherkat (1997); see also Ellison and Sherkat 1995; Sherkat and Wilson 1995. Supply-side influences are emphasized by Iannaccone (1991, 1992, 1994) and Finke and Stark (1992).
  It is important to note that the model of educational attainment used in this paper focuses on the demand and supply of funds for investments in schooling. In this context, "demand" and "supply" have a very different meaning, as elaborated in the text.
4 The possibility of discrimination has been discussed in the sociological literature in terms of the concept of "cultural capital" (Bourdieu 1977; DiMaggio and Mohr 1985). In this view, those privileged to have experiences with prestigious cultural resources are rewarded in the educational system; on the other hand, inferior cultural capital results in discrimination by the gatekeepers of social status. In the

5   economic model of human capital used in this study, discrimination in access to schooling or the quality of schooling results in a demand curve that is further to the left.

5   This survey was designed at the Center for Demography and Ecology at the University of Wisconsin-Madison under the direction of Larry Bumpass and James Sweet. The Institute for Survey Research at Temple University did the fieldwork.

6   Although the religion variables in this data set are considerably richer than those available in most other sources, they are not ideal. In particular, it would have been desirable to have information on the salience of religion in the family of origin and on the religious beliefs actually held by the various family members.

7   It would be inappropriate to lump all respondents together and simply include dummy variables for race/ethnicity and country of birth, because the effects of the explanatory variables may vary substantially across groups.

8   Individuals with no religion are not studied here as the NSFH does not distinguish between atheists, agnostics, and respondents who were raised without an affiliation for other reasons (e.g., being a child from an interfaith marriage). The implications for educational attainment may differ across these various groups. Mormons were not studied because of sample size limitations.

9   In his research on the classification of Protestant groups, Smith (1990) considers three main categories: fundamentalist, moderate, and liberal. He distinguishes between seven different Baptist denominations, classifying six of them as fundamentalist and one as moderate.

10 In preliminary runs, two categories of fundamentalist Protestant denominations were included separately – Baptists, on the one hand, and all the smaller exclusivist groups on the other. The sample sizes for the latter were very small, however, and it was not possible to discern significant differences between these two groups in any of the regressions. Thus, the analyses were conducted with all fundamentalist denominations included in one category.

11 Preliminary analyses suggested that cases in which the respondent did not know the parents' education are associated systematically with unusually low levels of respondent's schooling. Thus, no imputation is made for such cases and, instead, the sets of dummy variables for parents' schooling include a category for missing information. A separate dummy identifies cases where the father's education is unavailable due to the fact that, at age 16, neither the respondent's biological father nor a stepfather was present in the home.

12 See Chiswick (1998) for a detailed discussion of this issue and an analysis of the circumstances under which this interpretation of the coefficient on education is appropriate.

13 Respondents were asked about the form of compensation in their main job: by the hour, salaried (weekly, biweekly, monthly, or yearly), or on some other basis. For the first group, the definition of the wage is simple: it is the hourly amount indicated by the respondent. For the second group, the hourly wage is calculated as the amount earned over the relevant interval divided by the number of hours worked during the period. For the third group, the best wage measure available is the total annual earnings reported by the respondent divided by the total number of hours worked during the year (in the main job plus a second job, if applicable).

References

Alwin, D. F. (1984) "Trends in Parental Socialization Values: Detroit, 1958–1983." *American Journal of Sociology* 90(2):359–82.

Becker, G. S. (1967) *Human Capital and the Personal Distribution of Income.* Woytinsky Lecture No. 1, Ann Arbor: University of Michigan Press.

Becker, G. S. and Chiswick, B. R. (1966) "Education and the Distribution of Earnings." *American Economic Review* 56:358–69.

Bourdieu, P. (1977) *Reproduction in Education, Society, Culture.* Beverly Hills, CA: Sage.

Brenner, R. and Kiefer, N. (1981) "The Economics of Diaspora: Discrimination and Occupational Structure." *Economic Development and Cultural Change* 29(3):517–33.

Brinkerhoff, M. B. and MacKie, M. M. (1984) "Religious Denominations' Impact Upon Gender Attitudes: Some Methodological Implications." *Review of Religious Research* 25(4):365–78.

Brinkerhoff, M. B. and MacKie, M. M. (1988) "Religious Sources of Gender Traditionalism." Pp. 232–57 in D. Thomas (ed.) *The Religion and Family Connection.* Religious Studies Center, Salt Lake City: Brigham Young University.

Chiswick, B. R. (1983) "The Earnings and Human Capital of American Jews." *Journal of Human Resources* 8:313–36.

Chiswick, B. R. (1986) "Labor Supply and Investments in Child Quality: A Study of Jewish and Non-Jewish Women." *Review of Economics and Statistics* 68(4):700–3.

Chiswick, B. R. (1988) "Differences in Education and Earnings Across Racial and Ethnic Groups: Tastes, Discrimination, and Investments in Child Quality." *Quarterly Journal of Economics* 103(3):571–97.

Chiswick, B. R. (1993) "The Skills and Economic Status of American Jewry: Trends Over the Last Half-Century." *Journal of Labor Economics* 11(1):229–42.

Chiswick, B. R. (1998) "Interpreting the Coefficient of Schooling in the Human Capital Earnings Function." *Journal of Educational Planning and Administration* 12(2):123–30.

Chiswick, C. (1997) "Determinants of Religious Intermarriage: Are Jews Really Different?" Pp. 247–57 in S. Della Pergola and J. Even (eds) *Papers in Jewish Demography 1993, in Memory of U. O. Schmelz.* Proceedings of the Demographic Sessions held at the 11th World Congress of Jewish Studies, Jerusalem, June 1993.

Darnell, A. and Sherkat, D. E. (1997) "The Impact of Protestant Fundamentalism on Educational Attainment." *American Sociological Review* 62:306–15.

Della Pergola, S. (1980) "Patterns of American Jewish Fertility." *Demography* 17(3):261–73.

Desai, S., Chase-Lansdale, L. P., and Michael, R. (1989) "Mother or Market? Effects of Maternal Employment on the Intellectual Ability of 4-Year-Old Children." *Demography* 26(4):545–62.

DiMaggio, P. and Mohr, J. (1985) "Cultural Capital, Educational Attainment, and Marital Selection." *American Journal of Sociology* 90(6):1231–61.

Ellison, C. G. and Sherkat, D. E. (1993) "Obedience and Autonomy: Religion and Parental Values Reconsidered." *Journal for the Scientific Study of Religion* 32(4):313–29.

Ellison, C. G. and Sherkat, D. E. (1995) "Is Sociology the Core Discipline for the Scientific Study of Religion?" *Social Forces* 73:1255–66.

Featherman, D. L. (1971) "The Socioeconomic Achievement of White Religio-Ethnic Subgroups: Social and Psychological Explanations." *American Sociological Review* 36:207–22.

Finke, R. and Stark, R. (1992) *The Churching of America, 1776–1990: Winners and Losers in Our Religious Economy.* New Brunswick, NJ: Rutgers University Press.

Glenn, N. D. (1982) "Interreligious Marriage in the United States: Patterns and Recent Trends." *Journal of Marriage and the Family* 44:555–66.

Goldscheider, C. (1967) "Fertility of the Jews." *Demography* 4:196–209.

Greeley, A. M. (1976) *Ethnicity, Denomination and Inequality.* Beverly Hills, CA: Sage.

Greeley, A. M. (1981) "Catholics and the Upper Middle Class: A Comment on Roof." *Social Forces* 59(3):824–30.

Haveman, R. and Wolfe, B. (1995) "The Determinants of Children's Attainments: A Review of Methods and Findings." *Journal of Economic Literature* 33(4):1829–78.

Heaton, T. B. and Goodman, K. L. (1985) "Religion and Family Formation." *Review of Religious Research* 26(4):343–59.

Hill, M. S. and Duncan, G. J. (1987) "Parental Family Income and the Socioeconomic Attainment of Children." *Social Science Research* 16:39–73.

Iannaccone, L. R. (1991) "The Consequences of Religious Market Structure: Adam Smith and the Economics of Religion." *Rationality and Society* 3:156–77.

Iannaccone, L. R. (1992) "Sacrifice and Stigma: Reducing Free-Riding in Cults, Communes, and Other Collectives." *Journal of Political Economy* 100(2):271–91.

Iannaccone, L. R. (1994) "Why Strict Churches are Strong." *American Journal of Sociology* 99:1180–211.

Iannaccone, L. R. (1998) "An Introduction to the Economics of Religion." *Journal of Economic Literature* 36:1465–96.

Jones, E. F. and Westoff, C. F. (1979) "The End of 'Catholic' Fertility." *Demography* 16(2):209–18.

Kalmijn, M. (1991) "Shifting Boundaries: Trends in Religious and Educational Homogamy." *American Sociological Review* 56:786–800.

Lehrer, E. L. (1995) "The Effects of Religion on the Labor Supply of Married Women." *Social Science Research* 24:281–301. (Chapter 3 this volume.)

Lehrer, E. L. (1996a) "The Role of the Husband's Religion on the Economic and Demographic Behavior of Families." *Journal for the Scientific Study of Religion* 35(2):145–55.

Lehrer, E. L. (1996b) "Religion as a Determinant of Fertility." *Journal of Population Economics* 9:173–96.

Lehrer, E. L. (1998) "Religious Intermarriage in the United States: Determinants and Trends." *Social Science Research* 27:245–63.

Lehrer, E. L. (2000) "Religion as a Determinant of Entry into Cohabitation and Marriage. Pp. 227–52 in L. Waite, C. Bachrach, M. Hindin, E. Thomson, and A. Thornton (eds) *The Ties that Bind: Perspectives on Marriage and Cohabitation.* Hawthorne: Aldine de Gruyter.

Lehrer, E. L. and Chiswick, C. (1993) "Religion as a Determinant of Marital Stability." *Demography* 30(3):385–404. (Chapter 1 this volume.)

Lenski, G. (1961) *The Religious Factor.* Garden City, NJ: Doubleday.

Marcum, J. P. (1981) "Explaining Fertility Differentials Among U.S. Protestants." *Social Forces* 60(2):532–43.

McMurry, M. (1978) "Religion and Women's Sex Role Traditionalism." *Sociological Focus* 11(2):81–95.

Meng, R. and Sentance, J. (1984) "Religion and the Determination of Earnings: Further Results." *Canadian Journal of Economics* 17:481–8.

Mosher, W. D., Williams, L. B., and Johnson, D. P. (1992) "Religion and Fertility in the United States: New Patterns." *Demography* 29(2):199–214.

Newport, F. (1979) "The Religious Switcher in the United States." *American Sociological Review* 44(4): 528–52.

Roof, W. C. (1979) "Socioeconomic Differentials among White Socioreligious Groups in the United States." *Social Forces* 58(1):280–9.

Roof, W. C. (1981) "Unresolved Issues in the Study of Religion and the National Elite: Response to Greeley." *Social Forces* 59(3):831–6.

Sander, W. (1993) "Catholicism and Intermarriage in the United States." *Journal of Marriage and the Family* 55:1037–41.

Sander, W. (1995) *The Catholic Family: Marriage, Children, and Human Capital.* Boulder, CO: Westview Press.

Sherkat, D. E. (1997) "Embedding Religious Choices, Preferences and Social Constraints into Rational Choice Theories of Religious Behavior." Pp. 65–86 in L. A. Young (ed.) *Rational Choice Theory and Religion: Summary and Assessment.* London: Routledge.

Sherkat, D. E. and Darnell, A. (1999) "The Effects of Parents' Fundamentalism on Children's Educational Attainment: Examining Differences by Gender and Children's Fundamentalism." *Journal of the Scientific Study of Religion* 38(1):23–35.

Sherkat, D. E. and Wilson, J. (1995) "Preferences, Constraints, and Choices in Religious Markets: An Examination of Religious Switching and Apostasy." *Social Forces* 73(3):993–1026.

Smith, T. W. (1990) "Classifying Protestant Denominations." *Review of Religious Research* 31(3):225–45.

Steen, T. P. and Dubbink, K. S. (1994) "The Impact of Religion on the Earnings and Human Capital of Women." Presented at the meetings of the Midwest Economics Association, March 24–26, Chicago, IL.

Stevens, G. and Cho, J. H. (1985) "Socioeconomic Indexes and the New 1980 Census Occupational Classification Scheme." *Social Science Research* 14:142–68.

Thornton, A. (1985a) "Changing Attitudes Toward Separation and Divorce: Causes and Consequences." *American Journal of Sociology* 90(4):856–72.

Thornton, A. (1985b) "Reciprocal Influences of Family and Religion in a Changing World." *Journal of Marriage and the Family* May:381–94.

Tomes, N. (1983) "Religion and the Rate of Return on Human Capital: Evidence from Canada." *Canadian Journal of Economics* 16(1):122–38.

Tomes, N. (1985) "Religion and the Earnings Function." *AEA Papers and Proceedings* May:245–50.

Waters, M., Heath, W. C., and Watson, J. (1995) "A Positive Model of the Determination of Religious Affiliation." *Social Science Quarterly* 76(1):105–23.

7 Religion and high school graduation

A comparative analysis of patterns for white and black young women*

The far-reaching consequences of dropping out of high school are widely known: work careers characterized by low wages, high unemployment, and few opportunities for further training; unstable marital unions; and overall bleak prospects for economic well-being. Obstacles to the completion of secondary schooling include a range of often interrelated factors, including academic difficulties, the emotional turbulence that sometimes accompanies adolescence, substance use, pregnancy, violence in the neighborhood, poor schools, and dysfunctional homes. The central questions addressed in the present study are: are there differences by religion in the likelihood of successfully completing the transition to high school graduation? If so, how large are they? Do the patterns vary by race?

Previous studies have shown that two dimensions of religion – affiliation and participation – are systematically associated with years of schooling completed (see recent reviews of this literature in Lehrer 2004a, 2008). The present analysis employs data from a large-scale national survey addressed to women, the 1995 National Survey of Family Growth (NSFG), to study whether the differentials by affiliation and participation that have been documented in earlier research can be discerned already at the early stage of graduation from high school. This survey contains information on the religious affiliation in which the respondents were raised and their frequency of attendance to religious services at age 14, thus making it possible to examine how both of these dimensions of childhood religion are related to the probability of going on to successful completion of secondary schooling.

An attractive feature of the 1995 NSFG is that the number of respondents over age 20 is large enough to permit separate analyses of the religion–high school graduation relationship not only for non-Hispanic whites but also for black youth.[1] Because of sample size limitations, most previous studies in this area have either lumped all racial/ethnic groups together or have focused exclusively on non-Hispanic whites. Data from the 1995 NSFG make it possible to test the hypothesis, suggested by recent ethnographic research, that the beneficial effects of religious involvement for adolescents may be especially

* This chapter is reprinted from *Review of Economics of the Household* 4(3):277–293, 2006.

salient for disadvantaged minority youth (Williams and Warner 2001; Warner 2002). In addition, these data provide an opportunity to ascertain whether the patterns of education differentials by religious affiliation documented in earlier studies for non-Hispanic whites extend to black youth.

Analytical framework

A human capital model that analyzes the mechanisms through which religion may affect investments in education has been developed elsewhere (Chiswick 1988; Lehrer 1999). In this framework, religious affiliation is viewed as reflecting distinctive features of the home environment that can affect the supply and/or demand for funds for investments in schooling. On the demand side, religious affiliation can influence the returns from investments in education: among groups characterized by larger benefits from schooling, a higher level of attainment is expected, ceteris paribus. On the supply side, religious affiliation can affect the parents' willingness and ability to supply funds for such investments: a higher level of education is expected for religious groups in which the parents have a greater willingness and ability to supply funds for investments in schooling, ceteris paribus.

This model has been used to explain systematic patterns of differences across religious groups in years of schooling completed among non-Hispanic whites (Lehrer 2004a, 2008). Assuming that these patterns are already visible early in the educational process and that they also hold in the black population, I hypothesize that *the probability of graduation from high school is relatively low for conservative Protestants and Mormons; it is relatively high for Jews; and mainline Protestants and Catholics are at the center of the distribution.*

With regard to religious participation – another key dimension of religion – previous research has identified three main channels of causality linking it to beneficial outcomes: (a) a social capital effect (religion helps integrate youth into helpful social networks); (b) a regulative effect (religions generally encourage healthy, constructive behaviors); and (c) the direct psychological benefits that often stem from involvement in religious activities (Waite and Lehrer 2003). Youth who grow up with some religious involvement may thus be better able to benefit from investments in schooling. Within the human capital framework, their demand curve for funds for investments in education is farther to the right (Lehrer 2004b). Based on this theory and previous evidence in the literature confirming a positive effect of religiosity on years of schooling completed and other educational outcomes, I hypothesize that (a) *youth who grow up with no religious affiliation (and hence have zero involvement in religious activity, at least in the institutional context) are less likely to graduate from high school than their counterparts who grow up with some affiliation*; and (b) *among youth raised with some affiliation, a greater level of participation in religious activity during the adolescence years is associated with a higher probability of high school graduation.*

In an ethnographic study that is part of the broader "Youth and Religion Project," Williams and Warner (2001) suggest that the influence of religious participation is likely to be most pronounced for disadvantaged minority youth, who are at high risk of unfavorable outcomes (including non-completion of high school) and have limited access to helpful non-religious institutions and resources. As the authors note (2001, p. 3), for such youth:

> church is there to help them dodge both the real and figurative bullets of life in a major urban center. Adult leaders of the groups we observed could often name off very quickly the young people who had brothers in gangs, or who had family members with drug or alcohol problems. Part of the way religious involvement seems to help remove kids from risk is by the inculcation of values and ideals that urge them away from sub-stance abuse, crime, and so forth. But, more important in our view is the creation of an "alternative community" for youth who are sur-rounded by problematic or self-destructive behaviors in other parts of their lives [.]

These observations suggest that both the social capital and regulative effects associated with involvement in religious activities may be larger in the case of disadvantaged minorities. I thus hypothesize that *the beneficial influence of religious participation on the odds of high school graduation is more pronounced for black youth than for their white counterparts.*

Methods

The 1995 National Survey of Family Growth was conducted by the Research Triangle Institute under contract from the National Center for Health Statistics (see Kelly et al. 1997 for a description of the methodology). The questionnaires were addressed to a nationally representative sample of 10,847 civilian, non-institutionalized women ages 15–44 years of age of all marital statuses living in the United States. The interviews included questions on socioeconomic and family background variables, as well as information on religion, educational attainment, marriage, employment, and fertility.

To ensure that the sample used in the analysis does not include young women still working towards their high school degrees, respondents ages 20 or under were excluded. The sample was further limited to white and black non-Hispanic women who were raised in one of the following faiths: Roman Catholic, mainline Protestant (Presbyterian, Episcopalian, Method-ist, Lutheran),[2] conservative Protestant (Baptists and smaller denomina-tions associated with Pentecostal and fundamentalist movements, including Assembly of God, Church of Christ, and Holiness),[3] Mormon, and no religion. Jews were excluded from the sample as preliminary analyses revealed that among the 110 respondents raised in the Jewish faith there was virtually no variance in the outcome of interest: only three subjects had failed to graduate from high school. After excluding cases with missing information on key variables, the resulting sample size was 7,245.

The religious participation variable is based on information on the respondents' frequency of attendance to religious services at age 14. This is a measure, albeit an imperfect one, of the young women's involvement with religion at that age. Unfortunately, the survey does not contain information on other dimensions of religiosity at that time, nor does it contain any questions on the parents' religiosity. Religious participation is operationalized as a dichotomous variable. Individuals who attended religious services 1–3 times per month or more frequently are classified in the high religious participation category; others are placed in the low participation group.

Table 7.1 presents descriptive statistics for the religion variables by race. As expected, Panel A shows that mainline Protestants, conservative Protestants, and Catholics are the main groups among non-Hispanic whites; conservative Protestants are the dominant group in the black population. Panel B reveals a relatively high level of religious participation in black households, consistent with evidence from other studies (Taylor et al. 1996; Pattillo-McCoy 1998).

Definitions and means for the dependent and control variables are shown in Table 7.2. The dependent variable is dichotomous, equal to 1 for respondents who completed their high school education through regular schooling and earned a high school diploma, 0 otherwise.[4] The rate of completion is 0.86 for non-Hispanic white youth, compared to only 0.75 for their black counterparts. The controls include the parents' average years of schooling,[5] dummy variables for family structure at age 14, the size of the family of origin, whether the mother was 18 years of age or younger at the time of her first birth, maternal employment, and indicators of place of birth and birth cohort. These factors are included in the regressions because they are

Table 7.1 Descriptive statistics: religion variables

	White	*Black*
Panel A: Means of religious affiliation variables		
Mainline Protestant	0.30	0.11
Conservative Protestant	0.24	0.75
Mormon	0.03	–
Catholic	0.35	0.10
No religion	0.07	0.04
Panel B: Fraction in high religious participation category		
Mainline Protestant	0.74	0.86
Conservative Protestant	0.77	0.87
Mormon	0.80	–
Catholic	0.82	0.86
N	5,165	2,080

Table 7.2 Descriptive statistics: means of dependent variable and control variables

		White	Black
Dependent variable			
High school completion	= 1 if respondent (R) earned a high school diploma	0.86	0.75
Control variables			
Parental education	= 1 if the average years of schooling completed by R's father (or father figure) and mother (or mother figure) is in category indicated		
Less than 12 years (benchmark)		(0.35)	(0.55)
12 years		0.26	0.23
13–15 years		0.27	0.16
16 years or more		0.12	0.06
Family nonintact	= 1 if R's family was not intact at age 14 for the reason indicated		
Death of parent		0.05	0.09
Separation or divorce		0.21	0.22
Parents never married		0.04	0.26
Intact family (benchmark)		(0.70)	(0.43)
Family size	Number of siblings (including R)	3.80	5.24
Mother worked full-time	= 1 if R's mother worked full time during most of R's childhood	0.36	0.61
Mother <18 at first birth	= 1 if R's mother had first birth before age 18	0.10	0.33
Birth control instruction	= 1 if R said she had ever (by age 19) had any formal instruction regarding methods of birth control at school, church, community center, or some other place	0.59	0.66
Abstinence instruction	= 1 if R said she had ever (by age 19) had any formal instruction at school, church, community center, or some other place, about abstinence or how to say no to sex	0.52	0.59
Place of birth	= 1 if R's place of birth was in the region/ country indicated		
South (benchmark)		(0.26)	(0.54)
Northeast		0.22	0.15
Midwest		0.33	0.20
West		0.16	0.06
Foreign		0.03	0.05
Birth cohort	= 1 if R was born during the time period indicated		
1950s (benchmark)		(0.45)	(0.39)
1960s		0.40	0.45
1970s		0.15	0.16

expected to have an impact on the likelihood of high school completion.[6] The analyses also include variables for whether the respondent had ever been exposed to formal birth control instruction or abstinence instruction during the teenage years; such variables may influence the odds of completing high school indirectly through their impact on the probability of an unwanted nonmarital teen pregnancy. The models estimated are reduced form education equations – the estimates capture the direct effect of each variable on the likelihood of graduating from high school plus any indirect impact through teen fertility behavior.

Results

The effects of religious affiliation

Tables 7.3a and 7.3b present the results of logit regressions that estimate the effects of religious affiliation on high school graduation for white and black young women, respectively. The relative magnitudes of the effects can be assessed from the odds ratios reported therein. The absolute magnitudes of the influences may be ascertained from the predicted probabilities shown in Table 7.4. To facilitate comparisons with previous studies, mainline Protestants are used as the reference category in the white sample. In the black sample, the conservative Protestant category is by far the largest group and is used as benchmark.

Focusing first on the findings for white youth in Table 7.3a, consistent with the hypotheses, the zero-order regression reveals that conservative Protestants, Mormons, and the unaffiliated are significantly less likely to earn a high school diploma than mainline Protestants; no significant difference can be discerned between mainline Protestants and Catholics. All of the religion effects decrease in size when controls for family background variables (excluding parental education) are added in the next column, and decrease even further when parental education is added in the last column. Two effects remain significant in this last specification: ceteris paribus, relative to mainline Protestants, conservative Protestants and the unaffiliated are less likely to complete high school.[7] Additional pairwise comparisons were performed, changing the religious category used as benchmark. These ancillary analyses, based on the model in column 3, revealed that the following differences are significant at least at the 0.10 level: the likelihood of graduation from high school is lower for the unaffiliated than for Catholics and Mormons; it is also lower for conservative Protestants than for Catholics and Mormons.

Table 7.4 shows that the probability of high school graduation is 0.93 for a typical mainline Protestant respondent (with average characteristics for other variables); the estimates for Mormons (0.91) and Catholics (0.93) are in the same range. In contrast, the probabilities are only 0.86 and 0.84, respectively, for conservative Protestants and the unaffiliated, respectively.

The "true" effect of religious affiliation on the probability of high school

Table 7.3a Religious affiliation and high school graduation: white women. Logit regressions: coefficient (t-value) [odds ratio]

	(1) Zero-order effects	(2) Including background variables (except parental education)	(3) Including all background variables
Religion variables			
Mainline Protestant (benchmark)	—	—	—
Conservative Protestant	-1.323 (-11.9)** [0.266]	-1.000 (-8.2)** [0.368]	-0.771 (-6.9)** [0.463]
Mormon	-0.621 (-2.7)** [0.537]	-0.403 (-1.6)* [0.668]	-0.292 (-1.1) [0.746]
Catholic	-0.098 (-0.8) [0.907]	0.003 (0.02) [1.003]	0.011 (0.1) [1.011]
No religion	-1.297 (-8.6)** [0.273]	-1.033 (-6.4)** [0.356]	-0.938 (-5.6)** [0.391]
Control variables			
Family nonintact			
Death of parent		-0.535 (-3.1)** [0.585]	-0.471 (-2.7)** [0.624]
Separation or divorce		-1.008 (-10.1)** [0.365]	-1.016 (-9.9)** [0.362]
Parents never married		-1.275 (-7.5)** [0.279]	-1.206 (-6.9)** [0.299]
Family size		-0.187 (-9.6)** [0.830]	-0.158 (-7.9)** [0.854]
Mother worked full-time		-0.126 (-1.4) [0.881]	-0.122 (-1.3) [0.885]
Mother <18 at first birth		-0.695 (-6.2)** [0.499]	-0.389 (-3.3)** [0.678]
Birth cohort			
1960s		-0.136 (-1.4) [0.872]	-0.251 (-2.5)** [0.778]
1970s		-0.115 (-0.8) [0.891]	-0.384 (-2.6)** [0.681]
Place of birth			
Northeast		0.279 (2.0)** [1.322]	0.294 (2.0)** [1.342]
Midwest		0.247 (2.1)** [1.280]	0.249 (2.1)** [1.282]
West		0.290 (2.8)** [1.336]	0.133 (0.9) [1.142]
Foreign		0.036 (0.1) [1.037]	0.007 (0.3) [1.007]
Birth control instruction		0.290 (2.8)** [1.336]	0.261 (2.5)** [1.298]
Abstinence instruction		0.393 (3.8)** [1.482]	0.399 (3.8)** [1.490]
Parental education			
12 years			0.866 (7.8)** [2.377]
13–15 years			1.286 (9.9)** [3.617]
16 years or more			1.727 (7.7)** [5.637]
Constant	2.374 (26.3)**	3.064 (18.8)**	2.318 (13.4)**
Likelihood ratio chi square (df)	238.4 (4)**	604.6 (18)**	770.6 (21)**

N = 5,165
* p < 0.10; ** p < 0.05.

Table 7.3b Religious affiliation and high school graduation: black women. Logit regressions: coefficient (t-value) [odds ratio]

	(1) Zero-order effects	(2) Including background variables (except parental education)	(3) Including all background variables
Religion variables			
Mainline Protestant	0.769 (3.5)** [2.158]	0.698 (3.4)** [2.010]	0.631 (3.0)** [1.880]
Conservative Protestant (benchmark)	—	—	—
Catholic	0.175 (1.0) [1.191]	0.026 (0.1) [1.026]	-0.094 (-0.5) [0.910]
No religion	0.102 (0.4) [1.107]	0.169 (0.6) [1.184]	0.182 (0.7) [1.200]
Control variables			
Family nonintact			
Death of parent		-0.632 (-3.6)** [0.531]	-0.570 (-3.2)** [0.566]
Separation or divorce		-0.257 (-1.8)* [0.774]	-0.290 (-2.0)** [0.748]
Parents never married		-0.800 (-6.3)** [0.449]	-0.774 (-6.0)** [0.461]
Family size		-0.087 (-5.1)** [0.917]	-0.064 (-3.7)** [0.938]
Mother worked full-time		0.022 (0.2) [1.022]	-0.058 (-0.5) [0.944]
Mother <18 at first birth		-0.317 (-2.8)** [0.728]	-0.253 (-2.2)** [0.776]
Birth cohort			
1960s		0.075 (0.6) [1.078]	-0.040 (-0.3) [0.961]
1970s		-0.210 (-1.3) [0.811]	-0.411 (-2.4)** [0.663]
Place of birth			
Northeast		-0.373 (-2.4)** [0.689]	-0.444 (-2.8)** [0.642]
Midwest		-0.082 (-0.6) [0.921]	-0.148 (-1.0) [0.863]
West		0.154 (0.6) [1.167]	-0.133 (-0.5) [0.875]
Foreign		0.212 (0.3) [1.236]	0.143 (0.5) [1.154]
Birth control instruction		0.370 (2.7)** [1.448]	0.370 (2.7)** [1.448]
Abstinence instruction		0.164 (1.2) [1.179]	0.126 (0.9) [1.134]
Parental education			
12 years			0.426 (3.1)** [1.531]
13–15 years			1.305 (6.5)** [3.689]
16 years or more			1.281 (3.8)** [3.599]
Constant	1.012 (17.7)**	1.686 (8.6)**	1.439 (7.2)**
Likelihood ratio chi square (df)	18.1 (3)**	135.0 (17)**	196.9 (20)**

N = 2,080
* p < 0.10; ** p < 0.05.

Table 7.4 Predicted probabilities of high school graduation by religious affiliation[a]

	White	Black
Mainline Protestant	**0.93**	0.90
Conservative Protestant	0.86	**0.82**
Mormon	(0.91)	–
Catholic	(0.93)	(0.81)
No religion	0.84	(0.84)

Note

a These probabilities are based on the column 3 models of Table 7.3a and 7.3b. The number of siblings is set at the mean and the categorical variables are set at the modal group (for the specific racial/ethnic group). Figures corresponding to the category that was used as benchmark in each case are noted in bold; figures corresponding to coefficients that do not differ significantly from the benchmark at the 0.10 level are shown in parentheses.

The following differences are also significant: (a) in the white sample, the likelihood of completing high school is lower for the unaffiliated than for Catholics and Mormons; it is also lower for conservative Protestants than for Catholics and Mormons. (b) In the black sample, the likelihood of completing high school is higher for mainline Protestants than for Catholics.

graduation, net of other factors, can be thought of as being bracketed by the estimates in columns 2 and 3 of Table 7.3a. Parental education is the best proxy for socioeconomic status in these data, and the positive coefficient on this variable in part captures an income effect that should be controlled for. At the same time, however, the education differentials by religion in the respondents' generation are mirrored by corresponding differences in their parents' generation, which are due in part to the influence of religion.

Turning to the results for the black sample shown in Table 7.3b, youth raised as mainline Protestant are significantly more likely to complete their high school education than those raised as conservative Protestant, as expected; the magnitude of the effect diminishes somewhat when controls are added. Based on the model of column 3, additional pairwise comparisons among the religious affiliation categories were performed. They reveal one other significant effect: mainline Protestants are also significantly more likely to complete high school than Catholics (p < 0.10). This result – a departure from the non-Hispanic white pattern – had not been anticipated. Table 7.4 shows that for mainline Protestants the probability of high school completion is 0.90, compared to 0.81–0.84 for Catholics, conservative Protestants, and the unaffiliated.

These findings suggest that while the high school graduation outcome of Catholics is similar to that of mainline Protestants in the white sample, consistent with other results for non-Hispanic whites (Lehrer 2004a), it resembles that of conservative Protestants and the unaffiliated in the black population. Table 7.5, which reports tests of significance based on analyses of the pooled black and white samples shows that this pattern is indeed a statistically significant difference between the two racial groups. As Panel A shows, the outcomes of Catholics are less favorable in the black sample than in the

Table 7.5 Comparisons between white and black women in the religious affiliation–high school graduation relationship: logit regressions

	Coefficient (t-value)
Panel A: Interactions between race and affiliation	
Reference category: mainline Protestant	
Black * Conservative Protestant	0.139 (0.6)
Black * Catholic	−0.736 (−2.5)**
Black * No religion	0.490 (1.3)
Reference category: conservative Protestant	
Black * Mainline Protestant	−0.139 (−0.6)
Black * Catholic	−0.876 (−3.8)**
Black * No religion	0.350 (1.1)
Reference category: no religion	
Black * Mainline Protestant	−0.490 (−1.3)
Black * Conservative Protestant	−0.350 (−1.1)
Black * Catholic	−1.226 (−3.4)**
Panel B: Other variables in model with mainline Protestant as reference category	
Religious affiliation	
Conservative Protestant	−0.771 (−6.9)**
Mormon	−0.292 (−1.1)
Catholic	0.011 (0.1)
No religion	−0.938 (−5.6)**
Family nonintact	
Death of parent	−0.471 (−2.7)**
Separation or divorce	−1.016 (−9.9)**
Parents never married	−1.206 (−6.9)**
Family size	−0.158 (−7.9)**
Mother worked full-time	−0.122 (−1.3)
Mother <18 at first birth	−0.389 (−3.3)**
Birth cohort	
1960s	−0.251 (−2.5)**
1970s	−0.384 (−2.6)**
Place of birth	
Northeast	0.294 (2.0)**
Midwest	0.249 (2.1)**
West	0.133 (0.9)
Foreign	0.007 (0.3)
Birth control instruction	0.261 (2.5)**
Abstinence instruction	0.399 (3.8)**
Parental education	
12 years	0.866 (7.8)**
13–15 years	1.286 (9.9)**
16 years or more	1.727 (7.7)**
Black	−0.248 (−0.8)
Family nonintact	
Death of parent * Black	−0.099 (−0.4)
Separation or divorce * Black	0.727 (4.0)**
Parents never married * Black	0.432 (2.0)**

(*Continued Overleaf*)

Table 7.5 Continued

	Coefficient (t-value)
Family Size * Black	0.094 (3.5)**
Mother worked full-time * Black	0.064 (0.4)
Mother <18 at first birth * Black	0.136 (0.8)
Birth cohort	
1960s * Black	0.211 (1.4)
1970s * Black	−0.027 (−0.1)
Place of birth	
Northeast * Black	−0.738 (−3.5)**
Midwest * Black	−0.396 (−2.1)**
West * Black	−0.266 (−0.9)
Foreign * Black	0.137 (0.4)
Birth control instruction * Black	0.109 (0.6)
Abstinence instruction * Black	−0.273 (−1.6)*
Parental education	
12 years * Black	−0.440 (−2.5)**
13–15 years * Black	0.020 (0.1)
16 years or more * Black	−0.447 (−1.1)
Constant	1.548 (10.2)**
Likelihood Ratio chi square (df)	1078.05 (42)**

* $p < 0.10$; ** $p < 0.05$.
N = 7,245 (pooled sample of white and black women).

white sample relative to mainline Protestants, conservative Protestants, and the unaffiliated.

The estimates for the control variables in Tables 7.3a and 7.3b are generally consistent with expectations. For both racial groups, a nonintact family, a larger number of siblings, and having a mother who entered parenthood early influence the odds of high school graduation negatively; full-time maternal employment has no significant effect; parental education has a very large positive impact. Analyses of the pooled sample (Table 7.5) reveal that the adverse negative effects of a broken-home background and large sibsize, and also the favorable effect associated with higher parental education are significantly weaker for black youth than for their white counterparts.

Having been exposed to formal birth control instruction increases the odds of high school graduation for white and black youth and the size of the effect is similar for both groups. Exposure to abstinence instruction, however, is associated with an increased probability of high school graduation for white women only, consistent with research that suggests that the effectiveness of abstinence-only programs may be limited (Kirby 2001). This racial difference attains significance at the 10 percent level. The significant effects associated with programs that provide formal birth control instruction in both samples suggest that such programs help teenagers avoid pregnancies, which in turn makes it more likely that they will graduate from high school. More generally, these results highlight the role of fertility behavior in young women's completion of secondary schooling.

The estimates for the control variables help assess the relative importance of the religion variables. For example, Table 7.3a shows that for white youth, being raised with no religion has an effect on the odds of high school graduation similar in size to that of having parents who dissolved their marriage; for black youth, Table 7.3b indicates that the educational disadvantage of conservative Protestants relative to mainline Protestants is comparable to that associated with the death of a parent.

The effects of religious participation

In order to study the effects of attendance at religious services, each of the largest religious groups was subdivided into high- and low-participation categories. The column 3 models of Tables 7.3a and 7.3b were then reestimated with this more refined specification. Subdivision was feasible for conservative Protestants in the black sample and for both groups of Protestants and Catholics in the white sample. Based on these models, the estimated probabilities of high school graduation for each affiliation/religious participation category were computed. The results, along with t-tests for the comparisons of the underlying coefficients of interest, are reported in Table 7.6.

Table 7.6 Predicted probabilities of high school completion by religious affiliation and by high vs. low religious participation[a]

	White	t-value	Black	t-value
Mainline Protestant – low participation	0.88	3.9**	–	–
– high participation	0.94		–	–
Conservative Protestant – low participation	0.77	4.1**	0.76	2.5**
– high participation	0.87		0.83	
Catholic – low participation	0.86	4.7**	–	–
– high participation	0.94		–	–

* p < 0.10; ** p < 0.05.

Note

a These probabilities are based on models that include all the control variables shown in Tables 7.3a and 7.3b, column 3. The religion variables included are as follows: (a) for whites, the reference category is the group of high participation mainline Protestants; the model includes dummy variables for low participation mainline Protestants; high and low participation conservative Protestants, high and low participation Catholics, and controls for Mormon religion and no religion. The t-value of 3.9 reported above corresponds to the low-versus high-participation comparison within mainline Protestants. Additional pairwise comparisons of coefficients of interest were also performed and are reported above. (b) In the model for black women, high-participation conservative Protestants constitute the benchmark category. The model includes a variable for low-participation conservative Protestants, as well as controls for Catholic, mainline Protestant, and no affiliation.

The estimates for white youth show that for the three affiliations considered, members of the high-participation group are significantly more likely to complete high school than their counterparts in the low-participation group, consistent with the hypothesis that religious involvement has a beneficial effect on high school graduation. The gap between the high- and low-participation groups is 10 percentage points for conservative Protestants, 8 percentage points for Catholics, and 6 percentage points for mainline Protestants. It is noteworthy that a favorable effect of religious participation is observed for conservative Protestants. The relatively low educational outcomes of conservative Protestants have been interpreted in the literature as reflecting theological aspects of the faith that exert both supply- and demand-side influences (Darnell and Sherkat 1997; Lehrer 1999; Sherkat and Darnell 1999). Higher levels of involvement do not accentuate this pattern – to the contrary, the beneficial effects of such involvement are clearly dominant.

Because of limitations of sample size, patterns of high school graduation by high versus low religious participation can only be studied in the black sample for conservative Protestants, and a similar result is found here: a gap of 7 percentage points. As noted above, the corresponding gap in the white sample is 10 percentage points. Pooled analyses of the white and black samples reveal that the difference (which is in a direction opposite to that hypothesized) is not statistically significant (results not reported). Clearly there is no support for the hypothesis that the effect of religious participation is particularly large among black youth. Related to this, the results of the earlier religious affiliation analyses showed that the unaffiliated have a significantly lower graduation rate than mainline Protestants in the white but not in the black sample, although this difference between the racial groups does not attain statistical significance at conventional levels in the pooled analyses (t = 1.3, Table 7.5). Research in the area of sexual behavior has uncovered a parallel puzzle: although a high level of religiosity is a salient feature of most black households – with black youth at high risk of problem behaviors and little access to non-religious resources – religious involvement appears to have only a limited impact in promoting healthy behaviors such as delayed sexual debut and safer sex (Regnerus 2005). Perhaps the same factors reviewed by Regnerus – including more tolerant attitudes toward premarital sex and pregnancy, and congregations that are overextended – underlie in part the present results.

Unmeasured factors may bias the estimates of the effects of religious participation (and to a lesser degree, of religious affiliation) on high school graduation, and the results must thus be interpreted with caution. If church attendance is correlated with unobserved factors that are associated with positive educational outcomes, the present estimates would overstate the positive causal effect of religious participation on educational attainment. This would be the case, for example, if the more observant parents who encourage their children to attend religious services are also supportive of activities that are conducive to success in the secular arena. In interpreting his finding that churchgoing is positively associated with school attendance among black youth, Freeman (1986) has emphasized this type of bias: he cautions that the true causal impact of religious participation on educational outcomes may in fact be smaller than suggested by his estimates.

It is important to note, however, that the estimates may be affected by omitted variables biases that operate in the opposite direction (Waite and Lehrer 2003; Lehrer 2004b). There is some evidence that religious participation may be especially valuable for individuals who are more vulnerable for various reasons, including health problems or adverse economic circumstances (Hummer et al. 2002). To the extent that such individuals are aware of this and respond by embracing religiosity as a coping mechanism, the more religious homes would disproportionately have unobserved characteristics that affect educational outcomes adversely. If so, the estimated models would lead to an understatement of the true impact of religious participation on educational attainment. A priori, it is unclear which biases are dominant.

Conclusions

Using data from the 1995 National Survey of Family Growth, this study has quantified the association between religion and the likelihood of successfully completing the transition to a high school degree for non-Hispanic white and black young women in the United States. With regard to religious affiliation, among whites, youth who grow up with no religion and conservative Protestants are less likely than mainline Protestants to complete high school, consistent with the hypotheses. Although there is some evidence of a lower likelihood of completing high school for Mormons in the zero-order regressions, the Mormon coefficient becomes insignificant once background factors are held constant. Simple descriptive statistics for these data lend support to the hypothesis of elevated high school graduation rates among Jews.

As is the case for white youth, black youth raised in conservative Protestant denominations have a lower probability of graduating from high school than their counterparts raised as mainline Protestants, and the size of the effect is similar. However, statistical tests indicate that the patterns for Catholics are significantly different for the two racial groups. While the likelihood of high school completion for Catholics is the same as that for mainline Protestants in the white sample, it is significantly lower in the black sample. Earlier studies based on non-Hispanic whites have documented a convergence of Catholics to the mainline Protestant pattern in various dimensions of economic and demographic behavior, including fertility (Jones and Westoff 1979; Goldscheider and Mosher 1991), female labor supply (Lehrer 1995), and schooling (Lehrer 1999). The present findings suggest that this convergence has not extended to the black population, at least not in the area of early educational outcomes. Catholics represent only 10 percent of the black sample, and little is known about this small group. If the patterns found here are confirmed with other data, a fruitful avenue for further investigation would be to explore the extent to which they may be explained by black–white differences in the religion–nonmarital teen fertility connection. Although the role of fertility was not directly studied in this chapter, the significant effects associated with the birth control instruction variable in both samples suggest that mechanisms operating through behaviors related to teen pregnancies, abortions, and births are worth exploring.

Turning to the second dimension of religion considered in this paper, religious participation during childhood was hypothesized to have a positive impact on the probability of graduating from high school for a demand-side reason – the beneficial effects of religious involvement on children's ability to be productively engaged in schooling endeavors – and the effects were expected to be most pronounced for the minority group. The results show that for all the groups considered, frequent attendance at religious services at age 14 is indeed positively associated with the probability of completing high school, after controlling for a wide range of family background factors. The magnitudes of the influences are not trivial. Among mainline Protestants, conservative Protestants, and Catholics in the white sample, being in the high- rather than the low-religious participation group is associated with a gap of 6–10 percentage points in such probability. Among conservative Protestants in the black sample, the corresponding gap is 7 percentage points. Clearly the findings in this study do not support the hypothesis that the beneficial impact of involvement in religious activity is larger for black youth than for their white counterparts.

The 1995 NSFG contains a rich array of family background variables that were included in the analysis as controls; however, the results of this study must be interpreted with caution. To the extent that the more observant homes have unobserved characteristics that are positively correlated with favorable educational outcomes, the present estimates would overstate the beneficial influence of attendance to religious services; the opposite would hold if the correlations are predominantly negative. Our knowledge of the factors that underlie religious involvement is quite limited at present, and it is thus unclear whether the estimates in this and previous studies in the literature overstate or understate the positive causal impact of religious involvement. Progress in measuring this impact will involve analyses of rich data sets with instruments that make it possible to model religious participation as an endogenous variable; efforts in this direction have begun (Gruber 2005).

The present study specified religious participation as dichotomous: high vs. low frequency of attendance at religious services. Future research with larger sample sizes might refine this specification, as the effects of participation may be non-linear: higher levels of involvement in religious activities during childhood may have beneficial effects, but only up to a point. Beyond a certain level, participation in religious activities may crowd out investments in secular human capital. Furthermore, there may be important differences between those who never attended religious services during adolescence and those who did so infrequently. Our understanding of the religion–education linkage will increase as future research begins to address these various questions.

Acknowledgments

I am indebted to Shoshana Grossbard, Jennifer Glass, Donka Mirtcheva, and two anonymous referees for helpful comments and suggestions on earlier drafts. I also benefited from discussion with participants at the session on "Religious Commitment and Economic Development" at the annual meetings of the Association for the Study of Religion, Economics, and Culture, November 4–6, 2005, Rochester, New York, and at the session on "Religion, Religiosity and Family Behavior" at the annual meetings of the Population Association of America, March 30–April 1, 2006, Los Angeles.

Notes

1 Separate analyses by race/ethnicity are not feasible with the most recent round of the NSFG, conducted in 2002–3, due to sample size limitations – information on religious participation during the adolescent years was collected only for respondents who were under age 25 at the time of the interview.

2 One of the religious codes in the 1995 NSFG is "Protestant with no specific denominational affiliation." As Steensland et al. (2000) note, such individuals constitute a heterogeneous group that includes Protestants with no denomination along with nondenominational Protestants. Based on analysis of patterns of religious participation by race, respondents in this category were included with mainline Protestants in the white sample, and with conservative Protestants in the black sample.

3 The 1995 NSFG includes all Baptists in one category. In his research on the classification of Protestants into fundamentalist, moderate, and liberal, Smith (1987) distinguishes between seven different Baptist denominations, classifying six of them as fundamentalist and one as moderate. This limitation of the data implies that the respondents classified in the present study as conservative Protestants include some "moderate" religious groups.

4 See Heckman and LaFontaine (2006) for recent evidence on the low returns associated with achieving high school certification via the General Educational Development credential instead of regular schooling.

5 If the respondent was raised by some other "mother figure," such as a stepmother or grandmother, the information for this individual was used; the same was done in the case of the father. If educational attainment was missing for the father or mother, the value for the other parent was used.

6 It would have been desirable to control also for the rural–urban nature of the area where the respondent grew up, but unfortunately this information is not available.

7 In additional analyses, the conservative Protestant group was divided into two categories – Baptists and all other conservative Protestant denominations. No significant differences were found between these two groups. The same was true in the black sample. Recent research highlights the importance of considering more refined distinctions within the conservative Protestant group (Beyerlein 2004); unfortunately this was not possible given the information available in the 1995 NSFG.

References

Beyerlein, K. (2004) "Specifying the Impact of Conservative Protestantism on Educational Attainment." *Journal for the Scientific Study of Religion* 43(4):505–18.

Chiswick, B. (1988) "Differences in Education and Earnings across Racial and Ethnic Groups: Tastes, Discrimination, and Investments in Child Quality." *Quarterly Journal of Economics* 103(3):571–97.

Darnell, A. and Sherkat, D. E. (1997) "The Impact of Protestant Fundamentalism on Educational Attainment." *American Sociological Review* 62(April):306–15.

Freeman, R. B. (1986) "Who Escapes? The Relation of Churchgoing and Other Background Factors to the Socioeconomic Performance of Black Male Youths from Inner-City Tracts." Pp. 353–76 in R. B. Freeman and H. J. Holzer (eds) *The Black Youth Employment Crisis*. Chicago and London: University of Chicago Press.

Goldscheider, C. and Mosher, W. D. (1991) "Patterns of Contraceptive Use in the United States: The Importance of Religious Factors." *Studies in Family Planning* 22(2):102–15.

Gruber, J. (2005) "Religious Market Structure, Religious Participation, and Outcomes: Is Religion Good for You?" *Advances in Economic Analysis and Policy* 5(1):article 5. URL: http://www.bepress.com/bejeap/advances/vol5/iss1/art5

Heckman, J. J. and LaFontaine, P. A. (2006) "Bias Corrected Estimates of GED Returns." National Bureau of Economic Research, Working Paper 12018.

Hummer, R. A., Padilla, Y.C., Echevarria, S., and Kim, E. (2002) "Does Parental Religious Involvement Affect the Birth Outcomes and Health Status of Young Children?" Presented at the annual meetings of the Population Association of America, Atlanta, May 9–11.

Jones, E. F. and Westoff, C. F. (1979) "The End of 'Catholic' Fertility." *Demography* 16(2):209–18.

Kelly, J. E., Mosher, W. D., Duffer, A. P., and Kinsey, S. H. (1997) "Plan and Operation of the 1995 National Survey of Family Growth." *Vital and Health Statistics, Series I*.

Kirby, D. (2001) *Emerging Answers: Research Findings on Programs to Reduce Teen Pregnancy*. Washington, DC: National Campaign to Prevent Teen Pregnancy.

Lehrer, E. L. (1995) "The Effects of Religion on the Labor Supply of Married Women." *Social Science Research* 24:281–301. (Chapter 3 this volume.)

Lehrer, E. L. (1999) "Religion as a Determinant of Educational Attainment: An Economic Perspective." *Social Science Research* 28:358–79. (Chapter 6 this volume.)

Lehrer, E. L. (2004a) "Religion as a Determinant of Economic and Demographic Behavior in the United States." *Population and Development Review* 30(4):707–26.

Lehrer, E. L. (2004b) "Religiosity as a Determinant of Educational Attainment: The Case of Conservative Protestant Women in the United States." *Review of Economics of the Household* 2(2):203–19.

Lehrer, E. L. (2008) "Religious Affiliation and Participation as Determinants of Women's Educational Attainment and Wages." Forthcoming in C. Ellison and R. Hummer (eds) *Religion, Family Life, and Health in the United States*. Chapel Hill, NC: Rutgers University Press.

Pattillo-McCoy, M. (1998) "Church Culture as a Strategy of Action in the Black Community." *American Sociological Review* 63(December):767–84.

Regnerus, M. (2005) "Race, Religion, and Adolescent Sexual Behavior." Presented at the annual meetings of the Population Association of America, Philadelphia, March 31–April 2.

Sherkat, D. E. and Darnell, A. (1999) "The Effects of Parents' Fundamentalism on

Children's Educational Attainment: Examining Differences by Gender and Children's Fundamentalism." *Journal for the Scientific Study of Religion* 38(1):23–35.

Smith, T. W. (1987) "Classifying Protestant Denominations." General Social Survey Methodological Report No. 43. Chicago: National Opinion Research Center.

Steensland, B., Park, J. Z., Regnerus, M. D., Robinson, L. D., Wilcox, W. B., and Woodberry, R. D. (2000) "The Measure of American Religion: Toward Improving the State of the Art." *Social Forces* 79(1):1–28.

Taylor, R. J., Chatters, L. M., Jayakody, R., and Levin, J. S. (1996) "Black and White Differences in Religious Participation: A Multisample Comparison." *Journal for the Scientific Study of Religion* 35(4):403–10.

Waite, L. and Lehrer, E. (2003) "The Benefits from Marriage and Religion in the United States: A Comparative Analysis." *Population and Development Review* 29(2):255–75.

Warner, R. S. (2002) "The Black Church as the Village it Takes to Raise a Child." Youth and Religion Project, Module 1, URL (accessed February 2008): http://www.uic.edu/depts/soci/yrp/index1.html

Williams, R. S. and Warner, R. S. (2001) "Creating Urban Evangelicalism: Youth Ministry, Moral Boundaries, and Social Diversity." Youth and Religion Project, URL (accessed February 2008): http://www.uic.edu/depts/soci/yrp/simple/_pap3.html

Part IV

A revised analytical framework, conclusions, and directions for future research

8 The role of religion in union formation

An economic perspective*

This study examines the role of religion in two dimensions of women's transition to first union: the timing of such transition, and whether it takes the form of marriage or cohabitation. Previous research has shown that religious affiliation has important effects on economic and demographic behavior: it has an influence on educational attainment (Chiswick 1988; Darnell and Sherkat 1997; Lehrer 1999a, 2004), attitudes toward premarital sex (Sweet and Bumpass 1990), fertility (Thornton 1979; Lehrer 1996a, 1996b), female employment (Lehrer 1995; Sherkat 2000) and the prevalence of divorce (Lehrer and Chiswick 1993; Teachman 2002). Based on this evidence, the present study develops hypotheses regarding patterns of entry into marriage and cohabitation for the main religious groups in the United States: mainline Protestants, conservative Protestants, Catholics, Mormons, Jews, and the unaffiliated.

Much of what we know about the effects of religion on marriage and cohabitation is based on unions formed prior to the mid 1980s (Thornton et al. 1992; Sander 1993; Lehrer 2000). The present study uses more recent data on young women from the 1995 National Survey of Family Growth. This survey provides an opportunity to analyze entry into union formation for the post baby-boom cohort, a generation that has displayed a much higher prevalence of cohabitation and a tendency to delay formal marriage (Brien and Sheran 2003). This is also a generation that grew up after the end of the era of high Catholic fertility (Jones and Westoff 1979; Mosher et al. 1986; Goldscheider and Mosher 1991). With these data, it is possible to ascertain whether or not the distinctive Catholic pattern of delayed entry into marriage has also disappeared.

Another attractive feature of the 1995 NSFG is that it includes information on frequency of attendance at religious services during the years of adolescence. Previous data sets, including the widely used 1987–88 National Survey of Families and Households, have generally measured religious participation only at the time of the interview, a variable that is endogenous to

* Reprinted from *Population Research and Policy Review* 23:161–185, 2004.

union formation behavior. The present paper takes advantage of the information on religious participation during the formative years to study how it affects the linkage between religious affiliation and entry into first union, a question that has received little attention in the literature to date.

This study contributes to the ongoing debate regarding the overall importance of religion in society. The prevailing view until recently was that the process of modernization – with the accompanying increases in standards of living, the progress of science and technology, and universal education – should lead to a decline in the role of religion (e.g., Wilson 1976). A growing body of empirical research has challenged this secularization thesis: several studies document that the observed patterns of religious beliefs and practices are inconsistent with its predictions (Greeley 1972, 1989; Stark 1999). Rational choice theory has led to the formulation of an alternative thesis – the view that in the highly pluralistic religious market of American society, the expected condition of religion is one of vitality and vibrancy rather than decline (Iannaccone 1991; Finke and Stark 1992; Warner 1993). The analyses reported in this study provide insights as to whether religious affiliation and religiosity continue to play an important role in one aspect of young women's lives: their decisions regarding entry into cohabitation and marriage.

Analytical framework

The faith in which a young woman is raised is likely to affect the perceived costs and/or benefits of various decisions made over the life cycle. Religious beliefs may influence the subjective benefits of having a large number of children and staying home to take care of them; they may affect the psychic costs of sharing living arrangements with someone without the formality of a marriage contract; they may have an impact on the subjective costs of dissolving a marriage; the perceived benefits and costs of pursuing additional schooling may also be affected. The analyses in this study are based on the premise that members of the various religious groups make choices that are consistent with these differences in perceived benefits and costs. These responses, in turn, lead to various channels of causality from religious affiliation to patterns of union formation. Each of these mechanisms is explored below, using mainline Protestants as the reference group in all comparisons.

The focus of the analysis is on the linkage between religious affiliation and (a) the timing of the first legal marriage; and (b) the likelihood that the first union will take the form of cohabitation rather than formal marriage. The main difference between the two is the level of commitment that is involved: marriage is widely announced to all relatives and friends, the ceremony usually includes a statement along the lines of "until death do us part," and a legal document is signed, which makes dissolution of the union more costly (Willis and Michael 1994).

Fertility

Some religions provide psychic and social rewards to those who have many children, in the form of approval, social status, and blessings. As Stark and Finke (2000) have noted, the high fertility that Mormons have consistently displayed in the United States (Thornton 1979; Heaton 1986; Lehrer 1996b) can be interpreted as a rational response to such incentives. Similarly, the Catholic religion embodies strong pronatalist ideologies, which until the 1970s had also been manifested in a distinctive pattern of very high fertility. More recently, adherence to the teachings of the Catholic Church in this area has weakened markedly, with a corresponding decline in family size (Mosher et al. 1986; Goldscheider and Mosher 1991). Some aspects of conservative Protestant ideologies are also pronatalist, and the fertility of this group has been found to exceed that of mainline Protestants, but only by a small margin (Marcum 1981; Lehrer 1996b). At the other end of the continuum, Jews in the United States have consistently displayed unusually low fertility (Goldscheider 1967; Della Pergola 1980; Mosher and Hendershot 1984). It has been suggested that Jews have faced a higher price of having an extra child, and may have therefore chosen to substitute expenditures per child ("quality") for quantity (Chiswick 1988).

Individuals who report "no religion" constitute a relatively small and heterogeneous group: it includes atheists, agnostics, and respondents who were raised without an affiliation due to other circumstances (e.g., being a child from an interfaith marriage). Perhaps for this reason, results from earlier studies differ, some finding a pattern of low fertility for the unaffiliated (Mosher et al. 1992), others reporting a family size similar to that of mainline Protestants (Lehrer 1996b).

The optimal timing of entry into first union and the form such union takes are intimately related to plans regarding family size. Women who expect to have a large number of children have an incentive to marry earlier; they also have an incentive to avoid the more fragile cohabiting arrangements, as a stable two-parent household is the optimal institutional arrangement for the raising of children (Weiss and Willis 1985; Willis and Haaga 1996). This reasoning implies that Mormon women should have a low probability of cohabitation and a pattern of early first marriage, and the opposite should hold for their Jewish counterparts.

Educational attainment

Studies on the linkage between religious affiliation and years of schooling among non-Hispanic whites show that educational attainment is highest for Jews, lowest for conservative Protestants, with Catholics and mainline Protestants at the center of the distribution (Lehrer 1999a, 2004; see also Chiswick 1988, 1993; Darnell and Sherkat 1997; Sherkat and Darnell 1999). Recent research has interpreted these differentials within a human capital framework: religious affiliation is viewed as reflecting distinctive features of the home environment that affect both the returns and costs of additional investments in education (Chiswick 1988; Lehrer 1999a). Less is known about the relative schooling levels of Mormons. Analyses based on a sample of women suggest that their attainment is around the center of the educational distribution (Keysar and Kosmin 1995).

It is often difficult to combine the roles of student and spouse (Thornton et al. 1995), and women who pursue more advanced schooling levels generally delay their entry into marriage (Michael and Tuma 1985). Religious groups that promote high levels of investment in secular human capital thus also encourage, indirectly, a late transition to marriage. This channel of causality implies that Jews would delay entry into marriage, while conservative Protestants would tend to marry early.

At the same time, a high level of schooling does not necessarily imply late entry into an informal partnership. As Chiswick (1998) notes, adult characteristics that are important in the marriage market may not be fully revealed (to oneself or a potential spouse) until after entry to the labor force and acceptance of financial responsibility. Furthermore, high-level careers often involve an initial period of uncertainty that encourages young people to avoid the stronger commitment of a legal union (Oppenheimer 1988). If so, the prevalence of cohabitation should be relatively high among Jewish women and relatively low among conservative Protestant women.

Potential male earnings

In their analysis of union formation, Willis and Michael (1994) find that the better the economic prospects of the male partner at the time of the formation of the union, the more likely it is that the partnership will take the form of marriage rather than cohabitation. They interpret this result as consistent with the view that as the level of male earnings rise, the gains from the partnership increase, implying stronger incentives to choose the arrangement that involves more commitment, i.e., legal marriage. A complementary interpretation is suggested in the sociological literature: it is still culturally required in our society that prior to entering a formal union, the male partner should have the ability to provide steady earnings, and in the absence of such ability, cohabitation provides the closest substitute arrangement (Cherlin 2000).

Little research has been done regarding the earnings of men with various religious affiliations. Mirroring the patterns found for educational attainment, unusually high earnings have been reported for Jews (Chiswick 1983, 1988, 1993), and there is also some evidence that earnings are relatively low for conservative Protestants (Keister 2001). Previous research has also noted that religion is a trait for which there is positive assortative mating in the marriage market, although for many religious groups the tendency for religious homogamy has weakened over time (Kalmijn 1998; Lehrer 1998). This channel of causality predicts that cohabitation should be least likely for Jews and most likely for conservative Protestants.

Female employment

The Mormon and conservative Protestant faiths make a sharp distinction between male and female roles, encouraging the traditional division of labor within the household. Consistent with the view that such religions provide institutionalized moral support and psychic rewards to mothers who stay home with their children, previous research documents a lower level of female employment among members of these faiths when young children are present (Heaton and Cornwall 1989; Chadwick and Garrett 1995; Lehrer 1995, 1999b; Sherkat 2000). At the other end of the spectrum, although Jewish women are known to be very responsive in their labor supply to the presence of young children (Chiswick 1986), their overall commitment to labor market activities is stronger than that of women of other affiliations (Hartman and Hartman 1996).

With regard to Catholics, early studies found that they made a sharp distinction between appropriate male and female roles (Meir 1972; McMurry 1978). More recent analyses, however, suggest that Catholics have become more egalitarian (Brinkerhoff and MacKie 1984), and indeed somewhat less traditional in this regard than either group of Protestants (Brinkerhoff and MacKie 1985). The direction of this change mirrors transformations that have taken place in the behavior of Catholics in issues related to childrearing (Alwin 1984), and is also consistent with evidence on patterns of labor supply by religion. Data on married women with a child under age 6 from the 1987–88 National Survey of Family Growth show that the probability of being out of the labor force is lowest for Catholics (0.36) and highest for conservative Protestants (0.55), with mainline Protestants in between (0.43) (Lehrer 1995).

Young women who plan to orient their efforts to home rather labor market activities have incentives to form their unions early, and to do so via marriage rather than cohabitation, as the former provides greater economic security (Grossbard-Shechtman 1993). Willis and Michael (1994) find empirical support for the notion that women who are less involved in the labor market are indeed more likely to form marital rather than cohabiting unions. This line of reasoning predicts early marriage and a low probability of cohabitation for Mormon and conservative Protestant women, and the opposite pattern for their Jewish counterparts.

Costs of divorce

Since religions are generally family oriented, affiliation with any faith would increase the costs of marital dissolution. This effect should be particularly pronounced in the case of Catholicism, as it prohibits divorce. Empirically, most studies find that Catholic marriages are less likely to end in dissolution than other unions (Christensen and Barber 1967; Michael 1979; Sander 1993; Teachman 2002), although there is some evidence that this religious differential may be disappearing (Lehrer and Chiswick 1993). The higher cost of making a mistake for Catholics implies a tendency to search longer for a spouse and predicts a later age at entry into marriage.

Attitudes regarding premarital sex

While most religions encourage marriage and place a high value on family life, often with proscriptions against premarital sex, conservative Protestants and Mormons are most traditional in this regard. The level of approval of cohabitation has been found to be lowest for these groups, and highest for Jews and the unaffiliated (Sweet and Bumpass 1990). These differences by religion in the subjective costs of living with a partner without the formality of a marriage contract predict corresponding differences in the probability that the first union would take the form of cohabitation.

Summing up

The various mechanisms outlined above suggest several hypotheses regarding differences by religion in patterns of entry into formal marriage. Women brought up as conservative Protestants and as Mormons are expected to marry early, because their faith encourages an orientation to home activities, and also very high fertility in the case of Mormons. The relatively low schooling level of conservative Protestants is another factor operating in the same direction. At the other extreme, Jewish women are expected to delay entry into marriage for several interrelated reasons: their high educational attainment, their low desired level of fertility, and their strong commitment to the labor market.

Analyses based on earlier cohorts provide empirical support for these predictions and suggest that the magnitudes of the effects are sizable (Thornton et al. 1992; Sander 1993; Lehrer 2000). For the more recent post baby-boom cohort that is the focus of the present study, it is anticipated that the relationships outlined above will continue to prevail, although it is unclear a priori whether the magnitudes of the influences will remain large.

In the case of Catholics, however, the situation may have changed. Among earlier generations, the high cost of divorce for this group implied incentives for a longer period of marital search and a low probability of an early transition to marriage; at the same time, the pronatalist norms of the Catholic theology, which encourage marriage, suggested a low likelihood of a late transition. Based on these countervailing influences, Michael and Tuma (1985) hypothesized that affiliation with the Catholic faith should have a non-linear impact, promoting an intermediate timing of marriage as opposed to one that is very early or very late. Empirical analyses for a cohort of women born in the decade after World War II confirmed such non-linearity (Lehrer 2000). For the post baby-boom cohort studied in this study, the convergence of Catholic fertility with the mainline Protestant pattern suggests that the second of these effects no longer operates, implying that Catholics no longer avoid a very late entry to marriage. As to the first effect, it is unclear, based on the evidence to date, whether it is still relevant. Although the Catholic religion prohibits divorce, a recent study finds that Catholic individuals are dissolving their unions at the same rate as members of other religious groups (Lehrer and Chiswick 1993). To the extent that Catholics no longer perceive the costs of divorce as particularly high, there would be little reason to expect a continued pattern of delayed transition to first marriage.

Given that the behavior of Catholics has converged to the mainline Protestant pattern in virtually all other dimensions of family life, they are expected to follow roughly the same pattern of entry into cohabitation as mainline Protestants. A low probability of cohabitation is predicted for Mormons, because of their conservative attitudes toward premarital sex, their high fertility, and the tendency of mothers to stay home with their young children. At the other extreme, the subjective costs of sharing living arrangements without a legal contract are relatively small for the unaffiliated, implying a high level of cohabitation.

Countervailing influences are present for the other religious groups. In the case of Jews, their liberal attitudes toward premarital sex, low fertility, and high levels of female education and employment, all combine to predict a high prevalence of informal unions. However, the elevated earnings of Jewish men imply the contrary, and a priori the net effect is theoretically ambiguous. For the opposite reasons, the net impact is also ambiguous for conservative Protestants.

Empirically, an earlier analysis (which excluded individuals with no religious affiliation) found that cohabitation is least likely for Mormons and most likely for Jews (Lehrer 2000). Willis and Michael (1994) also report an unusually high rate of cohabitation for Jews.

The role of religiosity

The above discussion suggests that the doctrines of a particular religion influence union formation because they have an impact on the perceived costs and benefits of various decisions. The effects should therefore be stronger for those individuals who adhere more closely to the teachings of their faith. For example, the likelihood that a Mormon woman will have many children and stay home with them when they are young probably increases with commitment to the religion, implying a corresponding variation by religiosity in the effect of Mormonism on age at entry into marriage and on the likelihood of cohabitation.

Little empirical research has been done to quantify these relationships. An important exception is the case of attitudes toward premarital sex, which have been found to vary considerably by religiosity. In their analyses of mainline Protestants, conservative Protestants, and Catholics, Petersen and Donnenwerth (1997) find that for each of these religious groups, individuals who attend church frequently have a much more traditional stance regarding the acceptability of sex outside of marriage, implying a higher subjective cost of cohabitation. For members of these faiths, the probability of entering an informal union should thus vary inversely with religiosity.

Methods

Data and variables

The empirical analysis uses data from Cycle 5 of the National Survey of Family Growth (NSFG). The survey was conducted in 1995 by the Research Triangle Institute, under contract from the National Center for Health Statistics (see Kelly et al. 1997 for a description of the methodology). The questionnaires were addressed to a nationally representative sample of 10,847 civilian, non-institutionalized women ages 15–44 years of age of all marital statuses living in the US. The interviews included questions on socioeconomic and family background variables, as well as detailed cohabitation, marriage, and fertility histories.

The sample is restricted in three ways. First, patterns of union formation differ greatly by race and ethnicity (Brien 1998; Smock 2000); only non-Hispanic white respondents are included in the present analysis. Second, as already noted, the focus of this study is on the post baby-boom generation (women born after 1967). These respondents, ages 15–28 at the time of the survey, had not all experienced their first transition to a union, a factor taken into account by the Cox proportional hazards technique used in the empirical analysis. And third, the sample only includes individuals whose religion of upbringing is one of the six major religious groups in the US: Roman Catholic, mainline Protestant, conservative Protestant, Jewish, Mormon, and unaffiliated. The resulting sample size is N = 2,169.

The mainline Protestant group includes Episcopalians, Methodists, Presbyterians, and Lutherans; the conservative Protestant category includes Baptists and other, smaller fundamentalist Protestant groups. The 1995 NSFG uses the same code for all Baptists, so it is not possible to make finer distinctions. In his research on the classification of Protestants into fundamentalist, moderate, and liberal groups, Smith (1990) distinguishes between seven different Baptist denominations, classifying six of them as fundamentalist and one as moderate.

This limitation of the data implies that the respondents classified in the present study as conservative Protestant include a small number of non-fundamentalists, suggesting a bias toward zero in the coefficient on the conservative Protestant dummy variable. Thus the positive effect of membership in conservative Protestant denominations on the speed of entry into first marriage documented in the next section is more pronounced than indicated by the present estimates.

Previous research suggests that current religious affiliation and religiosity are determined simultaneously with education, fertility, and other economic and demographic variables (Sander 1995; Waters et al. 1995; Lehrer 1998). The variables used in this analysis, namely, the faith in which the individual was raised and religious participation measured at age 14, are less affected by problems of endogeneity.

Table 8.1 provides definitions and means for the religion variables as well as for the factors used as controls in the empirical analysis. These include the parents' average years of schooling, whether the mother worked on a full-time basis during most of the respondent's childhood, the size of the family of origin, dummy variables for family structure at age 16, and region of residence at the time of birth. It would have been preferable to control for region during the late adolescent/young adult years; it would also have been desirable to control for the rural–urban nature of the place of residence, as there are pronounced differences by religion in this distribution. Unfortunately this information is unavailable. To the extent that life in urban areas is conducive to later marriage, the present estimates may overstate the effect of affiliation with the Jewish and Catholic faiths in delaying marriage, as these groups are disproportionately represented in big cities and their suburbs; the coefficients of the other religion variables may likewise be affected by omitted variables biases.

The statistical model

The key variable in the Cox proportional hazards model is survival time, the interval until a certain event happens; in the present context, the time until union formation. The hazard function is expressed as follows:

$$h(t,z) = h_o(t) \exp(\beta'z)$$

where $h_o(t)$ is an unspecified time-dependent function, z is a vector of covariates, and β is a vector of unknown coefficients. The risk of union formation is thus allowed to vary with time and with the exogenous variables. When all the elements in z are 0, the hazard function equals $h_o(t)$. If β_k (the coefficient associated with explanatory variable z_k) is positive, an increase in z_k raises the value of the hazard function and therefore decreases survival time. A positive β_k thus implies that as z_k rises, the probability that union formation has taken place at each duration becomes higher. When the explanatory factor is specified as a 0–1 variable, a positive β_k means that when z_k takes the higher value, 1, the likelihood of union formation is greater.

The tables that follow report the estimated values of β, the corresponding t-statistics, and also the estimated value of $\exp(\beta)$. For continuous variables, the percentage change in the hazard associated with each unit change in the

Table 8.1 Definitions and means of explanatory variables

Control variables		
Parents' education	=1 if the average years of schooling completed by the respondent's (R) father (or father figure) and mother (or mother figure) is in category indicated[a]	
<12 years		0.21
12 years		0.26
(13–15 years, benchmark)		(0.34)
≥ 16 years		0.19
Mother worked full time	=1 if R's mother (figure) worked full time during most of R's childhood (ages 5–15)	0.46
Nonintact family	=1 if R did not live with both biological (or adoptive) parents at age 16 for the reason indicated:	
Death	death of one of the parents	0.05
Divorce or separation	parents' divorce or separation	0.33
Other	R never lived with both biological (or adoptive) parents	0.05
(Intact family of origin, benchmark)		(0.57)
Family size	number of children born to R's mother (or mother figure)	2.90
Residence at birth	R's region of residence at time of birth	
Northeast		0.19
(Midwest, benchmark)		(0.33)
West		0.18
South		0.28
Foreign		0.02
Religion variables		
Catholic		0.29
Conservative Protestant		0.25
(Mainline Protestant, benchmark)		(0.29)
Mormon		0.04
Jewish		0.01
No religion		0.12
N		2,169

Note

a If the respondent was raised by some other "mother figure," such as a stepmother or grandmother, the information for that individual was used, and the same was done in the case of the father. If educational attainment was missing for the father (figure) or the mother (figure), the value for the other person was used.

explanatory variable z_k (other covariates held constant), is equal to 100 (exp $(\beta_k) -1$). For dummy variables, the term $\exp(\beta)$ can be interpreted as the ratio of the estimated hazard for those with a value of 1 to the estimated hazard for those with a value of 0 (controlling for other factors) (Teachman 1982; Allison 1997).

The survival function in the Cox model is:

$$F(t,z) = (F_o(t))^{\exp(\beta'z)}$$

where

$$F_o(t) = \exp \{ - \textstyle\int_0^t h_o(u)du \}$$

Evaluating the survival function at specified durations and values of the covariates permits an assessment of the absolute magnitudes of the various effects. Exposure to the risk of union formation is assumed to begin at age 13.

Results

Following previous work by Thornton et al. (1992), four Cox proportional hazards models are estimated to study union formation. The first two panels of Table 8.2 present models of cohabitation and marriage, treating the other state as a competing risk. The marriage regression shown in the third panel ignores cohabitation; in this model those who first cohabited and then went on to formal marriage are included in the ranks of the married. The last model considers the hazard of union formation defined as either marriage or cohabitation, whichever happened first.

Table 8.3 shows predicted probabilities of early cohabitation and early marriage (by age 20) based, respectively, on the competing-risk models of panels 1 and 2 in Table 8.2. These estimates, obtained from the complement of the survival function evaluated at $t = 7$ for selected values of the covariates, illustrate the absolute magnitudes of the various influences.

Religion effects

Focusing first on the case of formal marriage, the results in panel 2 of Table 8.2 strongly confirm the hypotheses outlined in the previous section. Affiliation with the Catholic faith delays marriage ($t = -3.4$); the probability of having entered first marriage by age 20 is only 0.05 for Catholics, compared to 0.09 for mainline Protestants. The point estimate for a Jewish upbringing yields an even more pronounced effect: a probability of marriage by age 20 of only 0.02. However, the number of Jews in the sample is small ($N = 22$), and the coefficient attains significance only at the 15 percent level. In contrast, two groups display a pattern of very early entry into first marriage: conservative Protestants ($t = 4.3$) and Mormons ($t = 2.5$); the

Table 8.2 The effects of religious upbringing on union formation: Cox proportional hazards models

	Panel 1 Cohabitation (marriage as competing risk)			Panel 2 Marriage (cohabitation as competing risk)			Panel 3 Marriage (ignoring cohabitation)			Panel 4 Total union formation		
	β	t	$exp(\beta)$	β	t	$exp(\beta)$	β	t	$exp(\beta)$	β	t	$exp(\beta)$
Control variables												
Average education												
<12 years	0.407	4.0**	1.5	0.379	2.7**	1.5	0.266	2.7**	1.3	0.394	4.7**	1.5
12 years	0.209	2.1**	1.2	0.142	1.0	1.2	0.147	1.5#	1.2	0.188	2.3**	1.2
≥16 years	-0.491	-3.7**	0.6	-0.750	-3.8**	0.5	-0.767	-5.4**	0.5	-0.573	-5.3**	0.6
Mother worked full time	0.132	1.7*	1.1	-0.075	-0.7	0.9	-0.068	-0.9	0.9	0.068	1.0	1.1
Nonintact family												
Death	0.506	3.3**	1.7	0.169	0.7	1.2	0.172	1.0	1.2	0.402	3.1**	1.5
Divorce	0.587	6.9**	1.8	-0.235	-1.7*	0.8	0.176	2.1**	1.2	0.327	4.6**	1.4
Other	0.920	6.0**	2.5	0.411	1.7*	1.5	0.386	2.4**	1.5	0.741	5.7**	2.1
Family size	0.037	1.5#	1.0	0.057	1.6*	1.1	0.052	2.2**	1.1	0.043	2.1**	1.0
Residence at birth												
Northeast	-0.285	-2.5**	0.8	-0.185	-1.0	0.8	-0.332	-2.6**	0.7	-0.257	-2.6**	0.8
South	-0.298	-2.7**	0.7	0.253	1.7*	1.3	0.093	0.9	1.1	-0.105	-1.2	0.9
West	-0.049	-0.4	0.9	0.326	1.9*	1.4	0.165	1.4	1.2	0.071	0.7	1.1
Foreign	0.218	0.9	1.2	0.093	0.2	1.1	0.280	1.2	1.3	0.172	0.9	1.2
Religion variables												
Catholic	-0.259	-2.5**	0.8	-0.588	-3.4**	0.6	-0.296	-2.7**	0.7	-0.343	-3.9**	0.7
Conservative Protestant	-0.054	-0.5	0.9	0.644	4.3**	1.9	0.431	4.0**	1.5	0.221	2.4**	1.2
Mormon	-0.529	-1.9*	0.6	0.634	2.5**	1.9	0.548	2.8**	1.7	-0.011	-0.1	1.0
Jewish	-0.078	-0.2	0.9	-1.538	-1.5#	0.2	-0.993	-1.7*	0.4	-0.344	-1.1	0.7
No religion	0.230	1.8*	1.3	-0.111	-0.5	0.9	0.062	0.5	1.1	0.150	1.4	1.2
χ^2, 17 df	201.6**			177.0**			213.3**			262.4**		
N (% censored)	2,169 (69%)			2,169 (84%)			2,169 (68%)			2,169 (53%)		

# p < 0.15; * p < 0.10; ** p < 0.05.

Table 8.3 Predicted probabilities based on competing-risk models of Table 8.2[a]

	Cohabitation by age 20	*Marriage by age 20*
Reference case[b]	0.20	0.09
Selected cases:		
Parents' education		
<12 years	0.29	0.13
12 years	0.23	(0.11)
≥ 16 years	0.13	0.04
Mother worked full time	0.23	(0.09)
Nonintact family		
Death	0.31	(0.11)
Divorce or separation	0.33	0.07
Other	0.43	0.14
Family size		
2	0.19	0.09
4	0.21	0.10
Residence at birth		
Northeast	0.15	(0.08)
South	0.15	0.12
West	(0.19)	0.13
Foreign	(0.24)	(0.10)
Religion		
Catholic	0.16	0.05
Conservative Protestant	(0.19)	0.17
Mormon	0.12	0.17
Jewish	(0.19)	0.02
No religion	0.24	(0.08)

Notes

a Figures in parentheses correspond to coefficients that did not attain significance at the 15 percent level.

b The reference woman has the following characteristics: her religious affiliation is mainline Protestant; the average education of her parents is in the 13–15 years category; she grew up in an intact family; her mother did not work on a full-time basis during most of her childhood; residence at birth was in the Midwest; the total number of siblings in the family of origin is 3. The other cases differ from the reference case in only one characteristic, as shown in the stub.

probability of marriage by age 20 is fully 0.17 for members of these groups, almost twice the value for the reference category.

Panel 3 of Table 8.2 displays results for analyses that ignore cohabitation. Differences between the effects reported in panels 2 and 3 can be traced to (a) how the variable in question affects the probability of cohabitation (the sign and magnitude of the influence), and (b) the relationship between this variable and the likelihood that cohabitation is quickly followed by marriage. As Brien et al. (1999) observe, some cohabiting partnerships are quickly formalized into marriage, others are not. The results in panel 3 are qualitatively the same as those in panel 2, although the magnitudes of the influences differ somewhat. Overall, the estimated effects of religious affiliation on the timing of entry into formal marriage provide strong support for the hypotheses.

With regard to cohabitation, the first panel of Table 8.2 shows that this arrangement is most likely for the unaffiliated (t = 1.8); the probability of entering an informal union by age 20 is 0.24 for this group, compared to 0.20 for mainline Protestants. At the other end of the spectrum, informal co-residential arrangements are least likely for Mormons (t = −1.9), who have a probability of cohabitation by age 20 of only 0.12. Both of these influences are consistent with the hypotheses. Although this had not been anticipated, affiliation with the Catholic Church is also found to decrease the likelihood of cohabitation (t = −2.5), but not by as much: the probability of cohabitation by age 20 is 0.16. For conservative Protestants and Jews, the theoretical analysis identified countervailing influences. Empirically, the coefficients are found to be insignificant, suggesting that such effects are canceling each other out.

Two groups stand out in the union formation model. Catholics display a late entry into union formation (t = −3.9), reflecting their tendency to delay both cohabitation and marriage. Conservative Protestants have a pattern of early entry (t = 2.4), a result of the positive coefficient in the marriage equations and the insignificant effect in the cohabitation regression. Opposing influences are observed in the case of Mormons: a tendency to cohabit less but to enter marriage earlier; the net impact of affiliation with the Mormon faith on union formation broadly defined is zero. No significant effects are discerned for Jews or the unaffiliated.

Comparing the present results with those based on earlier generations, the post baby-boom cohort is characterized by a clear pattern of later entry into marriage for all religious groups. A study based on a sample of Jewish, Catholic, mainline Protestant, conservative Protestant, and Mormon women born in the decade after World War II, reports that the probabilities of early marriage (by age 18) are, respectively: 0.04, 0.08, 0.12, 0.20, and 0.23 (Lehrer 2000). Even though the corresponding figures in the present study are based on early marriage defined as marriage by age 20, they are uniformly lower: 0.02, 0.05, 0.09, 0.17, and 0.17.

Although members of all religious denominations are entering marriage later, the differences by religious affiliation in patterns of entry into marriage and cohabitation have remained remarkably stable. Conservative Protestants and Mormons continue to display an early entry into marriage, while Jews and Catholics continue to delay such entry. It is noteworthy that, although the behavior of Catholics has converged to the mainline Protestant pattern in fertility and most other domains of family life, their distinctive behavior in the area of union formation persists. The finding that Catholics continue to delay marriage, by a substantial margin, suggests that their marital search behavior is still influenced by their faith's proscription against divorce. Since this study follows women only up to their late twenties, it is not possible to ascertain here whether Catholic women are also avoiding a very late entry into marriage, as they used to.

As to cohabitation, the finding from earlier research that the prevalence is lowest among Mormons continues to hold (Lehrer 2000). The patterns of change over time for Jews are less clear. Analyses based on earlier cohorts had found that Jews stand out for their high prevalence of cohabitation (Willis and Michael 1994; Lehrer 2000). In contrast, the present results suggest that Jews do not differ from mainline Protestants in this area; however, these findings must be interpreted with caution because of the small sample size. Analyses of larger samples will be needed to establish whether the likelihood of cohabitation for Jews has indeed diminished over time.

Effects of the control variables

Cohabitation is found to be most common among women brought up in homes of low socioeconomic status, by parents with less than a high school education (t = 4.0). As the level of parental education rises, the likelihood of cohabitation declines (t = 2.1; t = −3.7). The daughters of highly educated parents tend to delay marriage as well (t = −3.8; t = −5.4). These effects reinforce each other, and produce a strong negative relationship between the level of parental education and age at entry into first union (t = 4.7; t = 2.3; t = −5.3).

Having a mother who worked full time has no impact on entry into formal marriage, but it does increase the likelihood of cohabitation (t = 1.7). A nonintact family of origin has a marked effect on the probability of cohabitation in the case of the death of a parent (t = 3.3) or divorce (t = 6.9); the influence is also significant (t = 6.0) and especially large in magnitude for respondents whose biological parents never married. Such respondents also have a pattern of early entry into marriage (t = 1.7; t = 2.4). While the variable for a parental divorce has a negative effect in the marriage equation when cohabitation is treated as a competing risk (t = −1.7), the coefficient is positive when cohabitation is ignored (t = 2.1). This result reflects in part the high prevalence of informal living arrangements among respondents who grew up in a home broken by separation or divorce; a large number of these unions appear to be quickly formalized into marriage.

The size of the family of origin has a positive coefficient in the cohabitation equation (t = 1.5), and also in the marriage models (t = 1.6; t = 2.2). Some of these influences are only marginally significant, and the sizes of the effects are small. The results also suggest variation in patterns of union formation by place of birth, with respondents born in the northeastern states having the latest entry into some form of union (t = −2.6).

The influences of the control variables noted above are generally consistent with results from earlier research (Axinn and Thornton 1992; Lehrer 2000; Smock 2000). These effects provide a way to assess the relative importance of religion as a determinant of entry into formal marriage. Among the family background factors, the parents' schooling and a non-intact family of origin have the largest influences. An increase in average parental education from under 12 years to 16 years or more lowers the probability that the first marriage will take place early, by age 20, from 0.13 to 0.04 – a difference of nine percentage points. Similarly, the probability of an early first marriage is 0.14 if the respondent never lived with both biological parents, compared to 0.09 if her family of origin was intact – a difference of five percentage points. By comparison, the corresponding difference between conservative Protestants and Catholics is 12 percentage points, and the difference between Mormons and Jews is fully 15 percentage points. The effects of religion rival in magnitude the influences associated with family structure and the parents' educational attainment. Similar types of comparisons reveal that the impact of religious affiliation on cohabitation is also substantial.

Variations by religiosity

The analyses that follow utilize information in the 1995 NSFG on the respondents' frequency of attendance at religious services at age 14. This is a measure, albeit an imperfect one, of commitment to religion during the adolescent years. Differences by religiosity can only be studied for mainline Protestants, conservative Protestants, and Catholics, as the sample sizes for the other religious groups are small. Individuals who attended religious services 1–3 times per month or more frequently are classified in the high religiosity category; others are placed in the low religiosity group. The percentage of respondents in the first category is 78 percent for conservative Protestants, 74 percent for Catholics, and 68 percent for mainline Protestants.

Table 8.4 reports the Cox models reestimated with the low religiosity, mainline Protestant group as benchmark. The corresponding probabilities in Table 8.5 show more clearly the magnitudes of each religiosity effect. The results indicate that patterns of entry into formal marriage do not vary significantly by frequency of attendance at services for any of the religious groups considered here. This finding marks a departure from results documented for earlier periods. In their (pooled) analyses of Catholics and Protestants, Thornton et al. (1992) report a pattern of delayed entry into marriage among those who are less religious.

Thornton et al. (1992) also found that a higher level of religiosity is associated with a lower rate of cohabitation, and the present results show that this effect continues to be strong. For each faith, the probability of cohabitation is lower by a wide margin for those in the high frequency group ($t = -3.2$; $t = -2.8$; $t = -4.3$). The difference is especially pronounced for conservative Protestants: the probability of cohabitation by age 20 falls by about half, from 0.31 to 0.16, when comparing conservative Protestants who attended church less than 1–3 times per month at age 14 to their counterparts who were more observant at that stage in life. This heterogeneity within religious groups highlights the importance of taking into account differences by religiosity in studying the linkage between religious affiliation and union formation.

Table 8.4 Variations by frequency of attendance to religious services: Cox proportional hazards models[a]

	Panel 1 Cohabitation (marriage as competing risk)			Panel 2 Marriage (cohabitation as competing risk)			Panel 3 Marriage (ignoring cohabitation)			Panel 4 Total union formation		
	β	t	$exp(\beta)$	β	t	$exp(\beta)$	β	t	$exp(\beta)$	β	t	$exp(\beta)$
Mainline Protestant – low (benchmark)	—			—			—			—		
Mainline Protestant – high	-0.457	-3.2**	0.6	0.148	0.6	1.2	-0.027	-0.2	1.0	-0.297	-2.4**	0.7
Catholic – low	-0.258	-1.5#	0.8	-0.414	-1.2	0.7	-0.222	-1.1	0.8	-0.263	-1.7*	0.8
Catholic – high	-0.687	-4.8**	0.5	-0.497	-1.9*	0.6	-0.349	-2.2**	0.7	-0.653	-5.2**	0.5
Conservative Protestant – low	0.194	1.1	1.2	0.857	2.8**	2.4	0.483	2.5**	1.6	0.367	2.4**	1.4
Conservative Protestant – high	-0.543	-3.5**	0.6	0.733	3.0**	2.1	0.392	2.5**	1.5	-0.075	-0.6	0.9
χ^2, 20 df	234.8**			177.7**			214.2**			285.2**		
N	2,168			2,168			2,168			2,168		

# p < 0.15; * p < 0.10; ** p < 0.05.

Note
a All the control variables are included in these regressions; the models also include dummies for Jewish, Mormon, and unaffiliated. Note that the t-statistics reported in this table refer to comparisons against the reference category, mainline Protestants who had a low level of attendance to religious services. Table 8.5 reports the t-values for low-high religiosity comparisons within each religious group.

Table 8.5 Predicted probabilities by frequency of attendance to religious services based on competing-risk models of Table 8.4

		Cohabitation by age 20		Marriage by age 20	
		probability	*t-test*[a]	*probability*	*t-test*[a]
Mainline Protestant					
Low frequency	*vs.*	0.27	−3.2**	0.08	0.6
High frequency		0.18		0.10	
Catholic					
Low frequency	*vs.*	0.21	−2.8**	0.06	−0.5
High frequency		0.14		0.05	
Conservative Protestant					
Low frequency	*vs.*	0.31	−4.3**	0.18	−0.3
High frequency		0.16		0.17	

** $p < 0.05$.

Note
a The t-tests are calculated by comparing the corresponding coefficients in Table 8.4, using information on the variance–covariance matrix.

Conclusions

A considerable body of literature documents that religion has important effects on the economic and demographic behavior of individuals and families. The present study has built on this earlier research to develop and test hypotheses regarding the role of religious affiliation as a determinant of union formation. The basic premise underlying the analysis is that religion has an impact on the perceived costs and/or the perceived benefits of various decisions that individuals make over the life cycle, including education, fertility, and employment. These decisions, in turn, influence choices regarding marriage and cohabitation. This perspective has shed light on the various channels through which religion may affect patterns of entry into union formation, and has provided a clearer interpretation of results previously reported in the literature.

Based on data on the post baby-boom generation, the present results show that religious affiliation continues to have a sizable effect on entry into marriage and cohabitation. The probability of having entered marriage by age 20 ranges from a low of 0.02 for Jews and 0.05 for Catholics, to a high of 0.17 for conservative Protestants and Mormons; mainline Protestants and the unaffiliated are at the center of the distribution, with a probability of 0.08–0.09. Although the behavior of Catholics has converged to the mainline Protestant pattern in most domains of family life, this group has retained its distinctive behavior in the area of entry into marriage. With regard to cohabitation, Mormons continue to display the lowest probability of entering an informal union by age 20. The results suggest that the tendency that Jews displayed in the past to cohabit at unusually high rates may have disappeared, but additional research based on larger data sets is needed to confirm this finding.

The present results underscore that religiosity also continues to be an important determinant of entry into cohabiting relationships. The analyses reveal that for both groups of Protestants and for Catholics, individuals who attended religious services frequently during their adolescent years have a relatively low probability of cohabitation by age 20, in the 0.14–0.18 range; for their less religious counterparts, the range is 0.21–0.31. The effect of religiosity is especially pronounced among conservative Protestants. The priority placed on religion during the formative years clearly affects the perceived costs of cohabitation, and plays a major role in the decision of whether or not to enter an informal union. In contrast, for individuals raised as Catholics, mainline Protestants, or conservative Protestants, differences in religiosity no longer have a significant effect on patterns of entry into formal marriage.

This study focused on women who were part of the post baby-boom cohort, following them up to their late twenties. With Cycle 6 of the National Surveys of Family Growth currently under way, it will be possible to observe this cohort into the thirties, and determine whether the patterns documented here follow a linear path, or whether significant non-linearities emerge (e.g., groups that delay marriage the most may not necessarily display the lowest probability of eventual marriage). Another important item in the agenda for future research will be to go beyond the reduced-form estimates presented in this study, which measure total effects, and begin efforts to quantify the relative importance of the various channels linking religious affiliation and religiosity to union formation within the framework of a structural model. Finally, very little is known at present about these relationships for the case of African Americans, Hispanics, and other racial and ethnic minorities. Work by Wilcox and Wolfinger (2006) is a recent effort to begin to fill this gap in the literature.

Acknowledgments

An earlier draft of this chapter was presented at the annual meetings of the Population Association of America, May 9–11, 2002, Atlanta. I am indebted to Barry Chiswick, Carmel Chiswick, Linda Waite, and anonymous referees, for many helpful comments and suggestions.

References

Allison, P. D. (1997) *Survival Analysis Using the SAS System: A Practical Guide.* Cary, NC: SAS Institute Inc.

Alwin, D. F. (1984) "Trends in Parental Socialization Values: Detroit, 1958–1983." *American Journal of Sociology* 90(2):359–82.

Axinn, W. G. and Thornton, A. (1992) "The Influence of Parental Resources on the Timing of Transition to Marriage." *Social Science Research* 21:261–85.

Brien, M. J. (1998) "Racial Differences in Marriage and the Role of Marriage Markets." *Journal of Human Resources* 32(4):741–78.

Brien, M. J., Lillard, L. A., and Waite, L. J. (1999) "Interrelated Family-Building Behaviors: Cohabitation, Marriage, and Nonmarital Conception." *Demography* 36(4):535–51.

Brien, M. J. and Sheran, M. E. (2003) "The Economics of Marriage and Household Formation." Pp. 37–54 in S. Grossbard-Shechtman (ed.) *Marriage and the Economy: Theory and Evidence from Industrialized Societies.* Cambridge: Cambridge University Press.

Brinkerhoff, M. B. and MacKie, M. M. (1984) "Religious Denominations' Impact Upon Gender Attitudes: Some Methodological Implications." *Review of Religious Research* 25(4):365–78.

Brinkerhoff, M. B. and MacKie, M. M. (1985) "Religion and Gender: A Comparison of Canadian and American Student Attitudes." *Journal of Marriage and the Family* 47(2):415–29.

Chadwick, B. A. and Garrett, H. D. (1995) "Women's Religiosity and Employment: The LDS Experience." *Review of Religious Research* 36(3):277–93.

Cherlin, A. (2000) "Toward a New Home Socioeconomics of Union Formation." Pp. 126–46 in L. Waite, C. Bacrach, M. Hindin, E. Thomson, and A. Thornton (eds) *The Ties that Bind: Perspectives on Marriage and Cohabitation.* New York: Aldine de Gruyter.

Chiswick, B. R. (1983) "The Earnings and Human Capital of American Jews." *Journal of Human Resources* 8:313–36.

Chiswick, B. R. (1986) "Labor Supply and Investments in Child Quality: A Study of Jewish and Non-Jewish Women." *Review of Economics and Statistics* 68(4):700–3.

Chiswick, B. R. (1988) "Differences in Education and Earnings across Racial and Ethnic Groups: Tastes, Discrimination, and Investments in Child Quality." *Quarterly Journal of Economics* 103(3):571–97.

Chiswick, B. R. (1993) "The Skills and Economic Status of American Jewry: Trends Over the Last Half-Century." *Journal of Labor Economics* 11(1):229–42.

Chiswick, C. U. (1998) "The Economics of Contemporary American Jewish Family Life." Pp. 65–80 in P. Y. Medding (ed.) *Coping with Life and Death: Jewish Families in the Twentieth Century.* Oxford: Oxford University Press.

Christensen, H. T. and Barber, K. E. (1967) "Interfaith Versus Intrafaith Marriage in Indiana." *Journal of Marriage and the Family* 29(3):461–9.

Darnell, A. and Sherkat, D. E. (1997) "The Impact of Protestant Fundamentalism on Educational Attainment." *American Sociological Review* 62(April):306–15.

Della Pergola, S. (1980) "Patterns of American Jewish Fertility." *Demography* 17(3):261–73.

Finke, R. and Stark, R. (1992) *The Churching of America, 1776–1990: Winners and Losers in our Religious Economy.* New Brunswick, NJ: Rutgers University Press.

Goldscheider, C. (1967) "Fertility of the Jews." *Demography* 4:196–209.

Goldscheider, C. and Mosher, W. D. (1991) "Patterns of Contraceptive Use in the United States: The Importance of Religious Factors." *Studies in Family Planning* 22(2):102–15.

Greeley, A. (1972) *Unsecular Man: The Persistence of Religion.* New York: Schocken Books.

Greeley, A. (1989) *Religious Change in America.* Cambridge, MA: Harvard University Press.

Grossbard-Shechtman, S. (1993) *On the Economics of Marriage: A Theory of Marriage, Labor, and Divorce.* Boulder, CO: Westview Press.

Hartman, M. and Hartman, H. (1996) *Gender Equality and American Jews.* Albany: State University of New York Press.

Heaton, T. B. (1986) "How Does Religion Influence Fertility? The Case of Mormons." *Journal for the Scientific Study of Religion* 25(2):248–58.

Heaton, T. B. and Cornwall, M. (1989) "Religious Group Variation in the Socio-economic Status and Family Behavior of Women." *Journal for the Scientific Study of Religion* 28(3):283–99.

Iannaccone, L. R. (1991) "The Consequences of Religious Market Structure." *Rationality and Society* 3:156–77.

Jones, E. F. and Westoff, C. F. (1979) "The End of 'Catholic' Fertility." *Demography* 16(2):209–18.

Kalmijn, M. (1998) "Intermarriage and Homogamy: Causes, Patterns, Trends." *Annual Review of Sociology* 24:395–421.

Keister, L. A. (2001) "Born to Pray and Save: An Investigation into the Role of Religion in Wealth Accumulation." Unpublished manuscript.

Kelly, J. E., Mosher, W. D, Duffer, A. P., and Kinsey, S. H. (1997) "Plan and Operation of the 1995 National Survey of Family Growth." *Vital and Health Statistics*, Series I. Hyatsville, MD.

Keysar, A. and Kosmin, B. A. (1995) "The Impact of Religious Identification on Differences in Educational Attainment Among American Women in 1990." *Journal for the Scientific Study of Religion* 34(1):49–62.

Lehrer, E. L. (1995) "The Effects of Religion on the Labor Supply of Married Women." *Social Science Research* 24:281–301. (Chapter 3 this volume.)

Lehrer, E. L. (1996a) "The Role of the Husband's Religion in the Economic and Demographic Behavior of Families." *Journal for the Scientific Study of Religion* 35(2):145–55.

Lehrer, E. L. (1996b) "Religion as a Determinant of Fertility." *Journal of Population Economics* 9:173–96. (Chapter 4 this volume.)

Lehrer, E. L. (1998) "Religious Intermarriage in the United States: Determinants and Trends." *Social Science Research* 27:245–63. (Chapter 2 this volume.)

Lehrer, E. L. (1999a) "Religion as a Determinant of Educational Attainment: An Economic Perspective." *Social Science Research* 28:358–79. (Chapter 6 this volume.)

Lehrer, E. L. (1999b) "Married Women's Labor Supply Behavior in the 1990s: Differences by Life-Cycle Stage." *Social Science Quarterly* 80(3):574–90.

Lehrer, E. L. (2000) "Religion as a Determinant of Entry into Cohabitation and Marriage." Pp. 227–52 in L. Waite, C. Bachrach, M. Hindin, E. Thomson, and A. Thornton (eds) *The Ties that Bind: Perspectives on Marriage and Cohabitation.* Hawthorne: Aldine de Gruyter.

Lehrer, E. L. (2004) "Religiosity as a Determinant of Educational Attainment: The Case of Conservative Protestant Women in the United States." *Review of Economics of the Household* 2(2):203–19.

Lehrer, E. L. and Chiswick, C. U. (1993) "Religion as a Determinant of Marital Stability." *Demography* 30(3):385–404. (Chapter 1 this volume.)

Marcum, J. P. (1981) "Explaining Fertility Differentials Among U.S. Protestants." *Social Forces* 60(2):532–43.

McMurry, M. (1978) "Religion and Women's Sex Role Traditionalism." *Sociological Focus* 11(2):81–95.

Meir, H. C. (1972) "Mother-Centeredness and College Youths' Attitudes Toward Social Equality for Women: Some Empirical Findings." *Journal of Marriage and the Family* 34(February):115–21.

Michael, R. T. (1979) "Determinants of Divorce." Pp. 223–68 L. Levy-Garboua (ed.) *Sociological Economics*. Beverly Hills, CA: Sage.

Michael, R. T. and Tuma, N. (1985) "Entry into Marriage and Parenthood by Young Men and Women: The Influence of Family Background." *Demography* 22(4):515–44.

Mosher, W. D., Williams, L. B., and Johnson, D. P. (1992) "Religion and Fertility in the United States: New Patterns." *Demography* 29(2):199–214.

Mosher, W. D. and Hendershot, G. E. (1984) "Religion and Fertility: A Replication." *Demography* 21(2):185–92.

Mosher, W. D., Johnson, D. P., and Horn, M. C. (1986) "Religion and Fertility in the United States: The Importance of Marriage Patterns and Hispanic Origin." *Demography* 23(3):367–80.

Oppenheimer, V. K. (1988) "A Theory of Marriage Timing." *American Journal of Sociology* 94:563–91.

Petersen, L. R. and Donnenwerth, G. V. (1997) "Secularization and the Influence of Religion on Beliefs about Premarital Sex." *Social Forces* 75(3):1071–89.

Sander, W. (1993) "Catholicism and Marriage in the United States." *Demography* 30(3):373–84.

Sander, W. (1995) *The Catholic Family: Marriage, Children, and Human Capital.* Boulder, CO: Westview Press.

Sherkat, D. E. (2000) "That They be Keepers of the Home: The Effect of Conservative Religion on Early and Late Transition into Housewifery." *Review of Religious Research* 41(3):344–58.

Sherkat, D. E. and Darnell, A. (1999) "The Effects of Parents' Fundamentalism on Children's Educational Attainment: Examining Differences by Gender and Children's Fundamentalism." *Journal for the Scientific Study of Religion* 38(1):23–35.

Smith, T. W. (1990) "Classifying Protestant Denominations." *Review of Religious Research* 31(3):225–45.

Smock, P. J. (2000) "Cohabitation in the United States: An Appraisal of Research Themes, Findings, and Implications." *Annual Review of Sociology* 26:1–20.

Stark, R. (1999) "Secularization, R.I.P." *Sociology of Religion* 60(3):249–73.

Stark, R. and Finke, R. (2000) *Acts of Faith: Explaining the Human Side of Religion.* Berkeley: University of California Press.

Sweet, J A. and Bumpass, L. L. (1990) "Religious Differentials in Marriage Behavior and Attitudes." NSFH Working Paper No. 15, University of Wisconsin.

Teachman, J. D. (1982) "Methodological Issues in the Analysis of Family Formation and Dissolution." *Journal of Marriage and the Family* 44(4):1037–53.

Teachman, J. D. (2002) "Stability across Cohorts in Divorce Risk Factors." *Demography* 39(2):331–52.

Thornton, A. (1979) "Religion and Fertility: The Case of Mormonism." *Journal of Marriage and the Family* 41(1):131–42.

Thornton, A., Axinn, W. G., and Hill, D. H. (1992) "Reciprocal Effects of Religiosity, Cohabitation, and Marriage." *American Journal of Sociology* 98(3):628–51.

Thornton, A., Axinn, W. G., and Teachman, J. D. (1995) "The Influence of School Enrollment and Accumulation on Cohabitation and Marriage in Early Adulthood." *American Sociological Review* 60(October):762–74.

Warner, S. R. (1993) "Work in Progress Toward a New Paradigm in the Sociology of Religion." *American Journal of Sociology* 98:1044–93.

Waters, M., Heath, W. C., and Watson, J. K. (1995) "A Positive Model of the Determination of Religious Affiliation." *Social Science Quarterly* 76(1):105–23.

Weiss, Y. and Willis, R. J. (1985) "Children as Collective Goods." *Journal of Labor Economics* 3:268–92.

Willis, R. J. and Haaga, J. G. (1996) "Economic Approaches to Understanding Nonmarital Fertility." Pp. 67–86 in J. B. Casterline, R. D. Lee, and K. A. Foote (eds) *Fertility in the United States: New Patterns, New Theories*. New York: The Population Council.

Willis, R. J. and Michael, R. T. (1994) "Innovation in Family Formation: Evidence on Cohabitation in the United States." Pp. 9–45 in J. Ermisch and N. Ogawa (eds) *The Family, the Market and the State in Ageing Societies*. Oxford: Clarendon Press.

Wilson, B. (1976) *Contemporary Transformations of Religion*. New York: Oxford University Press.

Wilcox, W. B. and Wolfinger, N. H. (2006) "Then Comes Marriage? Religion, Race, and Marriage in Urban America." *Social Science Research* 36:569–89.

9 Religion as a determinant of economic and demographic behavior in the United States *

A large body of literature documents that religion has widespread effects on the economic and demographic behavior of individuals and families in the United States, including the choice of marital partner, entry into cohabitation and marriage, divorce, fertility, women's work at home and in the labor market, education, wages, and wealth. Until now, these various relationships have been studied one at a time, in isolation. Using an analytical framework based on Gary Becker's theory of the economics of the family (1981), this paper critically reviews and synthesizes the theoretical and empirical research to date and identifies pathways through which religion has an impact on behavior. Gaps in knowledge are noted.

My main focus is on religious affiliation – the specific religious group to which an individual belongs – as a determinant of economic and demographic outcomes. I argue that religious affiliation matters because it has an impact on the perceived costs and the perceived benefits of various interrelated decisions that people make over the life cycle. In addition, for behaviors that pertain to married-couple households, as opposed to individuals, religion matters because it is a complementary trait within marriage, affecting many activities that a husband and wife engage in together.

Religiosity encompasses such dimensions as commitment to the religion, the strength of religious beliefs, and participation in religious activities individually or as part of a congregation. I contend that religiosity influences economic and demographic outcomes partly because it accentuates the effects of affiliation and partly because its generally positive influence on health and well-being can have repercussions for such outcomes.

The sections that follow review the role of religion in each of the economic and demographic outcomes cited above. The discussion focuses on the principal religious groups in the United States – mainline Protestants, conservative Protestants, Roman Catholics, Jews, and Mormons – as well as the unaffiliated.

* Reprinted from *Population and Development Review* 30(4):707–726, 2004.

Marital stability

In a pathbreaking paper, Becker (1973) developed an economic theory of marriage. One of his many useful insights is that in the optimal sorting in the marriage market, one finds negative assortative mating for traits that are substitutes and positive assortative mating for traits that are complements.[1] This idea has played a key role in subsequent economic analyses of the effects of religion on the behavior of married couples. Religion is a complementary trait within marriage, because it affects a large number of activities in which the spouses are involved together, as a couple, beyond the purely religious sphere. These include the education and upbringing of children, the allocation of time and money, the cultivation of social relationships, and often even the place of residence. As a result, there is greater efficiency in a household if husband and wife share the same religious beliefs. The other side of this argument is that a difference in religion between partners is generally a destabilizing force within a marriage. Several studies support the hypothesis that the probability of divorce is higher for religiously heterogamous couples (Bumpass and Sweet 1972; Becker et al. 1977; Michael 1979; Lehrer 1996c).

Not all religious intermarriages are the same, however. Analyses based on data from the 1987–88 National Survey of Families and Households (NSFH) reveal that the most unstable intermarriages include those in which (1) the beliefs of the two religious groups are very different (e.g., an interfaith union involving a Christian and a Jew); (2) one or both of the partners are affiliated with a religion that has sharply defined boundaries and has sought more separation from the broader culture (e.g., an interfaith union involving a conservative Protestant); or (3) one of the partners has no religious affiliation. The magnitude of the religious intermarriage effect is large. For a homogamous mainline Protestant couple with typical characteristics, the probability of marriage dissolution within five years is 0.20.[2] The corresponding probability for interfaith unions ranges from a low of 0.24 for those that are most stable to a high of 0.42 for the least stable (Lehrer and Chiswick 1993).

Among Catholics and Protestants in the United States, unions that achieve homogamy through religious conversion are at least as stable as those involving two partners who were brought up in the same religion (Lehrer and Chiswick 1993). An individual who switches to another faith to achieve religious homogamy usually does so following a process involving study of the new religion, and converts are often even more observant than those who grew up in the faith. The process of conversion appears to eliminate any destabilizing influences associated with husband and wife having grown up in different religious traditions. Whether conversion has a similar effect also for other groups, such as Jews and Mormons, is not known.

Beyond the distinction between heterogamy and homogamy, religion affects marital stability because the faith to which an individual belongs has an influence on the perceived costs of marital dissolution. Because virtually all religions are pro-family, affiliation with any faith should have a stabilizing influence, although the effect may be more pronounced in some cases than in others. Indeed, analyses of data from the 1987–88 NSFH reveal that by far the most unstable homogamous unions are those involving two religiously unaffiliated partners: for such unions the probability of dissolution by the fifth year is 0.36, compared to 0.20 for homogamous mainline Protestant unions. At the other extreme, homogamous Mormon marriages stand out for their high level of stability, with a probability of dissolution of 0.13 (Lehrer and Chiswick 1993). In the past, Catholic unions were unusually stable, a result attributed to the Catholic Church's prohibition against divorce (Michael 1979), but more recent work does not find a Catholic differential in this regard (Lehrer and Chiswick 1993).

Virtually nothing is known about the implications of religious heterogamy for children. Interfaith couples face three very different choices: to raise their children with no religion; to raise them in the faith of one of the parents; or to involve them to some degree in both religions. The first path may deprive children of the benefits associated with religious involvement during child-hood and adolescence, such as improved educational outcomes and fewer risky behaviors (Smith 2003; Waite and Lehrer 2003). While the other two paths provide such involvement, the implications for the children of possibly receiving conflicting messages, or of sharing religious activities with only one parent, have not been systematically studied.

The choice of marital partner

Given that marrying outside one's religion is generally destabilizing, why do so many people choose a partner of a different faith, often without a conversion? Becker (1981) was again the first scholar to address this question in the economics literature. He outlined various factors that would tend to make intermarriage more likely for a particular individual. His emphasis was on negative factors:

> The most plausible explanation is that persons enter mixed marriages even though they anticipate a higher probability of divorce because they do not expect to do better by further search and waiting. Perhaps they were unlucky in their search and became pregnant, or have aged and fear a diminishing market ... Some persons enter mixed marriages not because they are unlucky but because they are inefficient at discovering suitable prospects or have other characteristics that lower their expected gains from marriage.
>
> (1981, p. 232)

An extension of Becker's analysis considers a broader set of factors that influence the probability of entering an interfaith union (Chiswick and Lehrer 1991). The point of departure in this model is that religion is only one of many traits that are important in the marriage market, and tradeoffs are involved. Individuals face both benefits and costs from continued search for a same-faith partner; the optimal level of religious compatibility is that which equates the benefits and costs at the margin. This model predicts that a key determinant of the likelihood of intermarriage is the individual's commitment to the religion in which he or she was raised (which affects the benefits of continuing to search for a same-faith partner). Another determinant is the nature of the local marriage market: how difficult it is to find a coreligionist (which affects the costs of continuing to search for a same-faith partner). Subsequent empirical work has shown that those two factors are indeed important determinants of intermarriage (Lehrer 1998).

With regard to other factors, the effect of educational attainment on the probability of marrying outside one's religion is ambiguous a priori. Highly educated individuals generate marriage offers more easily and thus have lower search costs; this effect predicts a lower probability of intermarriage. At the same time, a higher level of schooling implies wider intellectual horizons and additional aspects of compatibility that may be traded off against compatibility in the religious sphere, implying a higher likelihood of intermarriage. Findings by Sherkat (2004) based on data from the 1973–94 General Social Surveys suggest that education is positively associated with the probability of intermarriage. Analyses conducted separately for Catholics, mainline Protestants, and conservative Protestants, using data from the 1987–88 NSFH, reveal a positive association only for the last of these (Lehrer 1998). Among the most highly educated conservative Protestants, higher levels of intellectual achievement and socioeconomic status (which may more easily be found by widening the search to include possible partners outside the religion) appear to represent an important aspect of marital compatibility that is traded off against religious compatibility.

Geographic mobility is another factor that affects the probability of religious intermarriage. Sherkat (2004) notes that migration increases the likelihood of marrying outside one's faith, because it provides opportunities to meet people of different backgrounds and disrupts social ties that constrain the choice of marital partner. At the same time, migration decisions may be endogenous: those who place a lower priority on religious homogamy may be more inclined to move. Sherkat (2004) also emphasizes the role of religious affiliation per se on the likelihood of placing an emphasis on religion when choosing a marital partner. He notes that intermarriage should be less common among people raised in traditions that claim exclusive access to supernatural rewards and traditions that impose high costs on members for marrying outside the faith.

The past several decades have witnessed an increase in the rate of intermarriage for mainline Protestants, Catholics, and Jews (Chiswick 1997; Lehrer 1998; Sherkat 2004). In contrast, the rate has remained remarkably stable for conservative Protestants (Lehrer 1998; Sherkat 2004). This pattern suggests a greater resistance over time to secularization among the stricter denominations, a behavior that may account in part for their continued strength (Iannaccone 1994).

Fertility

Some religions provide psychological and social rewards to couples who have many children, in the form of approval, social status, and blessings. As Stark and Finke (2000) have noted, the high fertility that Mormons have consistently displayed in the United States (Thornton 1979; Heaton 1986; Lehrer 1996a) can be interpreted as a rational response to such incentives. Similarly, Catholicism embodies strong pronatalist ideologies that raise the perceived benefits of having an additional child. Its teachings also forbid artificial forms of contraception, oppose abortion, and increase the costs of family planning (Sander 1995). Until the 1970s, these norms had been manifested in a distinctive pattern of high fertility. More recently, adherence to the teachings of the Catholic Church in these areas has weakened markedly, with a corresponding decline in family size (Jones and Westoff 1979; Mosher et al. 1986; Goldscheider and Mosher 1991).[3] Some aspects of conservative Protestant ideologies are also pronatalist, and the fertility of this group has been found to exceed that of mainline Protestants, though only by a small margin (Marcum 1981; Lehrer 1996a).

At the other end of the continuum, non-Orthodox Jews have consistently displayed unusually low fertility (Della Pergola 1980; Mosher and Hendershot 1984). In this case no doctrines in the religion per se encourage small family size, so explanations must be sought in other aspects of Judaism, the Jewish community, and its interactions with the broader society (Goldscheider 1971). The economics literature has suggested that, historically, Jews have faced a higher price of having an extra child (the reasons include higher rates of urbanization and female literacy) and may therefore have chosen to substitute expenditures per child ("quality") for quantity (Becker 1981; Chiswick 1988). In addition, as elaborated later in this chapter, Jewish women attain very high levels of schooling; the persistently low fertility in the Jewish community today is closely related to such attainment (Hurst and Mott 2003).

Most of what we know about fertility differences by religion is based on studies that use information on the religious affiliation of women. Yet the male partner's religion plays a role also, in part because the adverse effect of religious intermarriage on the stability of unions has implications for fertility – a point first noted by Becker et al. (1977). The authors observe that if the spouses are mismatched along some important dimension, such as education or religion, they may have reason to believe that their union is fragile. If so, both partners would have incentives to restrict their investments in spouse-specific human capital – children being the main form – because such investments decline irreversibly in value following the dissolution of the union. This "marital stability effect" is one pathway of causality linking the religious affiliation of both partners to fertility. It predicts that marrying outside one's religion depresses fertility.

There is a second pathway. If the spouses belong to different faiths, they may face conflicting incentives with regard to fertility. The resulting "bargaining effect," which refers to how the spouses negotiate these differences, may operate in the same direction as the "marital stability effect," or it may exert a countervailing influence, depending on the specific pair of religions involved. For example, if a Catholic woman marries someone affiliated with the Mormon faith (which has a more pronounced pronatalist theology), the bargaining effect suggests that her fertility will be higher than if she had married within her faith. The opposite would hold if she were to choose a partner who has no religious affiliation (and hence no pronatalist ideologies).

Evidence based on data from the 1987–88 NSFH suggests that both the marital stability effect and the bargaining effect play a role (Lehrer 1996a, 1996b). For example, for a couple with typical characteristics for all other variables, the predicted completed family size is 3.3 children if both spouses are Mormon, compared to 2.4–2.5 children if only the wife is Mormon. In this case, both the marital stability and bargaining effects imply that interfaith marriage has a negative impact on fertility. In contrast, when Protestant women marry outside their faith, there is no discernible influence on family size. In this case, although the intermarriage effect predicts, as always, that marrying outside the faith should depress fertility, the bargaining effect would exert an opposing force if the male partner is affiliated with the Catholic or Mormon faith. This discussion underscores the need to pay attention to the male partner's religion in future studies of fertility.

Women's work at home and in the labor market

The fertility differentials by religion discussed above may be expected to have implications for female time allocation patterns.[4] In addition, religious teachings influence such patterns directly. The Mormon and conservative Protestant faiths make a sharp distinction between male and female social and economic roles, encouraging the traditional division of labor within the household when young children are present. Consistent with the view that such religions provide institutionalized moral support and psychological rewards to mothers who stay home with their young children, previous research documents a lower level of female employment among members of these faiths (Heaton and Cornwall 1989; Chadwick and Garrett 1995; Lehrer 1995, 1999a). Along similar lines, Sherkat (2000) finds that young women who believe the Bible is the inerrant word of God are more likely than their nonfundamentalist counterparts to be housewives early in the life course. At the other end of the spectrum, although Jewish women are known to restrict their participation in the labor market when their children are young (Chiswick 1986), their overall commitment to labor market activities is stronger than that of women of other affiliations (Hartman and Hartman 1996).

Early studies found that Catholics emphasized the distinction between appropriate male and female roles (Meier 1972; McMurry 1978). More recent analyses, however, suggest that Catholics have become more egalitarian (Brinkerhoff and MacKie 1984) and indeed less traditional in this regard than both groups of Protestants (Brinkerhoff and MacKie 1985). The direction of this change mirrors transformations that have taken place in the behavior of Catholics on issues related to childrearing (Alwin 1984). Consistent with these changes, the patterns of employment for Catholic women today do not differ significantly from those of their mainline Protestant counterparts (Lehrer 1995).

As is the case for marital fertility, decisions regarding the allocation of married women's time are influenced not only by the wife's affiliation, but also by the husband's. To the extent that women in interfaith unions anticipate a higher probability of marital dissolution, they have incentives to invest more in skills that are specific to the labor market, as insurance against the possibility of a divorce. In addition, if the spouses are affiliated with different religions, they may face a dual structure of perceived costs and benefits associated with female employment, and may therefore need to resolve the resulting conflicts. Thus the "marital stability" and "bargaining" effects that apply to fertility also play a role in women's employment.

Analyses of data on married women with young children from the 1987–88 NSFH confirm the salience of these two effects (Lehrer 1995). For example, for women with typical characteristics for all other variables, the predicted probability of nonemployment is 0.55 in the case of a homogamous conservative Protestant union, compared to 0.35 if only the wife is a conservative Protestant. This pronounced difference reflects the fact that the bargaining effect reinforces the marital stability effect in this instance, and both effects lead the woman to work more in the labor market in the case of outmarriage. In contrast, the bargaining effect may work in the opposite direction in the case of Catholics (e.g., if a Catholic woman marries a conservative Protestant), and the probability of nonemployment for Catholic women in homogamous unions, 0.36, is the same as that of their counterparts in interfaith marriages.[5]

Ellison and Bartkowski (2002) examine the effects of religion on another aspect of time allocation, namely, the division of household work between husband and wife. Bivariate analyses reveal that homogamous conservative Protestant households are different from other homogamous households: in the former, the gender segregation of household work is greater, with women spending about 4.5 more hours per week performing tasks classified as typically female; the gap between the two types of households in the overall hours of household work is nearly identical. Couples in which only one partner is a conservative Protestant also display more traditional patterns than their homogamous nonconservative Protestant counterparts. The differences narrow somewhat but remain significant in regressions that include measures of the wife's education and of both partners' labor market activities.

Education, wages, and wealth

Research on the links between religious affiliation and educational attainment among non-Hispanic whites reveals that the mean years of schooling is highest for Jews (16.9 for males, 15.8 for females); lowest for conservative Protestants (13.3, 12.9), with Catholics (14.3, 13.7) and mainline Protestants (14.5, 14.0) at the center of the distribution (Lehrer 1999b; see also Chiswick 1988, 1993; Darnell and Sherkat 1997; Sherkat and Darnell 1999; Lehrer 2008).

A model of the supply of and demand for funds for investments in schooling, developed by Becker and Chiswick (1966) and Becker (1967), has been applied to interpret these differentials within a human capital framework: religious affiliation is viewed as reflecting distinctive features of the home environment that affect both the returns to and costs of additional investments in education (Chiswick 1988; Lehrer 1999b). On the demand side, religious affiliation can affect the returns from investments in education: among religious groups characterized by larger benefits from schooling, the incentives to pursue education are stronger and thus a higher level of attainment is expected, other things being equal. On the supply side, religious affiliation can affect parents' willingness and ability to supply funds for investments in schooling: a higher level of education is expected for religious groups in which parents have a greater willingness and ability to supply funds for such investments, other things equal.

More specifically, in this model, described in Figure 9.1, the demand curve (D) shows the marginal rate of return derived from each additional dollar spent on education. The slope is negative in part because of diminishing marginal returns to additional schooling. The supply curve (S) shows the marginal rate of interest on funds borrowed (or not lent) to finance investments in education. Its upward slope reflects the assumption that obtaining additional funds is increasingly expensive as more human capital investments are undertaken. The optimal level of investment in schooling is E_0. At this point, the marginal interest cost of funds is equal to the marginal rate of return (r_0.). This model yields predictions not only about the level of educational attainment, but also about the rate of return obtained from investments in schooling. The model thus makes it possible to ascertain the relative importance of demand and supply forces in causing unusually high or low schooling levels for various groups.

For the case of Jews, Chiswick (1988) presents arguments suggesting that both curves are further to the right than for other groups. On the supply side, the "diaspora hypothesis" posits that, historically, Jews have placed a high priority on making investments in the human capital of their children, as these are more portable than investments in physical capital (Brenner and Kiefer 1981).[6] This implies a willingness to invest more in human capital at any given interest rate, that is, a supply curve that is further to the right.

On the demand side, Chiswick (1988) notes that Jewish family size tends to

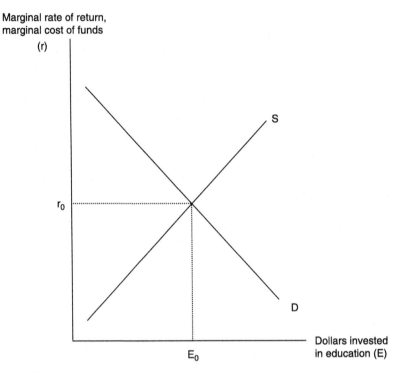

Figure 9.1 Demand and supply of funds for investments in schooling.

be small, and large amounts of resources, especially maternal time, are invested in each child during the early, formative years. These investments increase the productivity of formal education and lead to a demand curve that is further to the right. In addition, recent research has noted that Judaism, with its emphasis on the reading and analysis of Hebrew religious texts, is a human-capital-intensive religion, characterized by a high level of complementarity between religious and secular human capital (Chiswick 1999). These characteristics of Judaism also imply a demand curve that is further to the right.

Empirical analyses find that Jews not only have a high level of schooling but also earn a high rate of return on their investments (Chiswick 1988; Lehrer 1999b). These findings imply that the high educational attainment of Jews is primarily due to the demand-side forces outlined above.

With regard to conservative Protestants, there are reasons to believe that the level of schooling is low for both supply and demand reasons. As Sherkat and Darnell observe:

> the humanistic values openly taught or implied in secular curricula are frequently in conflict with conservative Protestants' conceptions of authority and submission – particularly the authority of the Bible as the

inerrant word of God, and the need for children to submit to the will of their parents.

(1999, p. 24)

Parents' reservations about the learning that takes place in secular institutions are particularly pronounced at the college level; at the same time, the opportunities to attend religious institutions of higher learning are limited and expensive. These concerns about possible negative effects of secular schooling imply that the supply curve for conservative Protestants is further to the left, because, at any given interest rate, parents would be willing to invest less in the education of their children.

On the demand side, a conservative Protestant upbringing may be associated with an authoritarian approach to knowledge and a rejection of critical inquiry and unconventional modes of thinking, implying lower levels of certain types of home investments in child quality (Sherkat and Darnell 1999). In addition, Darnell and Sherkat (1997) note that conservative Protestant parents often discourage their children from taking college preparatory courses, out of a concern that such courses may be harmful to them. As a result, children raised in conservative Protestant homes often acquire less human capital in their formative years and may thus be less able to benefit from college; hence the demand curve is further to the left.

Empirical analyses based on data from the 1987–88 NSFH show that the relatively low schooling level of conservative Protestants is accompanied by a rate of return that does not differ significantly from that of mainline Protestants, suggesting that in practice both the demand-side and supply-side forces described above play important roles (Lehrer 1999b).

Regarding the religiously unaffiliated, evidence is beginning to accumulate that they attain relatively low levels of schooling (Keysar and Kosmin 1995; Glass 1999; Lehrer 2008). Less is known about the educational achievement of Mormons; the studies to date report conflicting findings (Albrecht and Heaton 1984; Keysar and Kosmin 1995; Lehrer 2008).

Given that educational attainment is a key determinant of subsequent performance in the labor market, differences by religious affiliation in years of schooling should lead to corresponding differences in wages. The wages of Jews are indeed substantially higher than those of people affiliated with other faiths (Chiswick 1993; Lehrer 2008). In addition to their high level of education, other contributing factors include access to academic institutions of higher quality and a faith that emphasizes pursuits in this world as opposed to the afterlife.

The wages of conservative Protestant women have been found to be lower than those of their mainline Protestant counterparts (Lehrer 2008). This result has been interpreted as due in part to the relatively low level of schooling and labor market experience for this group. In addition, the greater asymmetry in the intrahousehold division of labor in conservative Protestant families noted by Ellison and Bartkowski (2002) decreases the amount of time and energy that women have for market work. The result may be lower productivity on the job and lower wages (Becker 1985). There is also evidence that the wages of Mormon and unaffiliated women are lower than those of mainline Protestant women (Lehrer 2008).

Another measure of economic well-being is wealth. Keister (2003) finds that the patterns of differences by religion in wealth closely mirror the differentials by education and wages described above. Jews have the highest level of wealth; conservative Protestants are at the other end of the spectrum, with mainline Protestants and Catholics at the center of the distribution. In explaining the unusually high levels of wealth among Jews, Keister notes that in addition to their high educational attainment, their low fertility contributes to wealth accumulation across the generations. The inter-generational transmission of skills conducive to financial success also plays a role, as does the strong emphasis placed by the Jewish theology on worldly pursuits. Keister suggests that a set of circumstances that is just the opposite explains in part the relatively low levels of wealth among conservative Protestants.

The timing of entry into first union and the choice of whether to cohabit

Religious affiliation has an impact on decisions related to entry into first union (e.g., whether it is a formal marriage or cohabitation; the timing of the union), largely because of its effects on the various outcomes reviewed above. Women raised as conservative Protestants and as Mormons have incentives to marry early, because their faith encourages an orientation to home-based activities and also promotes very high fertility in the case of Mormons. The relatively low schooling level of conservative Protestants is another factor operating in the same direction. At the other extreme, Jewish women have incentives to delay entry into marriage for several interrelated reasons: their high educational attainment, their low desired level of fertility, and their strong commitment to the labor market.

Empirical studies of unions formed before the mid-1980s find that religious differentials in this area are pronounced (Thornton et al. 1992; Sander 1993; Lehrer 2000). Analyses of the post baby-boom generation, based on data from the 1995 National Survey of Family Growth (NSFG), show that such differences remain large: for women with typical characteristics, the prob-ability of early marriage (by age 20) is 0.02 for Jews, compared to 0.17 for conservative Protestants and Mormons. Mainline Protestants and the unaffiliated are at the center of the distribution, with a probability of 0.08–0.09 (Lehrer 2004a). More recent studies also show that while the behavior of Catholics has converged to the mainline Protestant pattern in most domains of family life, their behavior has remained distinctive in the area of entry into marriage: their probability of having entered first marriage by age 20 is only 0.05. It appears that the Catholic proscription against divorce continues to exert some effect, encouraging Catholics to search longer and more carefully in the marriage market.

Cohabitation has been found to be least likely for Mormons and most likely for individuals without religious affiliation (Lehrer 2000, 2004a). Examination of data from the 1995 NSFG shows that for women with typical characteristics, the probability of having cohabited by age 20 is 0.12 for Mormons; for the unaffiliated, the probability is twice that amount (Lehrer 2004a). The low prevalence of cohabitation among Mormons is due in part to their conservative attitudes toward premarital sex, which imply high subjective costs associated with entering informal living arrangements (Sweet and Bumpass 1990). With their high fertility rate, Mormon women also have an incentive to avoid the more fragile cohabitation arrangements, given that stable two-parent households are the optimal institutional arrangement for raising children (Weiss and Willis 1985; Willis and Haaga 1996). Furthermore, marriage provides greater economic security (Grossbard-Shechtman 1993), making it especially attractive to Mormon women, who tend to orient their investments to home production when their children are young. At the other extreme, the unusually high levels of cohabitation among the unaffiliated reflect the low subjective costs for this group of sharing living arrangements without a legal contract.

Countervailing influences are present for Jews and conservative Protestants. The liberal attitudes of Jews toward premarital sex and their low fertility and high levels of female education and employment combine to produce a high prevalence of informal unions. However, the elevated earnings of Jewish men point in the opposite direction, since better economic prospects for the male partner imply stronger incentives to choose the arrangement that involves greater commitment, that is, marriage (Willis and Michael 1994). For the opposite reasons, the net impact is also ambiguous for conservative Protestants.

The empirical evidence for Jews is contradictory. While some studies find that they stand out for their high rate of cohabitation (Willis and Michael 1994; Lehrer 2000), no significant effect could be discerned in an analysis of a more recent data set, possibly because of small sample size (Lehrer 2004a). For conservative Protestants, the effects described above appear to cancel out, as their prevalence of cohabitation is not significantly different from that of mainline Protestants (Lehrer 2000, 2004a).

Given that the behavior of Catholics has converged to the mainline Protestant pattern in most aspects of family life, it is not surprising that they do not differ much from mainline Protestants in the area of cohabitation. One study (Lehrer 2004a) finds a small difference, with Catholics somewhat less likely to have cohabited by age 20 (a probability of 0.16, as opposed to 0.20); another finds no difference (Lehrer 2000).

The "no religion" category and the role of religiosity

Most research on the effects of religious affiliation has paid little or no attention to the role of religiosity, in part because the data sets employed have often lacked adequate measures of this dimension of religion. For example, the numerous studies reviewed above that used the 1987–88 National Survey of Families and Households were hampered by the fact that the survey only included a measure of religiosity as of the interview date, a variable that is endogenous to most outcomes of interest.

A main theme running through this note is that religious affiliation influences economic and demographic behavior because it has an impact on the perceived costs and benefits of various decisions made by individuals and families over the life cycle. The effects should therefore be stronger for those individuals who participate more frequently in religious observances and adhere more closely to the teachings of their faith. For example, the likelihood that a Mormon woman will choose to avoid informal cohabiting arrangements should be more pronounced if she is more religious. Studies that focus on religious affiliation and include analyses of the effects of religiosity generally make this argument either implicitly or explicitly (e.g., Lehrer 2004a; Read 2004).

Recently, however, it has become clear that the religiosity effects are more complex because, as a growing body of literature shows, participation in religious activities per se is associated with benefits in a wide range of areas (Smith 2003; Waite and Lehrer 2003). In particular, religious participation among young people has been linked to a lower probability of substance abuse and juvenile delinquency (Donahue and Benson 1995); a lower incidence of depression among some groups (Harker 2001); delayed sexual debut (Bearman and Bruckner 2001) and entry into cohabitation (Lehrer 2004a); more positive attitudes toward marriage and having children and more negative attitudes toward unmarried sex and premarital childbearing (Marchena and Waite 2002).[7]

The discussion above suggests that religiosity can have an impact on economic and demographic variables through two distinct channels. A higher level of religiosity may (1) accentuate the effects associated with religious affiliation and (2) lead to better outcomes because of its generally salutary effects on well-being and health. A recent study illustrates how these two channels may exert countervailing forces (Lehrer 2004b). As I noted above, conservative Protestants have a lower level of educational attainment than their mainline Protestant counterparts, because various aspects of conservative Protestant theology tend to discourage investments in secular education. Using the standard argument that religiosity should heighten the effects of affiliation, one would predict that among conservative Protestants, those who are most religious should be at the greatest educational disadvantage.

In fact, evidence suggests that the opposite is the case (Lehrer 2004b). Analyses based on data from the 1995 National Survey of Family Growth show that among young women raised as conservative Protestants, those who attended church at least once a month during adolescence attain more schooling than their counterparts raised in less observant homes. The zero-order effect is a difference of one year of schooling; the gap narrows to eight-tenths of a year when background factors are controlled. This result underscores the positive effects of religious involvement for children in the area of educational attainment: children who grow up in homes where there is some religious involvement have higher levels of social capital and mental well-being and are better able to benefit from investments in education; in the language of the human capital model presented earlier, they have a demand curve that is further to the right.[8] This finding also illustrates that one should no longer continue to assume that a higher level of religiosity merely accentuates existing differences across religious groups.

Just as the literature on the effects of religious affiliation on economic and demographic outcomes has paid too little attention to the role of religiosity, numerous studies on the effects of religiosity largely ignore religious affiliation. For example, in all of the research on how religiosity influences the quality and stability of marital unions, intra- and interfaith couples are lumped together (e.g., Glenn and Supancic 1984; Booth et al. 1995; Call and Heaton 1997). This approach does not consider that while a high level of religiosity among both partners may be a positive factor for homogamous marriages, it is most likely a negative factor for heterogamous marriages. If both partners are strongly committed to their own, distinct faiths, the consequences for marital quality and stability should be worse than if neither actively practices his or her religion (Waite and Lehrer 2003). The results from studies in this area thus reflect a mixture of positive and negative effects and allow no clear interpretation.

Yet another reason for seeking more integration between religious affiliation and religiosity in future research is that levels of religiosity are not uniform across the various groups. For example, conservative Protestants tend to participate in church services more frequently than members of most other religious groups. Thus, if analyses do not consider differences in religious involvement, some of the estimated "conservative Protestant" effect may actually be a religiosity effect.

Individuals who report "no religion" constitute a relatively small and heterogeneous group: it includes atheists, agnostics, and persons who were raised with no affiliation owing to other circumstances (e.g., being a child from an interfaith marriage). For this reason, many studies on the effects of religious affiliation on economic and demographic outcomes have omitted this group. The growing literature on the effects of religiosity helps interpret results from those studies that have included it. As Glenn (1987) has noted, it is useful to think of the "no religion" category as one extreme on the religiosity scale. Thus, the benefits typically associated with religious involvement are not available to the unaffiliated. This perspective provides a consistent interpretation for the findings about this group reviewed earlier, namely, that those with no religious affiliation tend to display lower levels of educational attainment and wages, and that rates of divorce are high among couples in which one or both partners are unaffiliated.

Conclusions

This chapter has underscored the fruitfulness of thinking about religious affiliation in terms of how it influences the costs and benefits of various interrelated decisions made over the life cycle by individuals and families; it has also shown that the complementarity of religion within the context of marriage makes it essential to consider the affiliations of both spouses. In addition, it has demonstrated that in interpreting the effects of religion, seeing the entire economic and demographic picture contributes significantly to a good understanding of any given piece.

Recent research has added to our knowledge of the conditions under which religion tends to exert the strongest effects on fertility. As McQuillan observes:

> [R]eligious values, while important, are likely to play a critical role in shaping demographic behavior only when religious authorities have at their disposal a menu of rewards and sanctions that will encourage the faithful to conform. This, in turn, is most apt to come about when churches are able both to build a network of religious institutions that play a formative role in the lives of members and to exercise influence over civil institutions in society as well.
>
> (2004, pp. 46–7)

It seems likely that such conditions are relevant not only to fertility, which is the focus of McQuillan's analysis, but also to other demographic and economic outcomes. Further research in this direction is likely to expand understanding of the pathways through which affiliation with various religious groups gives rise to differences in costs and benefits, and the circumstances under which such differences are most important.

Future studies should build on what we have learned in the process of integrating our knowledge of the effects of religious affiliation with the large and growing body of research on the generally beneficial influences of some religious involvement, whatever the faith may be. Future investigations should also pay more attention to the distinct patterns for minorities, including African Americans, Hispanics, and Asian Americans, as most studies to date have focused only on non-Hispanic whites. Efforts in this direction have begun (e.g., Read 2004; Wilcox and Wolfinger 2007). Another important avenue for future research is to compare the empirical regularities described here, for the case of the United States, with the patterns that prevail elsewhere, in other industrialized countries and in less developed economies.

Acknowledgments

Earlier versions of this chapter were presented at the 2002 meetings of the Society for the Scientific Study of Religion at a session honoring Gary Becker and his contributions to the economics of religion; at the seminar series of the Waterhead Center for International Affairs, Harvard University; and at Economics Department workshops at George Mason University and the University of Illinois at Chicago. For many helpful suggestions and comments, I am indebted to participants at these seminars, to Barry Chiswick, and to anonymous referees.

Notes

1   Substitute traits imply gains from a within-marriage division of labor; complementary traits are relevant to activities that husband and wife do jointly.
2   In the survival function, the control variables (which are all categorical) are set at the modal categories.
3   As discussed later in the text, the behavior of Catholics has also converged to the mainline Protestant pattern in many other areas. For a discussion of the role of the Second Vatican Council and Pope Paul VI's Encyclical *Humanae Vitae* in these transformations, see D'Antonio and Cavanaugh (1983) and Dolan (1985).
4   Causality also flows in the opposite direction. See Lehrer and Nerlove (1986) for a discussion of reciprocal causality between fertility and female employment decisions.
5   In a recent analysis along these lines, Read (2004) emphasizes the importance of gender role traditionalism and homogamy in the labor market decisions of women of Arab origin in the United States.
6   See Ayal and Chiswick (1983) for additional discussion of this hypothesis. The authors emphasize that only some investments in human capital are highly transferable, being equally productive in all locations. Others (such as an education in law) are not portable across national boundaries.
7   Under certain circumstances, the effects of religious involvement can be adverse; see Waite and Lehrer (2003).
8   Earlier research found beneficial effects of religious participation on other educational outcomes, including school attendance (Freeman 1986); test scores and educational expectations (Regnerus 2000); and time spent on homework, advanced mathematics credits earned, and the probability of earning a high school diploma, among other measures (Muller and Ellison 2001).

References

Albrecht, S. L. and Heaton, T. B. (1984) "Secularization, Higher Education, and Religiosity." *Review of Religious Research* 26(1):43–58.
Alwin, D. F. (1984) "Trends in Parental Socialization Values: Detroit, 1958–1983." *American Journal of Sociology* 90(2):359–82.
Ayal, E. B. and Chiswick, B. R. (1983) "The Economics of the Diaspora Revisited." *Economic Development and Cultural Change* 31(4):861–75.
Bearman, P. S. and Bruckner, H. (2001) "Promising the Future: Virginity Pledges and First Intercourse." *American Journal of Sociology* 106(4):859–912.
Becker, G. S. (1967) "Human Capital and the Personal Distribution of Income." Wotynsky Lecture No. 1. Ann Arbor, MI: University of Michigan Press.
Becker, G. S. (1973) "A Theory of Marriage." Pp. 299–344 in T. W. Schultz (ed.)

Economics of the Family Marriage, Children, and Human Capital. Chicago: University of Chicago Press.

Becker, G. S. (1981) *A Treatise on the Family.* Cambridge, MA: Harvard University Press.

Becker, G. S. (1985) "Human Capital, Effort, and the Sexual Division of Labor." *Journal of Labor Economics* 3(1):S33–S58.

Becker, G. S. and Chiswick, B. R. (1966) "Education and the Distribution of Earnings." *American Economic Review* 56 (May):358–69.

Becker, G. S., Landes, E. M., and Michael, R. T. (1977) "An Economic Analysis of Marital Instability." *Journal of Political Economy* 85(6):1141–87.

Booth, A., Johnson, D. R., Branaman, A., and Sica, A. (1995) "Belief and Behavior: Does Religion Matter in Today's Marriage?", *Journal of Marriage and the Family* 57(3):661–71.

Brenner, R. and Kiefer, N. M. (1981) "The Economics of the Diaspora: Discrimination and Occupational Structure." *Economic Development and Cultural Change* (April):517–33.

Brinkerhoff, M. B. and MacKie, M. M. (1984) "Religious Denominations' Impact Upon Gender Attitudes: Some Methodological Implications." *Review of Religious Research* 25(4):365–78.

Brinkerhoff, M. B. and MacKie, M. M. (1985) "Religion and Gender: A Comparison of Canadian and American Student Attitudes." *Journal of Marriage and the Family* 47(2):415–29.

Bumpass, L. L. and Sweet, J. A. (1972) "Differentials in Marital Stability: 1970." *American Sociological Review* 37(6):754–66.

Call, V. R. and Heaton, T. B. (1997) "Religious Influence on Marital Stability." *Journal for the Scientific Study of Religion* 36(3):382–92.

Chadwick, B. A. and Garrett, H. D. (1995) "Women's Religiosity and Employment: The LDS Experience." *Review of Religious Research* 36(3):277–93.

Chiswick, B. (1986) "Labor Supply and Investments in Child Quality: A Study of Jewish and non-Jewish Women." *Review of Economics and Statistics* 68(4):700–3.

Chiswick, B. (1988) "Differences in Education and Earnings across Racial and Ethnic Groups: Tastes, Discrimination, and Investments in Child Quality." *Quarterly Journal of Economics* 103(3):571–97.

Chiswick, B. (1993) "The Skills and Economic Status of American Jewry: Trends Over the Last Half-Century." *Journal of Labor Economics* 11(1):229–42.

Chiswick, C. (1997) "Determinants of Religious Intermarriage: Are Jews Really Different?" Pp. 247–57 in S. Della Pergola and J. Even (eds) *Papers in Jewish Demography, 1993, in Memory of U. O. Schmelz.* Jerusalem: World Union of Jewish Studies.

Chiswick, C. (1999) "An Economic Model of Jewish Continuity." *Contemporary Jewry* 20:30–56.

Chiswick, C. and Lehrer, E. L. (1991) "Religious Intermarriage: An Economic Perspective." *Contemporary Jewry* 12:21–34.

D'Antonio, W. V. and Cavanaugh, J. M. (1983) "Roman Catholicism and the Family." Pp. 141–62 in W. V. D'Antonio and J. Aldous (eds) *Families and Religions: Conflict and Change in Modern Society.* Beverly Hills, CA: Sage.

Darnell, A. and Sherkat, E. D. (1997) "The Impact of Protestant Fundamentalism on Educational Attainment." *American Sociological Review* 62 (April):306–15.

Della Pergola, S. (1980) "Patterns of American Jewish Fertility." *Demography* 17(3):261–73.

Dolan, J. P. (1985) *The American Catholic Experience: A History from Colonial Times to the Present.* Garden City, NY: Doubleday.

Donahue, M. J. and Benson, L. P. (1995) "Religion and the Well-Being of Adolescents." *Journal of Social Issues* 51(2):145–60.

Ellison, C. G. and Bartkowski, P. J. (2002) "Conservative Protestantism and the Division of Household Labor Among Married Couples." *Journal of Family Issues* 23(8):950–85.

Freeman, R. B. (1986) "Who Escapes? The Relationship of Churchgoing and Other Background Factors to the Socioeconomic Performance of Black Male Youths from Inner-City Tracts." Pp. 353–76 in R. B. Freeman and H. J. Holzer (eds) *The Black Youth Employment Crisis.* Chicago: University of Chicago Press.

Glass, J. (1999) "Growing Up Fundamentalist: Effects on Women's Early Life Course Transitions and Adult Attainment." Presented at the Annual Meeting of the Population Association of America, New York.

Glenn, N. D. (1987) "The Trend in 'No Religion' Respondents to U.S. National Surveys, Late 1950s to Early 1980s." *The Public Opinion Quarterly* 51(3):293–314.

Glenn, N. D. and Supancic, M. (1984) "The Social and Demographic Correlates of Divorce and Separation in the United States: An Update and Reconsideration." *Journal of Marriage and the Family* 46(3):563–75.

Goldscheider, C. (1971) *Population, Modernization, and Social Structure.* Boston, MA: Little Brown.

Goldscheider, C. and Mosher, D. W. (1991) "Patterns of Contraceptive Use in the United States: The Importance of Religious Factors." *Studies in Family Planning* 22(2):102–15.

Grossbard-Shechtman, S. (1993) *On the Economics of Marriage: A Theory of Marriage, Labor, and Divorce.* Boulder, CO: Westview Press.

Harker, K. (2001) "Immigrant Generation, Assimilation, and Adolescent Psychological Well-Being." *Social Forces* 79(3):969–1004.

Hartman, M. and Hartman, H. (1996) *Gender Equality and American Jews.* Albany, NY: State University of New York Press.

Heaton, T. B. (1986) "How Does Religion Influence Fertility? The Case of Mormons." *Journal for the Scientific Study of Religion* 25(2):248–58.

Heaton, T. B. and Cornwall, M. (1989) "Religious Group Variation in the Socioeconomic Status and Family Behavior of Women." *Journal for the Scientific Study of Religion* 28(3):283–99.

Hurst, D. S. and Mott, L. F. (2003) "Jewish Fertility and Population Sustenance: Contemporary Issues and Evidence." Unpublished manuscript, Ohio State University.

Iannaccone, L. (1994) "Why Strict Churches Are Strong." *American Journal of Sociology* 99(5):1180–211.

Jones, E. F. and Westoff, F. C. (1979) "The End of 'Catholic' Fertility." *Demography* 16(2):209–18.

Keister, L. A. (2003) "Religion and Wealth: The Role of Religious Affiliation and Participation in Early Adult Asset Accumulation." *Social Forces* 82:173–205.

Keysar, A. and Kosmin, B. (1995) "The Impact of Religious Identification on Differences in Educational Attainment Among American Women in 1990." *Journal for the Scientific Study of Religion* 34(1):49–62.

Lehrer, E. L. (1995) "The Effects of Religion on the Labor Supply of Married Women." *Social Science Research* 24:281–301. (Chapter 3 this volume.)

Lehrer, E. L. (1996a) "Religion as a Determinant of Fertility." *Journal of Population Economics* 9:173–96. (Chapter 4 this volume.)

Lehrer, E. L. (1996b) "The Role of the Husband's Religion on the Economic and Demographic Behavior of Families." *Journal for the Scientific Study of Religion* 35(2):145–55.

Lehrer, E. L. (1996c) "The Determinants of Marital Stability: A Comparative Analysis of First and Higher Order Marriages." Pp. 91–121 in T. P. Schultz (ed.) *Research in Population Economics* 8. Greenwich, CT: JAI Press.

Lehrer, E. L. (1998) "Religious Intermarriage in the United States: Determinants and Trends." *Social Science Research* 27:245–63. (Chapter 2 this volume.)

Lehrer, E. L. (1999a) "Married Women's Labor Supply Behavior in the 1990s: Differences by Life-Cycle Stage." *Social Science Quarterly* 80(3):574–90.

Lehrer, E. L. (1999b) "Religion as a Determinant of Educational Attainment: An Economic Perspective." *Social Science Research* 28:358–79. (Chapter 6 this volume.)

Lehrer, E. L. (2000) "Religion as a Determinant of Entry into Cohabitation and Marriage." Pp. 227–252 in L. Waite, C. Bachrach, M. Hindin, E. Thomson, and A. Thornton (eds) *The Ties that Bind: Perspectives on Marriage and Cohabitation.* Hawthorne, NY: Aldine de Gruyter.

Lehrer, E. L. (2004a) "The Role of Religion in Union Formation: An Economic Perspective." *Population Research and Policy Review* 23:161–85. (Chapter 8 this volume.)

Lehrer, E. L. (2004b) "Religiosity as a Determinant of Educational Attainment: The Case of Conservative Protestant Women in the United States." *Review of Economics of the Household* 2(2):203–19.

Lehrer, E. L. (2008) "Religious Affiliation and Participation as Determinants of Women's Educational Attainment and Wages." Forthcoming in C. Ellison and R. Hummer (eds) *Religion, Family Life, and Health in the United States.* Chapel Hill, NC: Rutgers University Press.

Lehrer, E. L. and Chiswick, C. U. (1993) "Religion as a Determinant of Marital Stability." *Demography* 30(3):385–404. (Chapter 1 this volume.)

Lehrer, E. L. and Nerlove, M. (1986) "Female Labor Force Behavior and Fertility in the United States." *Annual Review of Sociology* 12:181–204.

Marchena, E. and Waite, L. J. (2002) "Re-Assessing Family Goals and Attitudes in Late Adolescence: The Effects of Natal Family Experiences and Early Family Formation." Pp. 97–127 in R. Lesthaeghe (ed.) *Meaning and Choice: Value Orientations and Life Course Decisions.* Brussels: The Netherlands Interdisciplinary Demographic Institute.

Marcum, J. P. (1981) "Explaining Fertility Differentials among U.S. Protestants." *Social Forces* 60(2):532–43.

McMurry, M. (1978) "Religion and Women's Sex Role Traditionalism." *Sociological Focus* 11(2):81–95.

McQuillan, K. (2004) "When Does Religion Influence Fertility?" *Population and Development Review* 30(1):25–56.

Meier, H. C. (1972) "Mother-Centeredness and College Youths' Attitudes Toward Social Equality for Women: Some Empirical Findings." *Journal of Marriage and the Family* 34(February):115–21.

Michael, R. (1979) "Determinants of Divorce." Pp. 223–68 in L. Levy-Garboua (ed.) *Sociological Economics.* Beverly Hills, CA: Sage.

Mosher, W. D. and Hendershot, G. E. (1984) "Religion and Fertility: A Replication." *Demography* 21(2):185–92.

Mosher, W. D., Johnson, D. P., and Horn, M. C. (1986) "Religion and Fertility in the United States: The Importance of Marriage Patterns and Hispanic Origin." *Demography* 23(3):367–80.

Muller, C. and Ellison, C. G. (2001) "Religious Involvement, Social Capital, and Adolescents' Academic Progress: Evidence from the National Education Longitudinal Study of 1988." *Sociological Focus* 34(2):155–83.

Read, J. G. (2004) *Culture, Class, and Work among Arab-American Women.* New York: LFB Scholarly Publishing.

Regnerus, M. D. (2000) "Shaping Schooling Success: Religious Socialization and Educational Outcomes in Metropolitan Public Schools." *Journal for the Scientific Study of Religion* 39:363–70.

Sander, W. (1993) "Catholicism and Marriage in the United States." *Demography* 30(3):373–84.

Sander, W. (1995) *The Catholic Family: Marriage, Children, and Human Capital.* Boulder, CO: Westview Press.

Sherkat, D. E. (2000) "That They Be Keepers of the Home: The Effect of Conservative Religion on Early and Late Transition into Housewifery." *Review of Religious Research* 41(3):344–58.

Sherkat, D. E. (2004) "Religious Intermarriage in the United States: Trends, Patterns, and Predictors." *Social Science Research* 33:606–25.

Sherkat, D. E. and Darnell, A. (1999) "The Effects of Parents' Fundamentalism on Children's Educational Attainment: Examining Differences by Gender and Children's Fundamentalism." *Journal for the Scientific Study of Religion* 38(1):23–35.

Smith, C. (2003) "Theorizing Religious Effects among American Adolescents." *Journal for the Scientific Study of Religion* 42(1):17–30.

Stark, R. and Finke, R. (2000) *Acts of Faith: Explaining the Human Side of Religion.* Berkeley: University of California Press.

Sweet, J. A. and Bumpass, L. L. (1990) "Religious Differentials in Marriage Behavior and Attitudes." NSFH Working Paper No. 15, University of Wisconsin.

Thornton, A. (1979) "Religion and Fertility: The Case of Mormonism." *Journal of Marriage and the Family* 41(1):131–42.

Thornton, A., Axinn, W. G., and Hill, D. H. (1992) "Reciprocal Effects of Religiosity, Cohabitation, and Marriage." *American Journal of Sociology* 98(3):628–51.

Waite, L. J. and Lehrer, E. L. (2003) "The Benefits from Marriage and Religion in the United States: A Comparative Analysis." *Population and Development Review* 29(2):255–75.

Weiss, Y. and Willis, R. J. (1985) "Children as Collective Goods." *Journal of Labor Economics* 3:268–92.

Wilcox, W. B. and Wolfinger, N. H. (2007) "Then Comes Marriage? Religion, Race, and Marriage in Urban America." *Social Science Research* 36(2):569–89.

Willis, R. J. and Haaga, J. G. (1996) "Economic Approaches to Understanding Nonmarital Fertility." Pp. 67–86 in J. B. Casterline, R. D. Lee, and K. A. Foote (eds) *Fertility in the United States: New Patterns, New Theories, Supplement to Population and Development Review* 22.

Willis, R. J. and Michael, R. T. (1994) "Innovation in Family Formation: Evidence on Cohabitation in the United States." Pp. 9–45 in J. Ermisch and N. Ogawa (eds) *The Family, the Market and the State in Ageing Societies.* Oxford: Clarendon Press.

10 Recent developments in the field and an agenda for future research

The past few years have witnessed substantial progress in our understanding of how religious factors influence education, female employment, fertility, and union formation and dissolution. In this concluding chapter I highlight results from recent studies on the role of religion in these and related economic and demographic behaviors, updating the critical literature review presented in Chapter 9. Based on the theoretical framework developed in Chapter 8, I also suggest a reinterpretation of previous findings in the literature and identify promising avenues for future research. The focus of this review is on the United States, but a few closely related studies that employ data from other countries are also included.

A reinterpretation of previous findings

Analyses to date of how religion influences economic and demographic behavior have generally examined one relationship at a time, e.g., the religion–fertility linkage, the religion–female labor supply linkage, and so on. The broader perspective offered in Chapters 8 and 9, which emphasizes that in understanding any given relationship it is essential to consider the full picture, suggests a reinterpretation of previous findings in the literature and points towards a new direction for future analyses.

In his pioneering research and subsequent work, Goldscheider (1971, 1999, 2006) has made a distinction between fertility differences among religious groups that are attributable to (a) differences in socioeconomic and other demographic characteristics; and (b) specific teachings of the religion such as norms regarding contraception, and more importantly, broader value orientations and worldviews associated with the religion such as pronatalism or gender inequalities. Influenced by this theoretical framework, the approach that has generally been used in the literature to study how religion affects a particular demographic or economic outcome is to first estimate a zero-order regression model, including only religion variables, and then add controls for other demographic and socioeconomic factors. For example, Mosher et al. (1992) report results on overall differences in fertility between various religious groups, and the differences that remain after controlling for a series of demographic and socioeconomic variables including education. Yet as Chapters 6 and 7 illustrate, religious affiliation has a substantial impact on investments in human capital. Thus when a control for education is added to a fertility regression, the new, smaller coefficients on the religion variables leave out the indirect influence of religion on fertility via its impact on such investments.

This point applies to each of the other realms of economic and demographic behavior. For instance, in their analysis of the relationship between religious intermarriage and marital stability between waves I and II of the National Survey of Families and Households, Call and Heaton (1997) first report a zero-order regression, and then another with controls for socioeconomic and demographic variables, including the birth of a child between the waves. The coefficient on the religious intermarriage variable becomes smaller in magnitude and loses all significance in this second regression. But, as elaborated in Chapter 4, religious intermarriage may lead to a reduced level of investments in spouse-specific human capital, children in particular, thus increasing the probability of marriage dissolution. The small, insignificant coefficient on religious intermarriage in the second regression leaves out this indirect effect.

Future analyses should make a careful distinction between variables that are not influenced by religion, such as age, race, and ethnicity, properly held constant in the second regression, and those that are, such as investments in various forms of human capital, which should be excluded. This second regression would provide information on the total effects of religion. One might be tempted to go on to estimate a third regression including the latter variables so as to distinguish between direct and indirect influences, e.g., in the case of the religion–marital stability linkage discussed above, adding a variable for the birth of a child; however, marital stability and fertility are jointly determined. Thus this third step would generally be possible only when having access to a data set, or combination of data sets, rich enough to contain instruments that could be used to take these endogeneity issues into account.

Religion and demographic outcomes

An early study by Williams and Zimmer (1990) found that Catholics in Rhode Island had substantially higher fertility than non-Catholics, contrary to results that had begun to suggest an end to high Catholic fertility in the US as a whole (Westoff and Jones 1979). The Williams and Zimmer study was among the first empirical analyses to emphasize the importance of the community context: Rhode Island is different from other states in that Catholics there constitute a majority. Similar analyses would probably reveal that the influence of religious factors on the demographic behavior of Jews in New York or Mormons in Utah differs substantially from that for their counterparts in places with smaller concentrations of coreligionists. McQuillan's (2004) work is an effort to advance our understanding of why the effects of religion on fertility vary across locations and over time. He presents evidence suggesting that religion matters when the religious institutions are able to articulate norms that are relevant to fertility and have the means to enforce compliance, and when individuals have a strong sense of attachment to their religious community. Berman et al. (2006) also emphasize the critical role of religious institutions, in a different dimension, namely, the extent to which they provide health, education, and other social services that affect the monetary costs of having children.

Fertility in the US is considerably higher than that in most European countries, and indeed contrary to trends in other industrialized nations, the United States appears to be experiencing a baby boomlet; data for 2006 reveal the largest number of births since 1961 (Hamilton et al. 2007). Recent analyses of data for 13 developed countries show that the ideal family size of individuals who have some religious affiliation is higher than that of their unaffiliated counterparts (Adsera 2006a), and for the case of Spain, a higher level of religiosity is associated with a faster tempo of births and also with higher fertility, by a small margin (Adsera 2006b). Related work for the United States shows that among more religious individuals both current and intended fertility are higher (Hayford and Morgan 2008). Although these results must be interpreted as purely descriptive, because religiosity is measured as of the survey date in the three studies, the results are suggestive of a positive influence of religiosity on fertility. An interesting question is the extent to which the difference in fertility between the US and Europe is related to the much higher levels of religiosity and traditional family orientation that characterize the US. Analyses by Frejka and Westoff (2008) show that if the European countries had the same religiosity levels as the US, the fertility of women aged 18–44 would be higher than current levels by 13–14 percent (depending on the measure of religiosity used).

With regard to mortality, another major demographic outcome, previous studies have shown that some involvement in religious activities is generally associated with beneficial effects on health and survival rates, as discussed in Chapter 5. A recent critical literature review concludes that there is strong evidence supporting a connection between public religious attendance and mortality risk, with weaker evidence for the case of private religious activities (Hummer et al. 2004). However, the question of whether or to what extent participation in religious activities causes better health outcomes remains controversial (e.g., see Bagiella et al. 2005; Hummer 2005). Related work on self-reported happiness, a proxy for overall well-being, shows that attendance at religious services can help buffer an individual's happiness against income shocks – a finding that has implications for governmental provision of insurance (Dehejia et al. 2007). Although the linkages between religion and health/well-being can have other, potentially far-reaching economic implications, they have received virtually no attention in the literature to date.[1] It is noteworthy also that participation in religious activities has been found to promote cooperative behavior, enhancing well-being for the entire community (Sosis and Ruffle 2003).

Religion and socioeconomic outcomes

Chapters 6 and 7 discuss possible pathways of causality linking religious affiliation and participation to schooling outcomes and educational attainment, key determinants of economic well-being. Recent research suggests that religious factors are associated with the level of conflict between the parents (Curtis and Ellison 2002), domestic violence (Ellison et al. 1999), the degree of fathers' involvement with their children (King 2003; Wilcox 2004), the quality of mother–child relations (Pearce and Axinn 1998), and parenting styles and approaches to child discipline (Bartkowski and Wilcox 2000; Bartkowski et al. 2000). These studies suggest a number of other channels, which deserve further attention and quantification, through which religion may affect the home environment, the quality and quantity of informal investments in children's human capital, and educational outcomes.

Substantial progress has been made in recent years in understanding the effects of religion on other socioeconomic outcomes including labor supply, wages, and wealth. With regard to labor supply, conservative Protestant groups generally provide psychological rewards and institutionalized moral support to women who stay home with their young children, and consistent with this, Chapter 3 provides some evidence of relatively low levels of labor force participation among conservative Protestant women with children under the age of 6. Although there is heterogeneity within conservative religious groups regarding views on appropriate roles for women and men (Gay et al. 1996), there is growing evidence of a distinctive pattern of female labor supply behavior among such groups (Lehrer 1999; Sherkat 2000; Glass and Jacobs 2005; Glass and Nath 2006). Substantial, related differences in wages have also been found; thus future economic analyses of the male–female wage gap – its magnitude, causes, and changes over time – should consider the role of religious factors, including the growth of conservative Protestant denominations in the US (Glass and Nath 2006; Lehrer 2008a). The possible role of religion on the labor supply behavior of men has received less attention in the literature, as it is unusual for prime-aged men to depart from a pattern of full-time work. Research in progress is examining this issue (Civettini and Glass 2008).

Religion has also been found to have a large impact on wealth, both directly, by defining worthwhile objectives (oriented to this world and/or the afterlife) and providing tools for the development of savings and investment strategies, and indirectly, through its effects on education, fertility, and labor supply behavior (Keister 2003, 2005, 2008a, 2008b). Wealth differentials by religion mirror the patterns that have been found for education and wages: conservative Protestants have the lowest levels of wealth; Jews are at the other end of the spectrum, and mainline Protestants and Catholics are at the center of the distribution.

The implications of religious dissimilarity

The most recent study on this topic shows that the prevalence of religious intermarriage in the US has been rising for all groups except conservative Protestants (Sherkat 2004), confirming the patterns described in Chapter 2. As discussed in Chapter 1, differences in religious affiliation between husband and wife have repercussions for marital stability, depending in part on the ecumenical/exclusivist nature of the religions, and Chapters 3 and 4 discuss how such differences may also affect fertility and female labor supply. Recent studies have found further confirmation for the importance of religious heterogamy for marital stability (Kalmijn et al. 2005), fertility (Adsera 2006b, 2006c), and female labor supply (Glass and Nath 2006).

New findings on the age at marriage–divorce relationship suggest that the implications of religious intermarriage for marital stability (and hence also for fertility and female labor supply) may vary by age at marriage (Lehrer 2008b). In this recent work I found that women who are unconventional in marrying for the first time in their late twenties or thirties tend to be unconventional also in being more likely to wed partners who have had a previous marriage and who differ from them substantially in age, education, race/ethnicity, and also religion; yet their marriages are very stable. I interpreted these results as reflecting the importance of Valerie Oppenheimer's (1988) "maturity effect" – the greater emotional maturity that comes with older ages, the better self-knowledge, and the greater ability to assess the likely trajectory of potential partners. A greater appreciation of the benefits from marriage – especially having a partner with whom to have and raise a child – probably plays an important role also. Thus it seems likely that replication of the Chapter 1 analyses separately by age at entry into first marriage would reveal that the destabilizing effect associated with religious intermarriage is small or non-existent in the sub-sample of late entrants into first marriage. The potential fruitfulness of this line of investigation is suggested by the current trend towards increasingly delayed entry into first formal union (Lehrer 2008b).

Differences in religion between the parents lead to subsequent religious dissimilarity between at least one parent and the children, generating a potential source of conflict within the family; such intergenerational dissimilarity may arise also in households where the parents share the same religious affiliation, if a child chooses to follow a different path. Sherkat and Darnell (1999) find that conservative Protestant parents are less willing to make investments in higher education for children who do not follow their faith. Recent work has also found an association between parent–child religious dissimilarity and child's law abiding behavior: when the mother is very religious and the child is not, or vice versa, there is an elevated risk of adolescent delinquency (Pearce and Haynie 2004).

Two ways in which religiosity matters for demographic and economic behavior

Commitment to religion – in its various manifestations, including the strength of religious beliefs and the extent of participation in private and public religious activities – can affect demographic and economic behavior via two major pathways. First, a higher level of religiosity may be expected to accentuate the effects of religious affiliation, e.g., the tendency for conservative Protestant women to display low levels of employment when young children are present in the household should be most pronounced among highly observant conservative Protestant couples. Second, the generally beneficial effects of religiosity on health and well-being can have important implications for economic and demographic outcomes, e.g., children raised with some religious involvement in their lives tend to have better performance in school and to achieve a higher level of educational attainment. Analyses in the literature to date typically consider only one of these two pathways of causality. The arguments developed in Chapter 7 and in more recent work (Lehrer 2008a) emphasize the importance of taking both into account: the two pathways may exert countervailing influences, and in addition, the effects of religiosity may vary by religious affiliation.

The growing body of evidence showing that some involvement in religious activity is associated with better schooling outcomes has implications for the literature on the benefits of attendance to Catholic schools (e.g., Neal 1997; Altonji et al. 2005). Cohen-Zada and Sander (2008) note that most of these studies have failed to consider the comparatively high level of religiosity among children enrolled in Catholic schools, thus overstating the advantage associated with attendance to such schools with regard to test scores, high school graduation rates, and other educational outcomes.

Analyses that have found beneficial influences of religiosity on various health and economic outcomes have generally specified religiosity as either a continuous religious participation variable, or a dichotomous variable for high versus low attendance at religious services. Chiswick and Huang (2007) use a set of dummy variables for various levels of participation, thus allowing for the possibility of non-linearities. Based on data from the 2000/1 National Jewish Population Survey, they find that individuals who attend religious services weekly have significantly higher earnings than those who attend less frequently, supporting the hypothesis that some religious involvement has a beneficial effect on labor market outcomes; however, those who attend religious services more than weekly have lower earnings than those who attend weekly. The authors suggest that beyond a point, time and effort allocated to religious activities begins to crowd out time and effort that could be oriented to labor market activities. They also point out that discrimination in the labor market and lifestyle restrictions associated with the Orthodox denomination may play a role.

Unusually high rates of participation are often associated with extreme positions that may not be conducive to well-being, and non-linearities may emerge for this reason as well. A recent study of intimate partner violence in Chile finds that college women raised with some religious involvement in their lives are less likely to experience intimate partner violence, a result traced to their generally healthier, less risky lifestyles. However, there is no protective effect for women raised with high levels of religious participation. Such women probably include many raised with extreme views and role models, where the sacredness of family unity is seen as foremost even in the face of spousal abuse, and where submissiveness is viewed as a key female quality (Lehrer et al. 2007). Future research should use statistical specifications that allow for possible non-linearities. The key question is whether beyond a certain point, further increases in the level of religiosity have an insignificant or even adverse influence.

Related to this, although the US literature on religion and health overwhelmingly points towards benefits associated with religion, there are exceptions, particularly in the area of sexuality. The abstinence-only programs advocated by conservative religious groups have been found to be ineffective in reducing the risk of pregnancy or sexually transmitted diseases among teens (Kirby 2001; Trenholm et al. 2007), and while most studies have found that high levels of religiosity are associated with delayed sexual debut, results to date on the connection between religiosity and sexual risk behaviors among sexually active adolescents have been mixed (Whitehead et al. 2001). A better, more nuanced understanding of the effects of religion on health and economic outcomes requires further attention to these and other important exceptions.

Smaller religious and ethnic/racial groups

Most of the studies in this book and elsewhere in the US literature on the role of religion in economic and demographic behavior have been based on samples of non-Hispanic whites, with a focus on the large religious groups – Catholics, mainline Protestants, and conservative Protestants. Recent research has begun to analyze samples of racial/ethnic and religious minorities (Warner 2002; Read 2004; Glass and Jacobs 2005; Wilcox and Wolfinger 2006; C. Chiswick 2007, 2008; B. Chiswick 2008). Further research on these smaller groups would be desirable. The "no-religion" group, which grew in size from 8 percent of the population in 1990 to over 14 percent in 2001, also deserves additional attention (Kosmin and Keysar 2006).

Measurement and statistical issues

Much of what we know about the connection between religion and economic/demographic behavior is based on analyses that use only two indicators of religion: broad categories of religious affiliation and frequency of attendance at religious services, usually measured during childhood. Recent research suggests the fruitfulness of considering more detailed categories of religious affiliation (Barrett et al. 2007); a richer array of dimensions of religion, including beliefs (e.g., in the existence of God, miracles, the inerrancy of the Bible), the salience of religion, and private religiosity (Idler et al. 2003; Glass and Nath 2006; Kosmin and Keysar 2006); and measures of parental religious affiliation and participation (Branas-Garza and Neuman 2007; Pearce and Thornton 2007).

One of the main reservations expressed with regard to results that show beneficial effects of religious participation in various areas is that such effects may be overstated, because the estimates include the influence of unmeasured positive characteristics that are correlated with religiosity (e.g., Freeman 1986; Regnerus and Smith 2005). For example, if parents who encourage their children to attend religious services also tend to encourage them to do their homework and engage in other constructive behaviors, part of the observed positive association between religious participation and educational outcomes would reflect the influence of these other behaviors. As discussed in Chapter 5, however, to the extent that religious participation is especially beneficial for those who are more vulnerable (for reasons that might include poor health, unfavorable family circumstances, and adverse economic conditions), the estimated coefficients may actually understate the true effect of religiosity. Thus although the most serious concern expressed in this literature has been that the estimates overstate the effects, it may well be the case that the opposite is true.

Recent work by Barro and McCleary (2003) and Gruber (2005) uses instrumental variables methods to estimate the causal effects of participation in religious activities; additional efforts in this direction would be desirable. This approach offers promise in addressing endogeneity issues in connection with the effects of religious intermarriage (as discussed in Chapter 1, the same unobserved factors that lead an individual to enter an interfaith marriage may later influence the stability of the union), with the controversial religiosity–health relationship, and with the linkages between religiosity and each of the economic and demographic behaviors discussed in this book. While the theoretical arguments for these linkages are compelling and the evidence accumulated to date suggests that the magnitudes of the effects are likely not trivial, we need additional research that addresses concerns of reverse causality and confounding factors.

Concluding remarks

The studies in this volume describe the effects of religion on various economic and demographic behaviors, including education, female employment, fertility, and union formation and dissolution. Causality also flows in the opposite direction, and there is a growing literature that seeks to understand how economic and demographic variables influence the extent and form of involvement in religious activities, the process of switching from one religious affiliation to another, and other dimensions of religious behavior (for some recent contributions, see Branas-Garza and Neuman 2004; Barro and Hwang 2007; Zhai et al. 2007; C. Chiswick 2008; Waite and Lewin 2008). A major challenge that lies ahead is the need to do more to understand and model the reciprocal influences linking religion and economic/demographic behavior. The impressive recent advances in the field reviewed in this closing chapter bode well for continued progress.

Acknowledgments

I am indebted to Alicia Adsera, Carmel Chiswick, Chris Ellison, Jennifer Glass, and Lisa Pearce for valuable comments, and to Ramona Krauss and Zhenxiang Zhao for skillful research assistance.

Note

1   For an effort to begin to conceptualize some of these implications, for the specific case of Pentecontalism, see Woodberry (2006).

References

Adsera, A. (2006a) "Religion and Changes in Family-Size Norms in Developed Countries." *Review of Religious Research* 47(3):271–86.

Adsera, A. (2006b) "Marital Fertility and Religion in Spain, 1985 and 1999." *Population Studies* 60(2):205–21.

Adsera, A. (2006c) "An Economic Analysis of the Gap between Desired and Actual Fertility: The Case of Spain." *Review of Economics of the Household* 4:75–95.

Altonji, J. G., Elder, T. E., and Taber, C. R. (2005) "Selection on Observed and Unobserved Variables: Assessing the Effectiveness of Catholic Schools." *Journal of Political Economy* 113:151–84.

Bagiella, E., Hong, V., and Sloan, R. P. (2005) "Religious Attendance as a Predictor of Survival in the EPESE Cohorts." *International Journal of Epidemiology* 34:443–51.

Barrett, J. B., Ellison, C. G., and Grammich, C. (2007) "Religious Influences on American Opinion about Family Planning." Unpublished manuscript.

Barro, R. J. and McCleary, R. (2003) "Religion and Economic Growth." *American Sociological Review* 68(October):760–81.

Barro, R. J. and Hwang, J. (2007) "Religious Conversion in 40 Countries." Unpublished manuscript.

Bartkowski, J. P. and Wilcox, W. B. (2000) "Conservative Protestant Child Discipline: The Case of Parental Yelling." *Social Forces* 79:865–91.

Bartkowski, J. P., Wilcox, B., and Ellison, C. G. (2000) "Charting the Paradoxes of Evangelical Family Life: Gender and Parenting in Conservative Protestant Households." *Family Ministry* 14(4):9–21.

Berman, E., Iannaccone, L. R., and Ragusa, G. (2006) "From Empty Pews to Empty Cradles: Fertility Decline among European Catholics." Presented at the annual meetings of the Economic Association of America, Chicago.

Branas-Garza, P. and Neuman, S. (2004) "Analyzing Religiosity within an Economic

Framework: The Case of Spanish-Catholics." *Review of Economics of the Household* 2:52–44.

Branas-Garza, P. and Neuman, S. (2007) "Parental Religiosity and Daughters' Fertility: The Case of Catholics in Southern Europe." *Review of Economics of the Household* 5(3):305–27.

Call, V. R. A. and Heaton, T. B. (1997) "Religious Influence on Marital Stability." *Journal for the Scientific Study of Religion* 36(3):382–92.

Chiswick, B. (2008) "The Rise and Fall of the American Jewish PhD." IZA Discussion Paper, University of Illinois at Chicago.

Chiswick, B. and Huang, J. (2007). "The Earnings of American Jewish Men: Human Capital, Denomination, and Religiosity." Presented at the annual meetings of the Illinois Economic Association, Chicago.

Chiswick, C. (2007) "Judaism in Israel and the United States: An Economic Perspective." Pp. 131–54 in C. Chiswick, T. Lecker, and N. Kahana (eds) *Jewish Society and Culture: An Economic Perspective*. Ramat Gan, Israel: Bar-Ilan University Press.

Chiswick, C. (2008) *The Economics of American Judaism*. London: Routledge.

Civettini, N. H. and Glass, J. (2008) "The Impact of Religious Conservatism on Men's Work and Family Involvement." Unpublished manuscript.

Cohen-Zada, D. and Sander, W. (2008) "Religion, Religiosity and Private School Choice: Implications for Estimating the Effectiveness of Private Schools." Forthcoming in *Journal of Urban Economics*.

Curtis, K. T. and Ellison, C. G. (2002) "Religious Heterogamy and Marital Conflict: Findings from the National Survey of Families and Households." *Journal of Family Issues* 23(4):551–76.

Dehejia, R., DeLeire, T., and Luttmer, E. F. P. (2007) "Insuring Consumption and Happiness through Religious Organizations." *Journal of Public Economics* 91:259–79.

Ellison, C. G., Bartkowski, J. P., and Anderson, K. L. (1999) "Are There Religious Variations in Domestic Violence?" *Journal of Family Issues* 20(1):87–113.

Freeman, R. B. (1986) "Who Escapes? The Relationship of Churchgoing and Other Background Factors to the Socioeconomic Performance of Black Male Youths from Inner-City Tracts," Pp. 353–76 in R. B. Freeman and H. J. Holzer (eds) *The Black Youth Employment Crisis*. Chicago: University of Chicago Press.

Frejka, T. and Westoff, C. F. (2008) "Religion, Religiousness and Fertility in the US and in Europe." Forthcoming in *European Journal of Population*.

Gay, D. A., Ellison, C. G., and Powers, D. A. (1996) "In Search of Denominational Subcultures: Religious Affiliation and Pro-Family Issues Revisited." *Review of Religious Research* 38:3–17.

Glass, J. and Jacobs, J. (2005) "Childhood Religious Conservatism and Adult Attainment among Black and White Women." *Social Forces* 84(1):555–79.

Glass, J. and Nath, L. E. (2006) "Religious Conservatism and Women's Market Behavior Following Marriage and Childbirth." *Journal of Marriage and the Family* 68(August):611–29.

Goldscheider, C. (1971) *Population, Modernization, and Social Structure*. Boston, MA: Little, Brown.

Goldscheider, C. (1999) "Religious Values, Dependencies, and Fertility: Evidence and Implications from Israel." Pp. 310–30 in R. Leete (ed.) *Dynamics of Values in Fertility Change*. Oxford: Oxford University Press.

Goldscheider, C. (2006) "Religion, Family, and Fertility: What do We Know Historic- ally and Comparatively?" Pp. 41–58 in R. Derosas and F. van Poppel (eds.), *Religion and the Decline of Fertility in the Western World*. The Netherlands: Springer.

Gruber, J. (2005) "Religious Market Structure, Religious Participation, and Outcomes: Is Religion Good for You?" *Advances in Economic Analysis and Policy* 5(1): article 5. URL (consulted June 2008): http://www.bepress.com/bejeap/advances/vol5/iss1/ art5

Hamilton, B. E., Martin, J. A., and Ventura, S. J. (2007) "Births: Preliminary Data for 2006." *National Vital Statistics Reports* 56(7). URL (consulted February 2008): http://www.cdc.gov/nchs/data/nvsr/nvsr56/nvsr56_07.pdf

Hayford, S. R. and Morgan, S. P. (2008) "Religiosity and Fertility in the United States: The Role of Fertility Intentions." Forthcoming in *Social Forces*.

Hummer, R. A. (2005) "Commentary: Understanding Religious Involvement and Mortality Risk in the United States: Comment on Bagiella, Hong, and Sloan." *International Journal of Epidemiology* 34:452–3.

Hummer, R. A., Ellison, C. G., Rogers, R. G., Moulton, B. E., and Romero, R. R. (2004) "Religious Involvement and Adult Mortality in the United States: Review and Perspective." *Southern Medical Journal* 27(12):1223–30.

Kalmijn, M., de Graaf P. M., and Janssen J. P. (2005) "Intermarriage and the Risk of Divorce in the Netherlands: The Effects of Differences in Religion and in Nation- ality, 1974–94." *Population Studies* 59(1):71–85.

Idler, E. L., Musick, M. A., Ellison, C. G., George, L. K., Krause, N., Ory, M. G. et al. (2003) "Measuring Multiple Dimensions of Religion and Spirituality for Health Research: Conceptual Background and Findings from the 1998 General Social Survey." *Research on Aging* 25:327–65.

Keister, L. A. (2003) "Religion and Wealth: The Role of Religious Affiliation and Participation in Early Adult Asset Accumulation." *Social Forces* 82:173–205.

Keister, L. A. (2005) *Getting Rich: America's New Rich and How They Got that Way*. Cambridge: Cambridge University Press.

Keister, L. A. (2008a) "Childhood Religious Denomination and Early Adult Asset Accumulation." Forthcoming in C. Ellison and R. Hummer (eds.) *Religion, Family Life, and Health in the United States*, Rutgers University Press.

Keister, L. A. (2008b) "Conservative Protestants and Wealth: How Religion Perpetu- ates Asset Poverty." Forthcoming in *American Journal of Sociology*.

King, V. (2003) "The Influence of Religion on Fathers' Relationships with Their Children." *Journal of Marriage and the Family* 65:382–95.

Kirby, D. (2001) *Emerging Answers: Research Findings on Programs to Reduce Teen Pregnancy*. Washington, DC: National Campaign to Prevent Teen Pregnancy.

Kosmin B. A. and Keysar, A. (2006) *Religion in a Free Market*. Ithaca, NY: Para- mount Market Publishing, Inc.

Lehrer, E. L. (1999) "Married Women's Labor Supply Behavior in the 1990s: Differ- ences by Life-Cycle Stage." *Social Science Quarterly* 80(3):574–90.

Lehrer, E. L. (2008a) "Religious Affiliation and Participation as Determinants of Women's Educational Attainment and Wages." Forthcoming in C. Ellison and R. Hummer (eds.) *Religion, Family Life, and Health in the United States*. Rutgers University Press.

Lehrer, E. L. (2008b) "Age at Marriage and Marital Instability: The Becker-Landes- Michael Hypothesis Revisited." Forthcoming in *Journal of Population Economics*.

Lehrer, E. L., Lehrer, V. L., and Krauss, R. (2007) "Religion and Intimate Partner Violence in Chile: Macro- and Micro-Level Influences." Presented at the annual meetings of the Illinois Economic Association, Chicago.

McQuillan, K. (2004) "When does Religion Influence Fertility?" *Population and Development Review* 30(1):25–56.

Mosher, W. D., Williams, L. B., and Johnson, D. P. (1992) "Religion and Fertility in the United States: New Patterns." *Demography* 29(2): 199–214.

Neal, D. (1997) "The Effects of Catholic Secondary Schooling on Educational Achievement." *Journal of Labor Economics* 15(1):98–123.

Oppenheimer V. K. (1988) "A Theory of Marriage Timing." *American Journal of Sociology* 94:563–91.

Pearce, L. D. and Axinn, W. G. (1998). "The Impact of Family Religious Life on the Quality of Mother–Child Relations." *American Sociological Review* 63(6): 810–28.

Pearce, L. D. and Haynie, D. L. (2004) "Intergenerational Religious Dynamics and Adolescent Delinquency." *Social Forces* 82(4):1553–72.

Pearce, L. D. and Thornton, A. (2007). "Religious Identity and Family Ideologies in the Transition to Adulthood." *Journal of Marriage and the Family* 69:1227–43.

Read, J. G. (2004) *Culture, Class and Work Among Arab-American Women.* New York: LFB Scholarly Publishing LLC.

Regnerus, M. and Smith, C. (2005) "Selection Effects in Studies of Religious Influence." *Review of Religious Research* 47(1):23–50.

Sherkat, D. E. (2000) "That They be Keepers of the Home: The Effect of Conservative Religion on Early and Late Transition into Housewifery." *Review of Religious Research* 41(3):344–58.

Sherkat, D. E. (2004) "Religious Intermarriage in the United States: Trends, Patterns, and Predictors." *Social Science Research* 33:606–25.

Sherkat, D. E. and Darnell, A. (1999) "The Effects of Parents' Fundamentalism on Children's Educational Attainment: Examining Differences by Gender and Children's Fundamentalism." *Journal of the Scientific Study of Religion* 38(1):23–35.

Sosis, R. and Ruffle, B. (2003) "Religious Ritual and Cooperation: Testing for a Relationship on Israeli Religious and Secular Kibbutzim." *Current Anthropology* 44(5):713–22.

Trenholm, C., Devaney, B., Forston, K., Quay, L., Wheeler, J., and Clark, M. (2007) *Impacts of Four Title V, Section 510 Abstinence Education Programs.* Mathematica Policy Research, Inc. URL (consulted March 2008): http://www.mathematica-mpr.com/publications/pdfs/impactabstinence.pdf

Waite, L. J. and Lewin, A. C. (2008) "Religious Intermarriage and Conversion in the United States: Patterns and Changes Over Time." Forthcoming in C. Ellison and R. Hummer (eds) *Religion, Family Life, and Health in the United States.* Rutgers University Press.

Warner, R. S. (2002) "The Black Church as the Village it Takes to Raise a Child." *Youth and Religion Project, Module 1.* URL (consulted February 2008): http://www.uic.edu/depts/soci/yrp/index1.html

Westoff, C. F. and Jones, E. F. (1979) "The End of 'Catholic' Fertility." *Demography* 16:209–18.

Whitehead, B. D., Wilcox, B. L., and Rostosky, S. S. (2001) *Keeping the Faith: The Role of Religion and Faith Communities in Preventing Teen Pregnancy.* Washington, DC: The National Campaign to Prevent Teen Pregnancy.

Wilcox, W. B. (2004) *Soft Patriarchs, New Men: How Christianity Shapes Fathers and Husbands*. Chicago: The University of Chicago Press.

Wilcox, W. B. and Wolfinger, N. H. (2006) "Then Comes Marriage? Religion, Race, and Marriage in Urban America." *Social Science Research* 36:569–89.

Williams, L. and Zimmer, B. G. (1990) "The Changing Influence of Religion on U.S. Fertility: Evidence from Rhode Island." *Demography* 27(3):475–81.

Woodberry, R. D. (2006) "The Economic Consequences of Pentecostal Belief." *Society* 44(1):29–35.

Zhai, J. E., Ellison, C. G., Glenn, N. D., and Marquardt, E. (2007) "Parental Divorce and Religious Involvement among Young Adults." *Sociology of Religion* 68(2):125–44.

Author Index

Aiken, L. 30n8
Alwin, D. F. 149n1
Amato, P. R. 111
Axinn, W. G. 111, 119
Ayal, E. B. 213n6

Barber, K. E. 37
Barro, R. J. 110, 225
Bartkowski, P. J. 204, 207
Bean, F. 30n8
Becker, G. S. 3, 4, 30n13, 57, 75n5, 80, 81, 101n2, 130, 198, 199, 200, 202, 205
Berg, R. R. 48
Berman, E. 220
Booth, A. 119–20
Bracher, M. 30n12
Brien, M. J. 187
Bumpass, L. L. 30n13, 35, 49n5, 49n7
Bush, G. W. 122n4

Call, V. R. 119, 219
Cherlin, A. J. 111
Chiswick, B. R. 4, 74n4, 130, 132, 205–6, 213n6, 223
Chiswick, C. 1, 2, 33, 34, 35, 39, 60, 75n5, 81–2, 83, 95, 137, 178
Cho, J. H. 138, *139*
Christensen, H. T. 37
Cohen-Zada, D. 223
Cornwall, M. 56

Darnell, A. 129, 134–5, 144, 206–7, 222
Donnenwerth, G. V. 182
Durkheim, E. 113

Elder, M. D. 117
Ellison, C. G. 111–12, 113, 114, 204, 207

Finke, R. 177, 202
Foster, L. 23

Freeman, R. B. 111, 112, 167
Frejka, T. 220

George, L. K. 114
Glenn, N. D. 211
Goldscheider, C. 218
Gray, J. S. 117–18
Greeley, A. M. 113
Grossbard-Schechtman, S. 67
Gruber, J. 225

Heaton, T. 56, 119, 219
Horwitz, A. V. 109
Huang, J. 223
Hummer, R. A. 109

Iannaccone, L. R. 4
Idler, E. 116

Joyner, K. 112–13

Kasl, S. V. 116
Keister, L. A. 208
Kelley, D. M. 12, 16, 48n1, 101n1
Kiecolt-Glaser, J. 118
Koenig, H. G. 116
Korenman, S. 110

Lam, D. 29n5
Lambert, J. D. 109
Lehrer, E. 33, 34, 35, 39, 59, 60, 75n5, 81–2, 83, 95, 118, 137
Lenski, G. 149n1
Lillard, L. 75n5, 115, 122n5

Marks, N. F. 109
McCleary, R. M. 110, 225
McQuillan, K. 212, 219–20
Meng, R. 132
Michael, R. T. 14, 178, 179, 180, 181

Mosher, W. D. 30n12, 218–19
Muller, C. 111–12

Nerlove, M. 59
Neumark, D. 110

Oppenheimer, V. 222

Panis, C. 122n5
Pargament, K. I. 117
Pearce, L. D. 111, 119
Petersen, L. R. 182
Pullum, T. W. 48

Read, J. G. 213n5
Regnerus, M. D. 111, 117, 166

Sander, W. 93, 141, 223
Schneider, S. W. 13, 101n3
Sentance, J. 132
Sherkat, D. E. 129, 134–5, 144, 148, 201, 203, 206–7, 222
Simon, R. W. 109
Smith, J. E. 28
Smith, T. W. 150n9, 169n3, 182

Sobolewski, J. 111
Stark, R. 177, 202
Steensland, B. 169n2
Stets, J. E. 113
Stevens, G. 138, *139*
Sweet, J. A. 30n13, 35, 49n5

Thornton, A. 38, 128–9, 185, 190
Tomes, N. 74, 132
Tuma, N. 180

Vanderhart, M. J. 117–18

Waite, L. 4, 75n5, 112–13, 115
Warner, R. S. 156
Waters, M. 129
Westoff, C. F. 220
Wilcox, W. B. 120, 193
Williams, L. 219
Williams, R. S. 156
Willis, R. J. 178, 179, 181
Wilson, J. 148
Wolfinger, N. H. 193

Zimmer, B. G. 219

Subject Index

Note: *italic* page numbers denote references to Figures/Tables.

abortion 80, 202
abstinence instruction *158*, 159, *160*, *161*, *163*, 164, *164*, 224
age: fertility 87; husband's *61*, 62, *64*, 67, *68*, *71*; marital stability 13, 18, *19*, *20*, 25; "maturity effect" 222; women's labor force participation *61*, 62, *63*, 67, *68*, *71*
assortative mating 3, 29n5, 45, 47, 178, 199

bargaining effect 3, 33–4, 80, 81, *82*, 92–4, 99–100, 203; conversion 95; interethnic marriage 48; women's labor force participation 56–7, 58, 204
birth control instruction *158*, 159, *160*, *161*, *163*, 164, *164*, 168

Catholics: authoritarian values 149n1; cohabitation 188, 209; conversion 26–7, *27*, 94–5; divorce 42, 179–80, 181, 188; educational attainment 4, 44, 47, 128–9, *130*, 135, 137–47, 177, 205, 223; family size 40, 45; female earnings 74; fertility 3, 30n12, 80, 81, *82*, 84–5, 87–98, *99*, 100, 175, 177, 180–1, 202, 203, 219; gender roles 56, *57*, 204; high school graduation 5, 155, 156–7, 159–68; intermarriage 3, *17*, 24–5, *24*, 28, 34, 37, 39–48, 129, 201; marital stability 2, 16, *20*, *22*, 23–5, 26–7, 28, 81–2, 199–200; premarital sex 182; pronatalism 80, 177, 180, 202; socioeconomic distance 38; union formation 6, 180–1, 182, 183, *184*, 185–93, 208; wages *145*; wealth 208, 221; women's labor force participation

3, 56, 58, *61*, 62–7, 70–3, 74, *148–9*, 179, 204
childrearing 38, 59, 121, 149n1, 200, 204
children 79, 80–1, 100; benefits of marriage 110–11, 114, 116; economic well-being 116; intermarriage 200; out-of-wedlock 18, *19*, *21*, 25, 118; parent-child religious dissimilarity 222; religious participation 111–12, 114–15, 210–11; women's labor force participation 58–9, *61*, 62, *64*, 67, *68*, 70, *71*, 73, 75n5, *149*; *see also* human capital
cohabitation 6, 36, 181, 209; domestic violence 113; education 178; lack of research on 121; male earnings 178–9; marital stability 14, 18, 25; premarital sex 180; religiosity impact on 190, *191*, *192*; union formation 175, 176, 185–9; young people's attitudes towards 210
college degrees 141, *142*, *143*, 147
college preparatory courses 134–5, 207
conservative Protestants: classification of 169n3, 169n7; cohabitation 178, 179, 180, 181, 188, 193, 209; domestic violence 113; educational attainment 4, 117, 148, 177, 201, 205, 206–7, 210–11, 222; fertility 3, 177, 202; gender roles 179, 203, 204; high school graduation 5, 155, 156–7, 159–68; intermarriage 2–3, 201–2; male earnings 178; marital stability 2; parenting styles 111; premarital sex 182; religious participation 210, 211; union formation 6, 178, 180, 182–3, *184*, 185–93, 208; wages 207–8; wealth 208, 221; women's labor force

participation 3, 179, 204, 221, 223;
see also exclusivist Protestants;
fundamentalist Protestants
contraception 80, 202, 218
conversion 46, 60, 84; fertility 82–3, 94–5;
marital stability 13, 26–7, 28, 101n5,
119, 199
coreligionists 2, *41*, 42–3, *43*, *44*, *46*;
converts 13; cost of search for
marriage partner 36, 40, 201
cultural capital 149n4
cultural distance 38

discrimination 149n4
division of labor 55, 58, 60, 73, 74, 179,
203; fundamentalist Protestants 40–2,
134, 135, 144, 207; gains from
marriage 116; household work 204
divorce 15, 62, 80, 102n10, 118; broken-
home background impact on marital
stability 14, 25; Catholics 38, 42, 181,
188; cohabitation 189; conversion 95;
costs of 179–80; intermarriage 33, 79,
81, 83, 119; investment in children
75n5; mental health outcomes of
children 111; Mormons 28;
proscriptions against 12–13; religious
participation 120; unaffiliated couples
212; *see also* nonintact family of origin
domestic violence 113, 114, 221, 224
duration of marriage: definition of
102n10; fertility *86*, 87, 90–1

economic well-being 110, 113, 115–16,
117, 208, 221
ecumenical Protestants: classification of
39, 137; conversion 26–7, *27*; definition
of 12, 16; educational attainment 44,
47; fertility *82*, 84–5, *88–9*, 90–2, 93,
94, 100; gender roles 56, *57*;
intermarriage *17*, *20*, 23–5, *24*, 39–48,
60–1, 119; marital stability 12, 18, *20*,
21–5, 26–7, 60–1, 101n5; women's
labor force participation 56, 58, *61*,
62–7, 70–3, 74; *see also* mainline
Protestants
education 4, 128–53, 205–7, 221;
Catholics 38; conservative Protestants
117, 222; fertility *86*, 87, 202, 219; high
school graduation 5, 141, *142*, *143*,
154–71; intermarriage 2–3, 37, 40, *41*,
43–5, 46, 47, 201; investment in 130–2,
134, 135, 144, 146, 155, 205–6; marital
stability 13–14, 18, *19*, *20*, 25; religious

participation 5, 110, 111–12, 210–11,
213n8, 223; unaffiliated people 212;
union formation 177–8; women's labor
force participation *61*, *63*, 67, *68*, *71*;
see also parental education
elderly people 115
emotional well-being 114, 116
employment *see* labor force
participation; maternal employment
ethnicity 212, 224; high school
graduation 5, 154–5, 156, 157, 159–68;
interethnic marriage 48; union
formation 182, 193
exclusivist Protestants: classification of
39, 137; conversion 26, *27*; definition
of 12, 16; educational attainment
43–4, 45, 46, 47; fertility 80, *82*, 84–5,
88–9, 90–2, 100; gender roles 40–2,
55–6, *57*; intermarriage *17*, *20*, 23–5,
24, 39–48, 60; marital stability 12, *20*,
21–5, 26–7; pronatalism 80; women's
labor force participation 56, 58, *61*,
62–7, 70–3, 74; *see also* conservative
Protestants; fundamentalist
Protestants

family: Mormonism 23; norms of family
size 80; role of 12
family income: investment in education
132; marriage impact on 110; women's
labor force participation *61*, 62, *64*, 67,
68, *71*, 74; *see also* wages
family of origin size: high school
graduation 157–9, *160*, *161*, *163*, 164,
164; intermarriage 40, *41*, *43*, *44*, 45,
46; union formation 183, *184*, *186*,
187, 189
fertility 3–4, 33–4, 75n5, 79–104, 202–3,
212, 219–20; Catholics 30n12, 38, 175,
177, 180–1, 219; conversion 94–5;
differences between religions 218–19;
fundamentalist Protestants 38, 134;
high school graduation 164–5, 168;
Jews 132, 208; marriage cohorts 97–8;
Mormons 209; religiosity 95–7; union
formation 177; *see also* children;
human capital
fundamentalist Protestants 38–9, 128–9;
classification of 137–8, 150n9;
educational attainment 129, *130*,
134–5, *136*, 137–48, 148; wages *145*;
women's labor force participation
148–9; *see also* conservative
Protestants; exclusivist Protestants

gender: attitudes towards gender roles 38, 55–7, 60, 80, 134, 135, 179, 203–4; educational attainment 141–4, 147; intermarriage 37; *see also* men; women
General Social Surveys 109, 201
geographical factors *see* region of residence

happiness 109, 110, 220
health: economic well-being 116; marriage impact on 4, 108, 109, 113, 114, 115, 118, 122n5; mortality risk 220; religion impact on 4, 108–9, 115, 117, 220
heterogamous marriages *see* intermarriage
high school graduation 5, 141, *142, 143,* 154–71; religious affiliation impact on 159–65, 167–8; religious participation impact on 165–7, 168; *see also* education
homogamous marriages: classification of 39–40, 60; conversion 26–7, 28, 46, 60, 82–3, 84, 94–5, 119, 199; definition of 17; education 46, 47; fertility 3, 81, 85, 87–92, 94–5, 97, 99–100, *99;* marital stability 1–2, 12–13, 18, *20,* 21–3, *24,* 25, 28, 33, 199–200; religiosity 120, 211; women's labor force participation 3, 56–7, 58, 65–6, 67, 70–1, *72,* 73, 204
household work 204
human capital 3, 83, 100, 101n3; converts 13; educational attainment 130, 144, 147, 155, 177–8, 205; female earnings 74; fundamentalist Protestants 134; intermarriage 33, 57–8, 80–1; Jews 132, 205–6; marital stability 26–7, 202–3, 219; religious participation 4, 5; specialization 116; transferability 213n6; *see also* children

intermarriage: childrearing 59, 121, 200; choice of partner 200–2; determinants and trends 2–3, 33–52; fertility 33–4, 48, 80–3, *85, 88–9,* 90–9, 100, 202–3; human capital investment 57–8; increase in 129; marital stability 1–2, 11–12, 17–18, 23–9, 60–1, 81–2, 119, 199, 219, 222; measurement and statistical issues 225; religious participation 120, 121, 211; women's labor force participation 56–7, 58, *61,* 65–7, 70–3, 204

Jews: cohabitation 178, 179, 180, 181, 188, 189, 192, 209; educational attainment 4, 128, 129, *130,* 132–4, 138–47, 177, 202, 205–6; fertility 177, 202; high school graduation 155, 156–7; intermarriage *17, 24,* 25, 34, 37, 129, 201; labor market success 74n4, 223; male earnings 178; marital stability 2, 16, 17–18, *20, 22,* 23–5; union formation 6, 178, 180, 182, 183, *184,* 185–92, 208; wages *145,* 207; wealth 208, 221; women's labor force participation *148–9,* 179, 203

labor force participation 3–4, 55–78, 100, *148–9,* 179, 203–4, 221; attitudes towards gender roles 55–7, *57;* earnings 223; full-time or part-time employment 59–60, *59,* 65–7, *65, 66, 72;* human capital investment 57–8; intermarriage 33–4, 56–7, 58, *61,* 65–7, 70–3; Jews 132; "marriage premium" 116; *see also* maternal employment; wages
longevity 108–9, 114, 115, 116

mainline Protestants: classification of 39, 137; cohabitation 181, 188, 209; dominance of 27; educational attainment 4, 129, *130,* 135, *136,* 137–47, 177, 205; fertility 3; high school graduation 5, 155, 156–7, 159–68; intermarriage 3, 129, 201; marital stability 2, 199–200; premarital sex 182; single individuals 120; union formation 6, 182, *184,* 185–93, 208; wages *145,* 207, 208; wealth 208, 221; women's labor force participation 3, *148–9,* 179, 204; *see also* ecumenical Protestants
male earnings 178–9; *see also* family income; wages
marginal benefit (MB) of search for marriage partner 35–6, 37–9, 40, 49n4
marginal cost (MC) of search for marriage partner 35–7, 40, 47, 48n4
marital stability 1–2, 11–32, 33, 40, 199–200, 219, 222; decisions about children 59; ecumenical Protestants 60–1, 101n5; fertility 3, 48, 80–2, *82,* 93–4, 95, 99–100, 202–3; investment in children 79, 100; "marriage premium" 117–18; religious participation 97, 119–20; selection bias 118–19;

women's labor force participation 58, 204

marriage 1–6; benefits of 107–27; children 110–11, 114; choice of partner 200–2; domestic violence 113, 114; economic well-being 110, 113, 115–16; fertility 80; mental health 109, 118; physical health 108, 109, 113, 114, 115, 118, 122n5; promotion of 118, 122n4; religious participation 119–20; selection bias 118–19; sex 112, 114; social support 113, 114–15; union formation 5–6; young people's attitudes towards 210; *see also* previous marriages; union formation

marriage cohorts: fertility 97–8, *99*; intermarriage *41*, *43*, *44*, 45–6, *46*; marital stability 14

"marriage premium" 110, 116, 117–18

maternal employment: attitudes towards *57*; Catholics 38; educational attainment 138, *139*, *140*, 141; fundamentalist Protestants 39, 129, 134; high school graduation 157–9, *160*, *161*, *163*, 164, *164*; intermarriage 40–2, *41*, *43*, *44*, 45, *46*; Jews 132; marital stability 14, *19*, *21*, 25; union formation 179, 183, *184*, *186*, *187*, 189; *see also* labor force participation

"maturity effect" 222

men: domestic violence 113; educational attainment 13, 141–4, 147; intermarriage 37, *41*, *43*, *44*, 45, *46*; labor supply 221; longevity 108; marital stability *19*, *21*; "marriage premium" 110, 116; *see also* gender

mental health 109–10, 111, 117, 118

metropolitan areas *61*, *64*, *68–9*, 70, *71*

migration 201

mixed marriages *see* intermarriage

Mormons: cohabitation 180, 181, 188, 189, 192, 209; divorce 28; educational attainment 147, 178, 207; fertility 3, 80, 81, *82*, 84–5, 87–93, 100, 177, 202, 203; gender roles 179, 203; high school graduation 155, 156–7, 159, *160*, *162*, *163*, 167; intermarriage *17*, *24*, 25, 28; marital stability 2, 16, 17–18, *20*, *22*, 23–5, 28, 82, 199–200; pronatalism 80; union formation 6, 177, 180, *184*, 185–92, 208; wages 208

mortality 220

National Education Longitudinal Study (1988) 111–12

National Health and Social Life Survey (1992) 112

National Survey of Families and Households (NSFH): domestic violence 113; education 129, 135–8, 147, 148, 207; fertility 79–80, 83–4, 100, 203; intermarriage 34, 39–40; marital stability 2, 11, 15–18, 28, 119, 199, 200, 219; religiosity 210; women's labor force participation 55, 204

National Survey of Family Growth (NSFG): cohabitation 209; educational attainment 5, 210; high school graduation 154, 156, 167, 168, 169n2; marital stability 1; union formation 175, 182, 190, 193, 208; women's labor force participation 179

non-religious (unaffiliated) people 211; cohabitation 180, 209; educational attainment 207; fertility *82*, *88–9*, *90*, 91, *91*, 92–3; gender roles 56, *57*; growth in number of 224; high school graduation 155, 156–7, 159–67; intermarriage *17*, *24*; marital stability 16, *20*, *22*, 23, *24*, 28; union formation 182, *184*, 185–92, 208; wages 208; women's labor force participation *61*, 62–7, 70–1, *72*

nonintact family of origin: educational attainment 138, *139*, *140*, 141; high school graduation 157–9, *160*, *161*, *163*, 164; intermarriage *41*, 42, *43*, *44*, 45, *46*; marital stability 14, *19*, *20*, 25; mental health outcomes of children 111; union formation *184*, *186*, *187*, 189, 190; *see also* divorce

NSFG *see* National Survey of Family Growth

NSFH *see* National Survey of Families and Households

one-parent homes 14, 120

out-of-wedlock children 18, *19*, *21*, 25, 118; *see also* premarital pregnancy

parental education: educational attainment of children 138–41, *139*, *140*, 148, 150n11; high school graduation 157–9, *160*, *161*, 162, *163–4*; union formation 183, *184*, *186*, *187*, 189–90

parenting styles 111, 221

physical health: economic well-being 116; marriage impact on 108, 109, 113, 114, 115, 118, 122n5; religion impact on 108–9, 115, 117, 220

policy issues 118, 122n4

premarital pregnancy 36–7, 40, *41*, 43, *44*, *46*, 47, 166; *see also* out-of-wedlock children; teen pregnancy

premarital sex 166, 180, 181–2, 209, 210

previous marriages: fertility *86*, 87; marital stability 18, *19*, *21*, 25; women's labor force participation *61*, 62, *64*, 67, *68*, *71*

pronatalism 80, 81, 83, 177, 180, 202, 218

Protestants: classification of 137, 150n9, 169n3; conversion 26–7, 94–5; educational attainment 128–9, *130*, 134–5, *136*, 137–47, 148, 177; female earnings 74; fertility 81, 84–5, 87–98, *99*, 100, 203; gender roles 56, *57*; high school graduation 156–7, 159–68; intermarriage *17*, 23–5, *24*, 28, 34, 37, 39–48; marital stability 15–17, 18, *20*, 21–5, 26–7, 28, 81–2, 199; nondenominational 169n2; socioeconomic distance 38; union formation 182–3, *184*, 185–93; wages *145*; women's labor force participation 58, 204; *see also* conservative Protestants; ecumenical Protestants; exclusivist Protestants; fundamentalist Protestants; mainline Protestants

rational choice theory 38, 149n3, 176

region of residence: educational attainment 138, *139*, *140*; fertility *86*, 87; high school graduation 157–9, *160*, *161*, *163*, *164*; union formation 183, *184*, *186*, *187*, 189; wages *145*; women's labor force participation *61*, *64*, 68–9, 70, *71*, *148*

regulative effects of religion 4, 115, 155, 156

relationship skills 118

religiosity 95–7, 107, 121, 198, 210–11, 223; cohabitation 190, 193; domestic violence 113; educational attainment 110, 112, 210–12; fertility 220; marital stability 83; parenting styles 111; sexual risk 224; union formation 181–2, 190, *191*, *192*, 193; *see also* religious participation

religious compatibility 2, 34–5, 73, 83; choice of partner 36, 37, 45, 47, 201;

conversion 13, 60; marital stability 12, 13, 26; socioeconomic status 44

religious participation 4–5, 34, 40, 107, 210, 223–4; benefits of 107–27, 155, 212; children 111–12, 114–15; converts 13; domestic violence 113; economic well-being 110; educational attainment 111–12, 166–7, 213n8, 223; fertility 95–7; high school graduation 154, 155–6, 157, 165–7, 168; intermarriage 121; labor market outcomes 223; marital stability 12, 13, 18, 119–20; measurement and statistical issues 224–5; mental health 109–10, 117; physical health 108–9, 115, 220; sex 112–13; social support 114; spiritual benefits 113–14, 116; union formation 6, 175–6, 190, *191*, *192*, 193; *see also* religiosity

secularization 38, 48, 176, 201–2

selection bias 118–19

separation 15, 38, 102n10; *see also* divorce

sex 6, 224; marriage impact on 112, 114; premarital 166, 180, 181–2, 209, 210; religion impact on 112–13; young people's attitudes towards 210

siblings 138, *139*, *140*, 141

single individuals 120–1, 122n4

social capital 4, 114–15, 117, 155, 156, 211

social support 4, 113, 114–15

socioeconomic distance 38

socioeconomic status 44–5, 221; cohabitation 189; educational attainment 128, 138, *139*, *140*, 141, 201; parental education 162

South *61*, *64*, *69*, 70, *71*

specialization 116

teen pregnancy 157–9, *160*, *161*, *163*, 164, *164*, 168; *see also* premarital pregnancy

unaffiliated people *see* non-religious people

union formation 175–97, 208, 222; costs of divorce 179–80; educational attainment 177–8; female employment 179; fertility 177; fundamentalist Protestants 129; male earnings 178–9; religiosity 181–2; *see also* marriage

wages 110, 144, *145*, 150n13, 207–8;
education link 29n5; male-female wage
gap 221; non-religious people 212;
religious participation impact on
earnings 223; *see also* family income;
male earnings
wealth 208, 221
welfare recipients 138, *139*, *140*, 141
well-being 4, 118, 210, 220; children 111,
211; emotional 114, 116; mental
health 109–10; *see also* economic
well-being
widowhood 15, 102n10

women: domestic violence 224;
educational attainment 13–14, 25,
141–4, 147; fertility 81, 202;
fundamentalist Protestants 129, 135;
intermarriage 37; labor force
participation 3–4, 14, 55–78, 100,
148–9, 179, 203–4, 221; longevity 108,
116; marital loss 109; union formation
5–6, 175–97, 208; *see also* gender;
maternal employment

Youth Parent Socialization Panel 129
youths 114, 117, 155, 156, 210, 224

Printed in the United States
by Baker & Taylor Publisher Services